Selections from the Notebooks of
Edward Bond

Volume One: 1959 to 1980

Selections from the Notebooks of
Edward Bond

Volume One: 1959 to 1980

Edited and introduced by
Ian Stuart

Methuen

Published by Methuen 2000

1 3 5 7 9 10 8 6 4 2

First published in Great Britain in 2000 by Methuen Publishing Limited
215 Vauxhall Bridge Road, London SW1V 1EJ

Methuen Publishing Limited Reg. No. 3543167

A CIP catalogue record for this book is available from the British Library

ISBN 0 413 70500 5

Typeset by Deltatype Ltd, Birkenhead, Merseyside

Printed and bound in Great Britain by
Creative Print and Design (Wales), Ebbw Vale

Contents

Introduction

One benefit of working on Edward Bond's notebooks is that I have been able to follow in the footsteps of someone who, I believe, is one of the most interesting dramatists of our time. Whatever one feels about his plays, Bond's statement, in a 1985 letter to Terry Hands of the Royal Shakespeare Company: 'I may be a good or bad writer, but I am an innovative one', must be accurate.[1] In my notebook selections, I maintain that Edward Bond not only demonstrates that he is an innovative dramatist but also that he is one of the finest and most creative minds to have emerged in the twentieth century.

The entire notebook collection is stored at Doheny Library, University of Southern California, and the selections in this volume, and the later one, comprise about twenty per cent of Bond's writing.

London's Royal Court Theatre in the late 1950's was an exciting place for young writers. The English Stage Company, which bought the theatre's lease in 1955, had a different, more experimental philosophy than other London theatres. 'Ours is not to be a producer's theatre or an actor's theatre; it is a writer's theatre.'[2] The aim of the English Stage Company was 'to find a contemporary style in dramatic work, acting, décor and production. We hope to present exciting, provocative and stimulating plays . . . And we want to attract young people.'[3]

In 1955 Edward Bond left Vienna where he had spent two years on National Service with the Allied Army of Occupation. During his time with the army, Bond had started writing seriously and, upon returning to London, sent his plays to the Royal Court which had now established its reputation as the theatre for new writing. As a result of his submission, Bond was invited to meet George Devine, the Artistic

[1] *Edward Bond Letters II*, ed. Ian Stuart (London: Harwood Academic Publishers, 1995), 84.
[2] *New Statesman*, 24 March 1956.
[3] *The Stage*, 28 July 1955.

Director, and subsequently joined the newly formed Writers' Group at the Court in 1958 along with, among others, Ann Jellicoe, Wole Soyinka and Arnold Wesker. The theatre's approach was to expose writers to various acting techniques and, every two weeks, they would meet and improvise around a theme or an issue. (Examples of such a theme are Bond's comments on the eleven dead men at Hola Camp on 13 August 1959.)

The early, and unpublished, play of Bond's that had caught George Devine's attention was 'The Fiery Tree'. According to the first chapter in this volume, Bond wanted to establish in the next play that he had modified his philosophical position. He argues that with 'The Fiery Tree' he didn't make it clear 'that <u>men can be good</u>' (3 February 1960). By 8 February 1960, Bond had come to the realization that his approach to writing was new and that the style 'must be the truth'. And so, on 12 February 1961, he began to make notes for the 'Hermit Play', which became *The Pope's Wedding*, and was staged at the Royal Court, 9 December 1962 as a Sunday night production. These notes form Chapter Two of this volume.

As a result of *The Pope's Wedding*, Devine commissioned a new play from Bond on 24 April 1964. However, the notebooks reveal (in 'Public Garden' and 'Some Ideas') that, by the end of 1963, Bond was clearly beginning to think about *Saved*, the play which he eventually submitted to Devine to satisfy the commission on 18 September 1964. And by January 1964 Bond was composing the notorious scene of the play, 'the child killing'. The following year, 1965, saw Bond writing background notes for the play that took him two years to complete, *Early Morning*. Chapter Three consists of notebooks for *Saved* and *Early Morning* in addition to Bond's notes on theatre censorship.

Scholars have elsewhere gone into some depth about the Lord Chamberlain (whose power as theatre censor was removed in 1968) and so I will not go into the matter here other than to say that Bond's comments on censorship are particularly interesting.[4] Bond states:

> A play <u>may</u> corrupt someone, but a good play (and I will deal with bad plays later) has morally desirable effects. If someone will be corrupted anyway, one

---

[4] The reader is referred to, amongst others, John Johnston's *The Lord Chamberlain's Blue Pencil* (London: Hodder and Stoughton, 1990), Anthony Aldgate's *Censorship and the Permissive Society: British Cinema and Theatre, 1955–65* (Oxford: Clarendon Press, 1995) in addition to the *Report, together with the proceedings of the committee, minutes of evidence, appendices and index* (London: HMSO, 1967).

ought to risk corrupting him by a play if it is shown that other people benefit morally from the play.

Although Bond begins work on *Lear* on 3 June 1970, *Passion*, a short play written for the Campaign for Nuclear Disarmament's Festival of Life, interrupts his entries on 4 February 1971. And by 31 March 1971 the notebooks show in Chapter Four that Bond was working on both *Lear* and background notes and poems for *The Sea*, which Bond often refers to as the W[omb]A[nd]D[raper] play, simultaneously.

Chapter Five contains notes on art and the writer. Edward Bond believes that through politics, human beings attempt 'to cope' with their existential crisis. According to Bond, art, too, 'always gravitates towards the human crisis'. And so it is this meeting point, between politics and art, which Bond wants to explore. In his opinion, we cannot retreat into dreams or sentimentalism. 'Art can't escape from politics because society is the problem, the subject, of art.'

In the Great Wilbraham Papers of March 1974 that are Chapter Six, Bond argues that the artist needs to struggle with the problems of being human. Unlike the dramatists of the absurd, for example, Bond does not want writers to arrive at the conclusion that 'art is a cry of despair or pain, or a work of misery'. Instead he wants the writer to solve society's problems. Bond believes that writers should *actively* discuss the formation of a better society, a society that 'remains impracticable but which is an ideal in people which they can perhaps anticipate in the tension and repose of art, and which they can "keep alive" in themselves, so that the tradition is handed on to the generations who come after'.

Work on *Stone* began on 16 February 1976 and by 19 March 1976 Bond was at work on a new play called *The Swing*. At this point, though, I have to alert the reader to the potential difficulties that she/he may encounter in the date-order of the entries in Chapter Seven. Edward Bond has this practice of not following a strict chronological sequence and, occasionally, even finishing the notebooks some months later. Whilst completing the books is ecologically sound it is not editorially friendly so the reader will have to keep their wits about them. When this occurs, I have noted it but, in order to ensure accuracy, resisted, most of the time, the temptation to unite material that bears a common theme. Bond also keeps two or three notebooks concurrently therefore making chronology impossible without reorganizing the originals. This occurs with the notes at the beginning of this chapter. 'The New Road' or *The Bundle*, appears on 1 July 1977, before the 1976 notes on *Stone* and *The Swing*.

Editing 'The Rothbury Papers', which constitute the final chapter of this volume, was especially difficult as all the notes are socially relevant and provide useful insights on Brecht, art, dramatic method and acting.

My selections are divided into two volumes. Roughly speaking, the present volume contains Bond's early thoughts that span a twenty-year period from 1959. The second volume, also to be published by Methuen, will cover Bond's later work.

As I worked on the notebooks, it became clear that there are four types of entry: play drafts; commentary on the plays; Bond's thoughts on life and the play in particular; and stories and poems which may or may not have any direct relevance to the play in hand. In making my selections, I have tried to provide a balance between these different types of entries. My original thinking was to break the entries into their respective categories (with each play having sections on poetry, commentary on the plays, etc.). But having discussed the matter with Edward Bond, I decided not to tamper with the notebooks' original order of poems, stories, the philosophy and play drafts. Such an approach produces a very interesting result: a rare and extraordinary insight into the outlook of Bond and the workings of his creative mind.

In earlier versions of this manuscript, I liberally sprinkled the work with footnotes. Afraid these notes and lengthy explanations might become tedious for the reader and a distraction from the notebooks I reconsidered this thinking. Like the volumes of Edward Bond's letters, which I currently edit for Harwood Academic Publishers, instead I allow the notebooks to speak for themselves, keeping my editorial interference to a minimum, although providing the reader with a definition of terms or references to published texts. I have also indicated where I have edited the notebooks through the insertion of bracketed ellipses.

Edward Bond was born and educated in London. His plays include *The Pope's Wedding* (Royal Court Theatre, 1962); *Saved* (Royal Court, 1965); *Early Morning* (Royal Court, 1968); *Narrow Road to the Deep North* (Belgrade Theatre, Coventry, 1968; Royal Court, 1969); *Black Mass* (Sharpeville Commemoration Evening, Lyceum Theatre, London, 1970); *Passion* (CND Rally, Alexandra Palace, London, 1971); *Lear* (Royal Court, 1971); *The Sea* (Royal Court, 1973); *Bingo* (Northcott, Exeter, 1973; Royal Court, 1974); *The Fool* (Royal Court, 1975); *We Come to the River* (Covent Garden Opera, London, 1976); *The Bundle* (RSC Warehouse, 1978); *The Woman* (National Theatre, London, 1978); *The Worlds* (New Half Moon Theatre, London, 1981); *Restoration* (Royal Court, 1981); *Summer* (National Theatre, 1982); *Derek* (RSC

Youth Festival, The Other Place, Stratford-upon-Avon, 1982); *The Cat* (produced at the Staatstheater, Stuttgart, Germany, as *The English Cat* by the Stuttgart Opera, 1983); *Human Cannon* (Quantum Theatre, Manchester, 1986); *The War Plays* (*Red Black and Ignorant, The Tin Can People* and *Great Peace*) (RSC Barbican, 1985; Odéon Théâtre, Paris, 1995); *Jackets* (Haymarket, Leicester, 1989); *September* (Canterbury Cathedral, 1989); *In the Company of Men* (Théâtre de la Ville, Paris, 1992; RSC Barbican, 1996); *Olly's Prison* (BBC2 TV 1993; Berliner Ensemble, Germany, 1994); *Tuesday* (BBC Schools TV, 1993; Théâtre de la Colline, Paris, 1994); *At the Inland Sea* (toured by Big Brum Theatre-in-Education, 1995; Théâtre du Nord, Lille, 2000); *Eleven Vests* (toured by Big Brum Theatre-in-Education, 1997; Théâtre du Nord, Lille, 2000); *Coffee* (Théâtre de la Colline, Paris, 2000); *The Crime of the Twenty-first Century* (Théâtre de la Colline, Paris, 2000); *The Children* (Classworks, Cambridge, 2000); and *Chair* (BBC Radio 4, 2000). Bond's *Theatre Poems and Songs* were published in 1978, *Poems 1978–1985* in 1987 and *Edward Bond Letters* (Volumes I, II, III, 4, 5) in 1994, 1995, 1996, 1998 and 2000 (Harwood Academic Publishers).

Acknowledgments

I am very grateful to Edward Bond and Elisabeth Bond-Pablé for granting me permission to edit these notebooks and for correcting my typographical errors and many misinterpretations. My thanks to Michael Earley and Geoffrey Strachan of Methuen and Tom Erhardt of Casarotto Ramsay Limited for his help. I am especially grateful to Suzanne H. Kim for her patience in transcribing many of these notebooks and to Dr Hari Rorlich of the University of Southern California without whose support this study would not have been possible. Finally, I would like to express my appreciation to my parents who have followed my work with enthusiasm.

Ian Stuart
Los Angeles, California
January 2000

Editor's note

For readers who are unfamiliar with Edward Bond on the page, he has his own unique style of punctuation and spelling which I have tried to preserve. Any additional errors which have occurred while transcribing his notebooks are my responsibility.

Chapter One
The Early Period

30 January 1959

My appearance does not reflect what I am. This is very frightening: its as if I pushed something into my pocket, and the bulge it makes is of something completely different, it is the bulge of some other thing. The two eyes, peering solemnly out, or scurrying backwards and forwards like rats in the skirting between my cheeks and brow – never show the vast range of my vision as it darts over rivers or up mountains. My ears, which look like the fairy wings children wear at parties, silk stretched over wire frames, seem as unresponsive as wooden planks. My nose is like a tube of tin. And yet I hear a vast range of noises, and I can smell odours that can almost tell me the whole history of a place. Most surprising of all is the mouth, wet and soft and absurd; yet it opens and out pour ideas, lies, filth and bitterness. It is amusing and frightening to watch other people's faces: the lumps of putty stuck on the tops of bodies. It is absurd the way these lumps pucker and stretch and jerk, and all in response to whatever the person is feeling. If you drop a stone in water the surface ripples, and its the same with faces. Yet it is surprising it should be so. It betrays us, and yet it is important for society. We can, for instance, love only the things we know; could we love expressionless people? The essence of aristocracy is facial dissimulation; for this reason aristocracy is the suppression of love.

But most terrible of all – my body does not express the ache and bewilderment that lies inside it: my body is an ill-fitting garment. It is always a tramp; shuffling, dirty, diseased, lazy.

And how untrue are all the posed images that we connect with different sorts of personalities. Think of the solemn philosophical expression, the bright smile of the film star, the adenoidal, cold-in-the-head look of the tragedian! Or perhaps these poses do reflect the personality exactly, if they show the falseness of the personality imposed on the person behind it. The thing peering through the mask is completely different from the personality stamped on the mask; different in <u>kind</u>, as different as bread and tigers. And when the person sees this mask on a photograph or in a looking glass, there is another degree of falseness added. The person first looks at the stranger's mask and then goes on to find the person behind it: but he fails to do this, and the photograph feels absurd in his fingers, or the mask in the looking glass becomes so insolent that he has to turn away.

[. . .]

The Bog[1]

A mother said to her two children 'There is no bread in the larder, no fire in the grate. The river is frozen, the field is as hard as stone. You must go to your aunt and live with her for this winter. Be sure to cross the bog quickly, don't dawdle, and reach your aunt's before it grows dark.'

The children left the wooden hut and ran over the fields. They did not dawdle, but it was very hard going; the ground was wet and muddy, and the bog was treacherous.

Sometimes they found they were surrounded on three sides by oozy, black mud; and they had to retrace their steps for fifteen minutes before they found their way out and could go forward again.

By four o'clock they had barely gone half the distance to their aunt's. Now they were very hungry and cold, because they hadn't eaten properly for many weeks.

The younger child said to her brother 'O dear, I am tired. Please lets sit and rest here for a while.'

The big brother said 'No. <u>She</u> told us to reach our aunt's before the cold night came.'

Every few minutes the little girl asked to rest. She was crying now all the while, and both of them were walking slower and slower. At last, without a word they both sat down for a little rest. But at once they fell asleep because they were so tired.

The cold night came over the skies. Every thing was black. The wind whistled and rattled the bare leaves of the trees. The puddles [sic.] flew over the bog as if they were breathless with excitement.

In the morning the children were still lying where they had sat down. Their limbs were as black as bog water, and a little white frost had grown over them, over their hair, and eyes, and hands, and legs. A little white frost had stretched over patches of the bog and over the children, it was like spreading Columbine.

[1] 'The Bog' comes from an entry in Bond's notebook dated 3 February 1959.

14 February 1959

My play about the family was meant to ask this question: is it possible to do a good thing?[2]

I was not simply concerned with the way bad effects result from good causes; that is the sort of thing that happens in Synge's play about the blind who are made to see.[3]

I was concerned with something more sinister. If there is a good it must be something that makes life more abundant, something that increases the sense of life.

It struck me that excitement is concerned with just the opposite – the sense of death. Of course, excitement is a very crude way of being conscious; it even tends to negate self-consciousness.

And yet the risk in excitement is very real. It may be the risk involved in the roller coaster. It may be a risk acted out for us by other people. Nevertheless, danger was an important element in excitement. It maybe that this element – risk – infects many other forms taken by the search for a sense of being alive.

Thus, think of the risk in Ghandi's satyagraha.[4]

If this is true good is clearly a means to the sense of death.

Now, natural death is part of life. It does not smash the course of life, it completes it. But there are deaths that are for each individual accidental but which are statistically certain. The best example of this risk to the individual is a street accident.

5 February 1959

It is this death that has in it the element of risk. But for this risk to be truly menacing some people at least must succumb to it. Therefore we need some people to act out this risk by dying.

If all actions are turned towards one end, there is clearly no conflict between right and wrong, good and evil. But here are several explanations of the meaning of conflict, which do not include the idea of overcoming.

Conflict expresses dissatisfaction. It is dissatisfaction with the sense of life that turns men to the sense of death. But is conflict the urge to risk or the result of risk?

[2] According to Bond, 'the family play' was a work about Bill Sody, a trade unionist who had retired. In a letter to the editor, dated 21 January 1999, Bond observes, 'I cannot recall the title. I know the play was sent to the Royal Court and remember that John Arden said, 'I don't know who wrote this play (I hadn't put my name on it) but it's the sort of play we should be staging (at the R[oyal] C[ourt]).'' The play was not performed.

[3] *The Well of the Saints*, John Millington Synge.

[4] The term satyagraha, 'truth force', was first used by Mahatma Gandhi in 1906.

[. . .]

6 February 1959

A person is alienated from his own personality. In this mood consciousness is divided from the personality: consciousness watches the gimmicks and antics of its person.

And yet the whole of consciousness is focused on the personality. Personality is the expression of consciousness. Consciousness is not merely sick with its expression; it is sick with itself.

Personality is always unreal. Consciousness recognizes in its expression of unreality a parody of its own condition. The whole of man from the gesture of a little finger to the sighing of his soul, is unreal.

Reality is inevitable: it has no alternative forms, no unrealized possibility, no choice. On the other hand, man has endless alternative forms: his consciousness, that is, has moods. He can recognize his own inadequacy – therefore he has possibility. He is condemned to be free. Only nothing is real. Man is a mistake.

Man's reality is his death.

[. . .]

8 February 1959

The characters in Büchner's plays are not developed much.[5] They are not changed by events; they do not change events; events bring out what is in them.

Danton has no control over the revolution; Woyzeck has no control over Maria. And because they have no control over events, and because events bring out each character's truth, these characters have no control over themselves. They are puppets under the malignant hand of fate.

They are trapped by life. They are nailed up in their skins, and their skins are nailed down in glass cases. Their reality is like entries in a train timetable.

They have no option but to disassociate themselves from their essence; but they do not find freedom in existence. They cannot deny the reality of their own essence without denying the reality of all the world. The world becomes a printed railway catalogue.

They must therefore continuously tell one another what life is. And the more they tell, the further apart they are forced. Their knowledge reveals nothing more than the absurdity of their situation.

[5] Georg Büchner (1813–1837), playwright, author of *Danton's Death*, *Woyzeck* and *Leonce and Lena*. Some of these plays are mentioned subsequently by Bond.

This is because their existence is trapped in their essence.

They are strangers with little stories – their past – and pictures – their physiques – and with these they have vouchsafed themselves personalities.

It is the uncontrolled record of events – which they begin by defining as crises and end by ignoring as phantoms – which shows them the hollowness of their disguise. It is a disguise which hides nothing.

[. . .]

17 February 1959

If writing depended on choice I would not write.

. . . Why live until the holocaust? I must have a group to which I can belong; this is a basic need of being deeply grounded in existence. One does not always have to be in a company, but one must know that somewhere there are friends who know us intimately and to whom we are not afraid to make ourselves known: that is the meaning of group.

The arrow that will kill me has already been released. It was released long ago. It will not be a tragic or a heroic death. It will be a choked and managed death. A brief visit from the district nurse. The pulling down of the blinds. People walking softly in the house for three days. The coffin sliding on well-oiled castors. Ashes thrown on the breasts of the wind.

21 February 1959

People should create their society; but what happens is the reverse, society creates people. What ought to be is this: people should create society by the projection of their ability to be virtuous.

. . . Society is like an empty, dry, dead, crocodile sleeping on a river bank, yet all over its inside there are little people moving, and their movements cause the lifeless hulk to move. It ambles forward with lifeless, slow twists off its stomach, and its short feet rise and fall like dead grass in the wind. Inside there is intense activity, but it does not choose a direction; this is left to gravity and the heavy snout and belly of the crocodile.

Yet the people do not create this crocodile; the crocodile is the form, and the form defines the nature of the contents.

22 February 1959
The Maids [6]

Madame is kind, maternal to the maids. When the maids act Madame they celebrate the meaning of this maternalism: Madame thinks her maids are dirty sluts. But this is also how the maids experience themselves, they feel themselves to be full of spit – sluts full of spit. They venerate madam – her scented bosom, her beautiful clothes, her powerful lover. (This lover is full of menacing power.) It is this beauty which makes them dissatisfied with their own experience of themselves; Madame is their foreboding of what might be.

Yet the maids are powerless to become Madame, they are not successful.

This is, I think, because they act in terms of Madame's world – the personae group. In this group there is no escape for them. The more they struggle the more withering the real Madame becomes, and the smaller and more ludicrous they become. They even turn against each other: the two maids love each other and flagellate each other. It is the love of slaves.

To establish themselves as something permanent, as something that exists in its own right in society, as a success – they kill themselves. Madame Claire dies in order that she may live on with Solange, the Lemercier woman, the prisoner. It is the escape from dreams into reality, it is an act, it is a choice . . .

It is the story of Cinderella – from rags to riches. The walls of her palace will be obscured by shit.

Madame and Monsieur will envy madam. Her dissent will invigorate society. The union boss reduces himself to something that society cannot envy; that is one half of his success. And because she remains in society.

Madame Solange will enjoy their envy; this makes personal freedom impossible for her.

[. . .]

2 March 1959

Theatre can serve one of two purposes. It can be an act of social therapy – Aristotle's catharsis. Or it can be propaganda – Euripides' plea for rationalism . . .

Drama must create society; it must not let itself be dictated to by its audience. Ultimately this attitude will draw its audience.

[. . .]

[6] *The Maids* by Jean Genet (1910–1986)

18 March 1959

Goodness isnt related to any particular actions. If I am Robinson Crusoe and I have a tree full of pineapples, my action, if I eat the pineapples, is ethically neutral. If I live in a street, and I am well fed while my neighbour is tortured by starvation, my action, if I eat two pineapples and give none to my neighbour, is ethically bad. Good is something introduced into the world by people; obviously, in one sense, good is a social thing – it concerns the behaviour of man to man. But there is a second sort of good which is purely personal: Crusoe, on his Island, isn't entirely cut off from ethical problems just because he is cut off from other people. There is the good which concerns man in his relation to 'God' – that is, to himself.

If Robinson Crusoe has a humped back, this doesn't upset him at all, so long as he's on his Island. But in a group, Crusoe will notice that he is different. He feels that this hump is a bad thing that has happened to him. This badness is not intrinsically repulsive – on the island it was unnoticed. It is repulsive because it is not normal. This badness can't be blamed on the group; nor can it be blamed on god. If it is blamed on god the social judgement must be twisted. 'The hump is for the humpback's good. God visits those he loves, etc.' But it is still <u>bad</u>, otherwise God would not be testing the humpback; and it still remains true that this judgement of <u>bad</u> is passed by the group. Badness, in this example, is only possible within the group. All lesser deformities are judged in this way, because the group has a standard of physical excellence. This standard is set by choice pieces of humanity and by the pictures, sculptures etc. of artists.

Sexually, some people are attracted by stumps, squints, crookbacks and so on. This is similar to a psychotic attraction to dirt. It is a desecration of the group idea of beauty. It is 'bad' because it is not normal, but it is not harmful. It is probably self-desecration more than group-desecration. (This <u>is</u> all I am good for . . . etc). You can teach children nothing by fear, except to <u>be afraid</u>.

Suppose. Good is a thing fabricated by the group. This doesn't mean that the Good may be an inferior sort of thing. A rich man may feel impelled to give alms to a beggar, because even a rich man knows what it is to want <u>something</u>. Such habits of mind would become part of an inherited make-up. The rich man would not reason about giving, he would feel an impulse to give, which might amount to no more than buying off the gods. This instinct may be debasing. Thus, an influential Aztec would, before going on a journey, sacrifice a human slave.

Can you say that the massacre of the Jews was ethically bad? If good is a group convenience, no. But it is essential that the group should always know what its up to. So one can say the massacre was bad because the reasons for the massacre were bad. It is not true that the brains of an Einstein, or the hands of an Epstein, would debase deutsche kultur.[7] This is what happens when one says that good is a superstition; you get into this theoretical difficulty.

[. . .]

2 April 1959

I am not a materialist. I don't think that men can be explained away by their metabolism, their physiology, their biology. I think the spiritual and artistic moods that occur in man are prompted by his physical condition, in as much as this is the sum total of his being. Gods and types of beauty are no more than his interpretation of this condition. That is, consciousness has risen out of and superseded matter. It is rooted in matter, but it has progressed beyond it, and this gives it a final absolute command over <u>itself</u> but not over matter: consciousness can cease to be. There is now no longer any 'proper' place for matter; it is entirely comparable with the bourgeois who has risen above his station. He has been squeezed out of the tight little world of atoms, he cannot return to them without literally ceasing to be what he is: death. But there is nothing into which he can become, his isolation is complete. A metaphor: he shouts out of the earth into empty space. There are no gods waiting to make him an angel. There is no condition called <u>good</u> into which he can transpose himself. I am not a materialist because man has ceased to be material. His condition is deeply tragic. But there is no rite that can reconcile him to his condition: he can only stare at the bleakness into which he is projected.

If the group is a comforter, a protection from this bleakness, this vastness, then the group is a dangerous hindrance. It will corrupt men until they conform to its patterns, and it will punish them if they are non-conformist; it sets up standards of its own that are completely irrelevant to man.

Now, <u>man has an inclination to tragedy</u>. His natural condition is to be tragic in relation to vastness, bleakness. If man is removed from his tragic setting and transplanted to the group, he will create his tragedy in new terms that are viable in the new setting. But this new tragedy is vulgar – group tragedy is pseudo-tragedy.

---

[7] Jacob Epstein (1880–1959).

Dream: night 2–3 April 1959
3 April 1959

Divided into three parts; only the last part is at all detailed in my memory. Something happened in the house or the place, and because of this I was sent away. This land was a lawn with paths round it. There was a green house with dull glass windows, I could not see what went on inside; besides, I had my head bent down. It was the sort of lawn on which Alice played croquet with flamingos. I think they dug graves there. The lawn could almost have been in a house, there was so little light. I think I didn't cast a shadow, but the whole place was in half-shadow. There were box hedges and perhaps a wall.

When they sent me up from my ward to the children's section (Truro, 1941) I stared one whole morning at a model garden-farm on a table. I was too shy to look up and talk. Later, at Shipee-hill I made gardens out of printed cut-out sheets; there was a green-house there.

I returned to the house. My reasons for returning or going back aren't clear. I had a date with my mother. I know I met her in the house, but this was all forgotten when I found myself in the family bedroom. The details of the room, my father's dress, and the props I used, were all historic. I was sitting on a stack of things: a chest, a case, finally a chair. In my hand a heavy cricket bat. I remember the weight from my childhood. I lent on the marble mantelpiece end against the ugly, old clock (added later) – like either night or day by Michelangelo as they lean over the door. I couldn't see the face. It moved. Perhaps I touched it. It was important. The door up left was open. I heard my father outside. Angry. He comes in as I look down towards the door. Black mack, hat pulled down to ears, carries long thin stick. He looks like a schoolboy but is obviously old.

I am pretending I havent seen my mother. It's a question who speaks to whom first. I'm probably waiting for her to make the first move, I have some sort of historic precedent to justify my attitude. Some other writer took this attitude. My father says: alright, she's getting ready, she's waiting outside there. Also, I have just heard her voice in the hall. Then many things happened at once. I shout: you – its you – you've killed her. I know I've killed her. I'm coming down from my pile of things by the empty fire. He threatens me with his stick. At the same time he crumbles in an absurd, grotesque way, and says: I didn't mean to do it – honest. He is very dangerous, yet with a few swipes I manage to lop off large pieces of his stick: it's child's play. I peer terrified through the French windows. Half-pause. I am playing in the garden. I ask a neighbour. Two things have happened. A something has been got hold of by the lettuce; or the lettuce has been got hold of by a something. I see the lettuce: it is like a twisted green belt. The other thing is that the cat's got the child. My sister is now up the garden, it is her child. I urgently go into the house – to rescue? I can do this now because I have my sister with me. Front room. It is dark. The light is on, but the shade is too thick to let much through. My sister says would you believe it, this is summertime. She doesn't seem to understand the urgency. The pile of bones on the carpet has already reared up and spoken. It can do this because it doesn't have to rise up far: it's only a child – partly my sister's child and partly my mother. But my father, the menace, is still there. Just before the light goes on I know he's behind the armchair. I bring my bat down heavily between the armchair and the wall. I know that's where he's lying. He is another pile of bones. I don't want to see what I've done, but the light comes on as I bring the bat down – perhaps this is a second time. I see his white face, beaked nose. Because his head is bald I call it a skull. My bat smashes through it. It is like an egg shell. I think the house is now safe. I haven't yet seen my mother.

His bones were lying there like a heap from a Roman burial. I'd seen this in the museum at Saffron Walden. Towards the end of the dream I think there were other people in the front room, but I didn't have parts for them all.

The main thing about the dream – in the house, on the lawn, and perhaps in the lost early section – is the menace. I feel I am in the house in Rillington Place where Christie murdered his women. He put some of them in a cupboard, shut it, and wall-papered over the door. The other main thing is the gloom, none of the things reflected light. It was a horrible dream; when I woke (middle of the night) my mind, for a second, seemed to stop belonging to me. It went across the room and belonged to the wall. I think I had a dream once in which I planned the play; in the play I went to Rillington Place and asked to be shown the house; I gave some reason, I was a sociologist or something. The man I had asked said: O yes, they all give that excuse. Some short time before dreaming this I read that years after Christie was hanged there were still sightseers at his house. The council had changed the street name. To what, I wonder?

[. . .]

10 April 1959

A story of a little boy who is taken to a funeral. He is struck by the great attention given to the little girl in the box: this veneration even stops uncle smoking, auntie joking, makes his mother cry one or two tears, subdues his father's voice and so forth. Even better, the hearse is heaped with hundreds of flowers, the car moves as slowly as a coach, and instead of the snatch of a lullaby three hymns are sung right through. So the little boy wants to die, to be dead as the little girl in the box. He asks his mother how can he die? He cries when she scolds him and tells him he must wait.

[. . .]

23 April 1959

There was a mother whose child was dead in her womb.

A great doctor had come to the town a few weeks before. He had cured a child of beriberi, cured an old woman on her deathbed, and quieted a mad dog by smiling at it. The mother asked the doctor to bring the child in her belly alive.

The doctor said: I will, but I must warn you of this. The child will live but you will go blind.

The mother worked it out: I have no one to love, and so I hoped to love my child, and I know my child would love me. If I bear him he will soon grow up and then he can lead me and help me with his eyes. I shall have his eyes and his love; for, because I am blind, he will have a way in which he can show me even more love than if I could see.

So the doctor made the child live (by spitting in the mother's mouth), and it soon grew up. It was very helpful in the home, it swept the floor, cut up its mother's meat, chopped the wood, hung the curtains and picked the apples.

But it also had to go to school, and so the mother spent the bigger part of every workday sitting by the window in the front of the house. When the child came home from school he could see her sitting inside this window even when he was a long way down the road; and – this was the odd thing – she was talking. He was afraid to ask her what she was saying because he thought: she will think I spy on her.

He tried creeping up the path, silently opening the door, turning his key in the lock, and tiptoeing up the stairs to her door. But when he gently pushed her door open she had always stopped talking; she sat in the window with her hands in her lap and with her mouth shut and sometimes smiling a little. She knew her child was in the house.

The child wanted very much to know what his mother said, and so he worked out a plan. The next day when he came home from school he didn't go into the house. Instead he very carefully and slowly climbed up the drain pipe. When he was level with her window he reached across and pulled himself onto the sill.

But his mother talked very softly and the glass was thick – he couldn't make out a single word. After a while he decided to climb down to the earth. But when he reached out to the drainpipe it seemed to have moved away from him, and the drop from the sill to the ground had become ten times as big. He turned to tap on the window – but no, she would think he was spying; she wouldn't say anything angry or unkind, but she would be deeply hurt. He looked at her face. The mouth was opening and shutting, the Adam's apple jerked and swung and bulged, he could see little furrows in the enamel of her teeth, her skin glistened.

He sat on the sill with his back to the window. Once a man passed in the street, but the child didn't dare to shout: If only I hadn't left my school books on the ground by the drain I could throw those at him! He pulled a button from his trousers and threw it, but the man had passed by and the button didn't reach him.

It got dark, and the child was hungry and cold. He screwed up his courage and clawed out to grab the pipe, he missed it, fell to the ground and broke his neck.

The mother went on talking. After a while she began to worry: What has become of my child?

Still talking she stood up and groped her way round the room. She knocked a chair down.

O dear, I am hungry!

She opened the door and groped her way down the dark stairs. Still talking she crept into every room and felt the surfaces of the pots, the backs of the chairs, the tabletops, feeling for his face.

She opened the front door and felt the cold air on her face and hands. She put one hand out to touch the wall and groped her way right round the house. She was still talking. She felt the rough brick on her fingers, and sometimes the smoothness of paint or wire.

She came to the drain and stumbled over the child's legs. She knelt down and felt his clothes and his hard shoes. She poked a finger into the coils of his ear. Then she just knelt by him and talked and talked and talked.

27 April 1959

Is it possible for an act within the group to be a good act? As people are not always at their worst there must be a scale of goodness. But this is a very limited statement; it loses most of its meaning if there is a strict, uninterrupted historical decline in the group.

If a man is cured of cancer his doctor has performed a good act: this is not necessarily a true statement. It sometimes happens that a man who is to be hanged is given medical treatment to make him fit for hanging.

Then, also, there is the story of the Bad Samaritan. He went to the man set upon by thieves and took him to an inn, but there he held him kidnapped for a ransom; and when he received the ransom he killed the man so that he could not tell the authorities the whereabouts of the hideaway. No act can in itself be called <u>good</u>. If society is preparing for its final immolation, then all acts in society are bad.

No act is good. But if there is goodness the goodness is not something added to an act by the actor. This is because the intention behind an act is irrelevant. An old woman bends down and helps up a boy who has slipped over; the little boy thinks the woman is a witch; he dashes out into the road and is killed by a lorry. <u>The Well of the Saints</u> is another example of this sort of tragedy. Objectively a good act can only be judged by its effect. It follows, then, that there is no such thing as a good act; and, at its best, doing good is accidental.

Yet it is certainly possible for good to occur in society; some people who are in society wish to leave it, and this is a good thing. Goodness is not an intention, it is an attitude. A thing can only be good for oneself, and anything can be good for oneself. But there can be no good unless it is outside of the group or part of the mechanics of escape from the group. This is because the final stage of society is bad – it is the immolation, and remaining in society makes the immolation your intention.

[. . .]

Things 7 May 1959

If emotions are grounded in the personality, and one chooses one's personality, obviously one isn't a slave of one's emotions. But what is 'it' that chooses the personality? When nothingness is in the world it necessitates the creation of an instrument by which it may inhabit the world (this is the body). This is putting the cart before the horse. One is aware that one is not really here, the body is not an adequate explanation; one is also aware that one is not oneself, personality is not an adequate explanation. What one is essentially only becomes a problem because one finds oneself, one knows oneself, as a category which one is not. It may be that what one is not precedes what one is; that is, one has outgrown oneself. If that is so the wish to return to the simplicity of things is reactionary, a desire to abdicate from increased awareness. But if what-one-is-not is the consequence of what-one-is <u>being here</u>, then what-one-is is responsible for one's <u>being here</u>, and what-one-is-not is the form in which it expresses itself: things are the creation of one's nothingness, in the sense that they become created for our awareness by the 'pressure' of the nothingness of what one is. If this is true, then in order for one's awareness to become aware of the nothingness of what one is, one should get to know <u>things</u>. Things, as it were, project our nothingness back to us. There is a slight confusion here about the genesis of <u>awareness</u>. We become peculiarly <u>aware</u> of things in the movement of consciousness; yet I have also said that this awareness is as a result of the pressure of nothingness; but if, in order to accommodate the first form, I say that our nothingness created our awareness in order that we should know things, and so know itself, I am cancelling out the direct relationship between our nothingness and things, expressed in the statement: 'things are created by the pressure of our nothingness', and so it is difficult to see the validity of the second form; since if one is aware of things (through the pressure of nothingness) but these things are <u>not</u> there through the pressure of nothingness, becoming aware of them does not teach us anything about, or put us into a relation with, our nothingness.

11 May 1959

I don't think it is possible for a member to leave the group without damaging it. People even within the group remain free in a certain sense – we cannot make their choices for them. If they choose to be hurt, offended or angered by our departure – that is their choice. And the group has chosen that out of every event it will make the capital of misery and violence. Our rejection of society is bound to be interpreted by society as an attack upon itself.

The problem of disassociation is therefore left to the individual; how he solves it, or rather whether he solves it, will be an outward proof of his freedom. If he thinks he can leave society by making a scene, by staging an attack, he clearly isn't free; his action is dictated by the pleasure he gets from leaving; he will go away and sulk or scream in a corner; he is very much a member of the group.

The free departure isn't ironical, either. Irony is a defence for the freeman when he finds himself in the serf-society, it tides him over. A man converted to Christianity is exhorted to repent <u>at once</u>; because in the next second the last trumpet may have sounded and it will be too late; this is a sort of debasement of Kierkegaard's <u>instant</u>. The convert throws himself into the arms of god; the freeman doesn't have this refuge; he is forced to calculate, and this calculation is the first use he makes of his freedom.

Why can't he stay in the group even after he has seen its rottenness? The answer to this implies an absolute standard of values: he wishes to be better than the group; that means he <u>is</u> better than the group and he wants to have the chance for his goodness to operate. He can't help anybody else (qualify this) because this would be an interference with their freedom, but he can help himself; his attitude to the group is positive, not an attitude of disgust, but an attitude of boredom. He is measurelessly fatigued if he has to go through the shallow, meaningless rituals of the group. Freedom implies not merely freedom of the mind but also freedom of the body. If he remains in the group he can exercise his mental freedom, but his body is surrendered to economic and social slavery; and this is equally true of his spoken and published ideas. The freeman, then, sets about rescuing his body; he wishes to own his body; in the group it is mortgaged out to others.

[. . .]

15 May 1959

Every man is a perfect individual, because he is what he is, but all societies are hell.

[. . .]

What should be the purpose of plays? Obviously this is about the effect the play should have on the audience. Serious theatre cant be concerned only with entertainment: we only have time for entertainment in Utopia, and then we don't need it. People must relax sometimes; but the very nature of theatre precludes mere entertainment. Theatre engages its audience; and while they are in the theatre the dramatist (and his assistants) is responsible for them.

The classical theatre tried to give its audience an emotional experience (catharsis). But this experience is not merely emotional – and this is a very important point. Classical theatre was intensely serious, and Euripides, Sophocles and Aeschylus all presented their audience with a mature philosophy which taught them how to act the business of their lives. But there are two ways of presenting this philosophy. The Aristotelian theatre of Aeschylus, Sophocles and Aristophanes committed the audience in the action of the play, a direct appeal was made to their emotions, and this was meant to convince the audience of the truth of the intellectual superstructure of the play; simply, brainwashing by laughter or terror . . .

20 May 1959

Theatre should demonstrate the action of emotions and show the group personality, but it should not do this by preying on the audience's emotional susceptibility. It is a question of object; I (the writer) want to contact the self behind the emotions and make it articulate, embody it in intention. I assume that I can only do this by <u>going through</u> the screen of emotions which surrounds each member of the audience. The events on the stage must not be so compulsive that they compel emotion in the audience, the spectator mustn't be the passive part of a joint orgasm; the play must not be a record of what the audience secretly want to be, but do not dare to be, this would be fulfilment and make the theatre an end in itself. The stage must show people what they are, and show them that this isnt good enough. The audience should be brought face to face with the hollowness of their personalities and the mediocrity of their condition.

The Fascist – 21 May 1959

There was a dwarf. When he was a boy he grew slower than other boys; so he liked to mix with strangers who thought he was younger than he was in fact, and took him to be normal size. His doctor had said, when the boy was only a baby, that he would stop growing altogether on his 17th birthday, and he would never grow taller than a 12-year-old boy. How bitterly and happily he lived his youth and first manhood; other people let this time slip by, but for him every moment was frantic and beautiful and tense; people were dazzled by the beauty that shone in him. And years later, when people despised him, kids jeered at him, dogs barked at him, and babies were afraid of him, he looked back on this time very often. He carried it about with him like an unshareable secret. He was a special person: he had lived in the golden age. He was a fascist.

Theatre can use emotions, but emotional stimulation should not be the object of theatre. Theatre is sanitation, it should flush away the emotional excesses that cling to people like clinkers on a sheep's arse. How is this different from the aristotelian purging? Empathy is the identification of the emotional self with the emotions that are symbolized in the actors' faces and gestures, and the play's plot and staging; it is therefore an articulation of the emotional self, it confirms and strengthens the emotional self. The 'free' theatre does just this, it wants to reach the no-centre of the individual so that his emotional pretence falls like rotten hoardings. It isnt, then, simply a critical scientific theatre; it is a 'spiritual' theatre, a philosophical theatre, a desperate theatre, which wishes to make men concrete instead of – as the aristotelian theatre makes them – vapid, stinking marsh gasses, latrine odours, or – as the scientific theatre makes them: automatic hardening [of] their jungle instincts under a veneer of boredom or logic. It doesn't want to make him think – thinking is too often vitiated by logic-emotion; it wishes to do something – it is a catharsis, or rather a <u>marking</u> of intellectual intention. It must make everything strange, it must make man a stranger to himself.

[. . .]

23 May 1959

Being amused, entertained, <u>diverted</u>, takes one away from oneself. Now this doesn't mean taking persona away from itself: it means diverting attention from 'urge' that nags persona on to destruction. The nagging is the sense of the bogusness of the activity. This is an instructive point: obviously the awareness of this bogusness can never be removed while the bogus activity is performed. Entertainment is something after this sort: instead of undertaking the bogus activity oneself one for the time being allows it to be acted out by the entertainment and the entertainers. Obviously this 'passing the buck' is itself fraudulent and bogus; it is a further instance of self-deceit.

But there is another possibility. Revolutionaries sing revolutionary songs: these keep up their fervour. And some sorts of entertainment or all sorts in some ways, do this. They crystallize the normally diffuse and slip-shod self-destruction of the group. How does this divert? It does not divert the nagging; the persona has become completely identified in itself, it is as if one had a picture taken of oneself and this picture then took on a life of its own: the role is this animated picture. The more stimulated and active the role the more it becomes itself – the sense of alienation from its true self; in other words, it is more itself (<u>happy</u> – happiness is the extent to which one becomes what one is) when it is nagged more. And it is the job of entertainment to do this: take one-self out of oneself into the picture. Objectively speaking, then, the more one is entertained the unhappier one is.

Entertainment is a leprosy. Entertainment diverts us from the activity of being with things: it makes everything old, because when one is aware of things they are new.

There is no God, and Why this is Good

If there was a God he could not be the God of Love. He would be a perverted, obscene, wicked, vindictive thug. Only such a person would let omnipotence be degraded by the filth of this world. Look at the rotten limbs of a little paralytic. It is much better for us that there isn't a God. If there was a God we would be the toys – not even the guinea pigs – of a perverted, evil monster; we would not stand a chance of being good. If there was a God we would all be predestined for sin; we would be crushed before we took our first breath; we would be his excrement; no man, or God, can create something that is not in him; if we were created by a God we would faithfully mirror his personality. It is no solution to emasculate God and give people the free choice of evil and good: we would still have to have derived our freedom from God. This would mean, then, that not merely would God be free to do evil, but also that in creating man he had done it. Anyway, God could not create freedom and only a monster would create freedom if it meant giving men the possibility of doing evil. Freedom is a blessing to man because it means that it is possible for him to be good. But the first creator would not have been troubled with this – unless he was mad. Or you could say: good = not doing evil, therefore the choice is necessary to being good. So it is, for men – but <u>again</u> not for God. God could not create men, he could only create other Gods. Therefore there is no distinction between men and God; and since all men are limited by finitude, and God isn't, it follows that there is no God.

It's better for us that there is no God: man still has a chance.

25 May 1959

I have had difficulty in choosing a title for my play. I started by calling it: <u>Refusal to Mourn</u>, but I have rejected it because it is romantic. I next called it: <u>Part</u>.[8] This was an apology, I wanted to defend the play against left-wing critics; I also felt bound to defend political and social action. In doing this I was justifying my own conduct: I organized an appeal for Peter Manuel and I have done some work for the Campaign for Nuclear Disarmament.[9]

A title is not only a convenient reference for the play; it also indicates the author's attitude to the play. <u>Chicken Soup with Barley</u> is a good title: it indicates the author's rational attitude to his characters and plot.[10] This title is descriptive of something ordinary; the characters in the play are ordinary, and the author doesn't comment on them, he describes them. This description is so accurate, and is so turned towards the essential, that the characters, and <u>their</u> plot, themselves become

---

[8] In a letter to the editor, 21 January 1999, Bond states: "*Refusal to Mourn*" (glad I rejected that) "*Part*" (I quite like this) I don't know what play it refers to . . . I think it may well be the "family" play . . .'

[9] Peter Manuel was hung for murder. Bond describes his CND work as 'driving round in a van with a loudspeaker on top announcing meetings and rallies'.

[10] *Chicken Soup with Barley*, by Arnold Wesker, was first performed on 7 July 1958 at the Belgrade Theatre, Coventry.

comment. <u>Hamlet of Stepney Green</u> is a vulgar, romantic title; it is meant to have the shock effect of the cynical overlapping of a standard association; the whole play is like this, bringing a few jerks back into a corpse by pulling its leg. (It is a pity, but you can't bring a corpse to life by pulling its leg.)

26 May 1959

I have reached the point where I ought to make some general statements and hope they mount up to a point of view.
1. There is no God.
2. The creation of life was fortuitous.
3. Man has grown out of himself.
4. Because of 3. he is isolated.

These four articles describe man's situation. Man has evolved from the thing-elements that litter the universe, and he has developed consciousness just as a man who rises to his feet sees to a greater distance; as he sees his environment he sees his detachment from it, he is completely isolated in himself, there is no beneficent deity to help him and no devil to damn him. (God is a metaphor.) He is the product of the sequence of events that have led to him, and in this way he <u>is</u> all that has been. Yet consciousness is not a piercing light: man is in doubt about the nature of his awareness. Evolution is no answer, because awareness enables men to take charge: they are no longer the tools of blind instincts, they have to choose. Undoubtedly consciousness would evolve into a greater clarity, perhaps it would percolate through all things until the whole world became a group-awareness. But speculation of this sort is pointless. People don't want to lose their individuality; although there are no grounds for supposing that an evolution of consciousness would result in a greater sense of individuality; the time that we have to measure the trend, whichever way it is, is far too short to make any honest decision possible.

Consciousness should increase as men make more choices. The developing body is like a horse-shoe fashioned by the hammer blows of its environment; but consciousness is like a bellows that blow on a fire. Consciousness is (that means, <u>should be</u>) active, the body is passive.

There are two stages (at least) of development in a person. The passive body which is beaten by the hammers, and the active mind.

Psychosomatic action. Is it the old problem of soul versus body?

[. . .]

War Story 29 May 1959

The mother had a child who yelled and screamed and kicked. How can I describe it? He called up the big men in the German forest, and they came over the sea and flew through the air and attacked the city. The other little boy and the two sisters were sent to the country, where it was safe. They were at the station sitting in a train; the little boy wanted to get out of the carriage, toddle up to the train and drive it away; probably he'd have driven it off the track and straight through the city. But he stayed in the carriage with his two little sisters.

In the country he wanted to look after them, he wanted to protect them; but they were older and bigger than he and so they mothered him. The water was bad and many people died in the village. They opened up new cemeteries full of mass-produced, commercial graves; and flowers that came from behind the glass windows of town shops: they were not a bit like the flowers of the fields or the poppies or blue stars the gypsies sold.

The little boy often saw big silver balloons in the sky, tied to the earth by a black steel hawser. Once he found the concrete emplacement where a balloon had been fastened to the ground. There were barbed-wire fences, and a red board with white letters stencilled on it: DANGER – KEEP OUT. There was a derelict wooden mission hut; the hot sun made the paint smell like an animal. A window had been broken; and there was fresh water in a rough-made tin bird bath. Through the water he saw the bright rusty sides.

The wind blew over the heath and through his hair: it was warm. The sun bleached the growing grass until it looked and smelt like hay. The big men in blue had driven off in a large, snorting lorry. He found an empty cigarette packet and a page of Blighty.[11] The lorry tracks had crushed the grass.

The site was deserted; there wasn't even a bird in the blue sky. On the ground he found concrete stumps; a wide concrete platform that had been set into the grass; iron rings plugged deep into cement; and the grass fluttered around the edge; he lay flat in the grass, reached out and pressed his palm on the concrete base: it was hot and had the texture of goose-pimples.

[. . .]

---

[11] Bond observes in a letter to the editor, 21 January 1999: ' "Blighty" was, I think, the name of a magazine – it had been popular with soldiers in the war and was probably tottering on in a last after-life. I imagine it's the sort of magazine described in the cellar at the end of [*In the*] *Company* [*of Men*].' *In the Company of Men* is published in *Edward Bond Plays: 5* (London: Methuen, 1996).

Paper – 16 June 1959

The sheet of thin tissue paper was about 12 by 18 inches. A young girl, with big brown hands, wrapped two grapefruit in it, and packed them in a box with other grapefruit. The box then went by train to London – it was just wooden slats fastened by wire onto a wooden frame: it smelt very strongly of wood.

In the large central market. The grapefruits were laid out for display on a ramp. The gold peel and the white tissue were very beautiful. Soon the grapefruit were bought, and the paper was put into the basket with them. The woman started to carry the basket through the street. Suddenly two of her red, fat fingers jabbed into the basket, ripped the paper from the fruit, and threw it into the gutter.

It would have been hosed into the sewer, or swept up and burnt, but a boy found it. He said 'This is just what I needed for my new kite'. He had already made the kite frame. This was made of thin strips of wood nailed together; and a brand new cord had been fastened at the corners. The boy carefully glued the paper to this frame; and then, when the glue had dried, he took his new kite to the fields and flew it. The kite rushed higher and higher in the air. The paper could hear the wind rushing under its feet: it was very proud and excited. Sometimes the kite lurched violently down, but always it landed safely in the wind and rose even higher.

Blackbirds. They were far away. Suddenly they were very close. To see the paper they had to face away from it because their eyes were in the side of their heads. Wings up, wide-spread feathers; then down, black, hitting, angry. Yellow beaks. They all peck. They scream and fly in and rip and tear and puncture the paper. The kite sinks. The little boy hates his kite; he throws it away.

The wind blows the kite up the hill into a thorn bush. The kite frame spreads the paper out over the thorns and the wind tears it.

A poet, who has forgotten his books, takes the kite from the bush. He rips the paper from the frame. He is going to write on it. He is going to write a poem to his girl. Then the girl comes over the hill. She wears a white dress and has golden hair. The poet throws the paper away. He hasn't written a word on it. He runs to the girl. I think they are like young lambs.

The paper is by itself for a month. It blows through many fields, a village and a wood. A sheep gobbled it and spat it out. Then two little boys find it. They set it up on their boat. It is a white sail. The boat slips over the rippling water, like a mouse cautiously coming out of its hole in brisk little darts. The boys throw stones at the ship. It is broken and sinks. The paper is rushed along through the river.

A huge iron sheet with a great iron fist. The fist falls on the river. It is like the collapse of a city. The river screams and leaps up. The water is white hot. The fist buries itself in the heart of the mud. It rips out a chunk of river bed and stuffs it away in the iron hold. The paper is in this mud. It is ferried out to the deep.

A Sea Story

A man stepped into a boat and started his journey. When he was far out at sea a great storm began. The waves and the wind ripped off the deck and the cabin. They even ripped off the plank sides, so that the man was sailing in the cage of wooden ribs.

He was quite safe. The sharks had flat bull snouts, which they could not poke in between the ribs. They could not even nibble through the wood because they had thick, quivering lips, and their teeth were set far back behind these. All they could do was worry their snouts against the wood. Some of them bled. The blood came in little brown spurts in the water. They had eyes that were like heel marks in muddy puddles.

The boat came to an island. It was a beautiful, fruitful island. The man fed and slept well and played in the lagoon. There were bright corals at the mouth to keep the sharks and stingrays out. He decided to continue his journey. He cut planks from fallen trees and nailed these on in the inside of his old hull frame.

He went to sea again. Again the storm blew up and ripped off the deck and a little tent he had made. It also ripped off the side planks; but as the planks were nailed to the inside of the frame so that the ribs were nailed to the outside of the planks, the ribs were ripped off with the planks. The man fell into the sea and the sharks ate him.

[. . .]

21 June 1959

I have come across this idea before, in a different form. The stage event is orderly, there is no real danger of Hamlet being poisoned and stabbed by the same blade (notice how Hamlet suffers both his father's and his mother's deaths in the one cut, and how he then identifies his father with himself by making his father's death a double-death), and his genuine security is emphasized by all the nice calculation of the stage designing and lighting and the careful patterns of movement that the actors make. No drama is probably far more powerful as <u>total emotion</u> than western drama; this is because the mockery, the element of order, is emphasized. Even chaos, when it is represented onstage, is really order, because it is there, it is captured; and it is almost certainly more drilled than a static scene which on the face of it represents true order. It is right that drama is traditionally represented by the two faces.

There is ambivalence. The tragic mask grimaces at the jeering mask: it is the symbol of insecurity. And the jeering mask laughs at the tragic mask: it is the symbol of security. This is the idea I have come across before – order is chaos. This isn't merely because we never quite feel secure, we do not believe that our good luck, or whatever it is, can last. A mask is a face that has laughed its head off and cried its eyes out: that is drama, the total experience. The mask – the papiermâché – hiding real horror, either in the form of the clown (the false smile) or in the form of the tragedian (to whom we relate ourselves as the clown). It deliberately brings to the boil all our emotions, which are certainly violent, but lets us experience them in a safe form. Cartharsis is not the washed-out, hopeless feeling of the condemned cell: it is vicious, we have taken out the god in us for an airing, and instead of acting out our urges in a moment of violence, we let them go on simpering inside us just off the boil – with disastrous results to society. Admittedly the results are not as disastrous as the results of giving way to our emotions: it is better to watch a play-acted mockery of a crime than to do the crime, at least from society's point of view. But this is a false alternative. This acting-out in mockery reconciles us to the violence in our nature, it even tones it up. It is like religion, it reconciles men to evil. There is no place for emotion in the theatre; the theatre can be more constructive than that.

I cannot solve the problem just like that; but there is a solution as long as you don't hinder yourself with the theory of dialectical materialism, as Brecht did; but the present school of young writers has not even faced up to the problem – Arnold Wesker writes like a disciple of Arthur Miller, John Arden is looking back to the Elizabethans, which will turn out to be as abortive as the attempts of the bright young things to make this glorious reign a second Elizabethan age (we have the pirates but not the ships), and Ann Jellicoe sums up the new plays, including her own, as a direct appeal to our emotions.

The new drama should not be an arid, unpopular experience; it was Brecht, and not the neo-Ibsens, who found a role for music and poetry on the modern stage. And his music and poetry are not merely decorative, they are a functional part of the play.

[. . .]

6 July 1959

I am attracted by bomb sites and building sites. The symbolism of the straight walls has not completely overcome the lush 'chaotic order' of nature: nature is romantic, if it is to be classical it must be seen from a distance.

I am also attracted by wide, concrete motor roads, with little strips on either side for the pedestrians: it is the immense commerce and industry that has gone into making the vacant through-way. If the road is crowded with cars there is no attraction, it is the desolation that attracts me, and one or two lonely cars – or better still, lorries – roaring past. Railway tracks also have this atmosphere. This is true even of city railway tracks. They bring in to the city some of the unruly country, it is heaped up on either side of the track: there are pebbles, and tough oily grass; at the top of the bank are hedges and a few trees, and streaking through the leaves and grass there are the electric cables and the iron guard fences.

[. . .]

Trip [12]

Odyssey. Go on. Set out. Put one foot before the other. Push the door back on the stiff hinge. Look down carefully. Watch the foot on the step. Shuffle it forward. Slowly, slowly – it'll wait. Is it possible that I ever tied those laces? Those <u>hawsers</u>. And the great welt of the boot like a raft.

I have been on this street for a long time. Perhaps fifty years. I don't know. Sometimes I turn my head back and look. I see the open door. All I see of the inside of that house is the black strip of the open door. At the top the black strip is like a short pennant pointed towards the hinge. I have left the door open. I want the wind to slam it shut. There is a key under the hair doormat. Even if the key has gone there is its impression in the dust. I can make a wax pattern. You can easily buy candles. From the wax pattern cut a metal key. That is locksmith's work. It would be easy if the wind slammed the door. As it is I worry. And another thing, the birds nest in my hair. My hair is caulked and petrified with their limings. They do not even build a nest in my hair, my hair is shaped like an iron nest. White, grey, streaks of black, and a few pale blue shadows. They seem to be comfortable. Sometimes they fight and break the eggs. The yellow yoke has trickled down my neck and behind my ears. It is dry now.

I must look a sight. The rain has made my cheeks black. I wear my

[12] 'Trip' comes from an entry in Bond's notebook dated 7 July 1959.

long silk house coat. I stole it from the French brothel where they overcharged me. It was Madam's. There are velvet cuffs. They are worn; the velvet is threadbare; they are like the cassocks where men kneel, old men with wispy hair and shiny knees. I have many large rings screwed in my fingers. They are my knuckle dusters. I have a white stick. If ever someone does come I shall poke him. Let me tell you some more about my face. My mouth is pursed like an ancient anus and the old hair on my cheeks streaks down like the water stains from gutterings. But if I excite myself I can make my lips deep mauve and oily. They split and smile charmingly like an erotic Buddha. There is a mystery about my eyes. If you glance at them you see a few white lashes protruding from pink hoods that look like uninflamed styes. You would think that the eyeballs are dry. No, they are doey, velvety eyes, with sweeping, oily, black lashes on the upper and lower lids. They are soft eyes. Moist. The pupils are deep violet. And look how perfect my cuticles are, and my nails are so clean. Well they were. Now they look like the stumps of weather-beaten fencing, I have been on the street too long. Old goat's neck, I have worn out my soles. Someone stole my lace-ups. I was sleeping at the time. He had the greater need, he was in carpet slippers. He left the slippers for me. There are still a few shreds about the toes. The uppers have rotted away. The little leather rims round the holes for the feet are there. They are still round my ankles. I don't know what I wear under my black robe. How the birds have soiled the back! Fortunately, I stoop over the front. If I meet someone I can meet them face to face. Look them straight in the eye. Keep a firm grip on the stick. I don't let the weather upset me. Whatever it is I wear it against my skin like underclothing. I feel the weather against my skin. But perhaps I don't like the rain. I have been on the street too long.

One day I shall reach the lamppost. The dogs piss there, why can't I? Green. Ornate. Victorian. Which reminds me, I must look very superior. It is the glass bowl that draws me. All the metal is painted green. At the head of the post a gallows beam juts over the pavement. In the angle of the bracket metal curlicues. More bunchy curlicues support the light box. The floor of the light box is a dusty, oily metal square. From its four corners rise thin strong supports up to the top square. The top square is larger than the bottom square. Between these supports are the four glass sheets. I'll tell you about those. But first, the top square. The four segments of the diagonals rise to the raised intersection. At the intersection there are more metal curlicues above the floor. And will they have taken away the streetlamp? I don't want them to light it. I don't ask them to squander their taxes. But it costs nothing to leave it where it is. It does no one any harm.

Perhaps it is so.

[. . .]

Notes for report on Eleven Men Dead at Hola Camp[13]
13 August 1959

You are dealing with two separate things: the presentation of actual political events (all social events are political events) and an attempt at elucidating the characters of the improvisers. The question which you ask – and which is meant to unite these two things, factual and fantastic, is this: what is it in people that results in certain political actions?

If you use the personalities of the improvisers to create an authentic presentation of a political event, you are putting the cart before the horse; this is because an improviser doesn't work outward to the factual event, but inward to his fantasy. The improviser cannot act out a factual event – if he does this he becomes an actor. The actor needs a dramatist and a producer, at the very least; nothing should be left to his fantasy, because this will always result in the distortion or obscuring of the facts. The improviser, on the other hand, cannot act out a factual event; he can only be given a situation to start from, and he then develops this as a fantasy.

The factual actors' presentation can never be social therapy, in the meaning of a curing process. Empathy is not therapeutic. As far as the audience goes, there is no difference between a staged mock-lynching and an actual lynching, except that one is safe. The ultimate empathetic situation is to actually be a member of a lynching crowd, and no one would say that this is a therapy; the mock-lynching is only as far as we dare go; the mistake is to imagine that when we only go as far as this we are in some way refraining from going any further; sublimation is training for the real thing. Do you think that the Nazis took a fetid interest in sport because it would sublimate the animal instincts of their young men and make them less warlike?

The improviser doesn't perform on the grand scale of political events, his improvisations must be essentially domestic and intimate. His character must be given free run, and this should result in virile social comment. The problem is to develop a technique for projecting the improvisation to a paying audience without at the same time spoiling the spontaneity of the improvisers. In the first two paragraphs of your

---

[13] According to Bond, Hola Camp was a prison camp in Rhodesia/Zimbabwe where an atrocity was committed that resulted in the death of eleven prisoners. These notes relate to a one-off performance at the Royal Court, which included improvisation and rehearsal pieces.

conclusions you speak of rehearsing your actors for three months because without this the improvisations are not dramatically satisfying, and at the same time of wanting people to come straight out of the audience and improvise. Of course an audience would be more tolerant of its own members who came forward and so their inefficiency at improvising would be excused: but this isn't the point, the point is: which method will most fully reveal the character of the improviser? I think that rehearsing does not increase the therapeutic value of improvising (if there is any), probably it does just the opposite.

The great value – for us now – of improvisation is that it breaks up the rigor mortis of the theatre.

Four half hour periods are too long. Three half hour periods with two intervals – at any rate to begin with. The audience should be asked to buy season tickets for a series of three performances – so that the audience can be conditioned to what goes on.

If you are going so far as to introduce the audience to the stage I can't see why your permanent team of improvisers all have to be actors. Actors, when they improvise, tend to be sloppy and wet – they find it difficult to stop acting; they don't always grasp the point of an improvisation – this is especially true if you don't just give them an initial situation, but tell them to act out an event; this is what was going wrong with the Man's imitation. Keith was absolutely right to interrupt this – but he lost the sympathy of the audience because they did not understand what an improvisation is, and because anyway Keith and Bill were asking the improvisers to improvise something that could not be an improvisation – it had to be a fact.[14] You need one or two writers in the team. Cf Wolly.[15]

If you rehearse a permanent team for any length of time the members of the team will invent stock types and conventions. C[ommedia] d[ell]'A[rte]. If this happens you have excellent theatre but no therapy. This is because when the improviser acts inward to his fantasy, the context of the improvisation must create its own form; what is important, as therapy, is to watch this character created, not to see the improviser adopt the particular character that will get the most out of a situation. (This growing into a character might be therapeutic for the actor but not for the audience. Who is your therapy supposed to benefit?)

Obviously you haven't the time for this in the theatre; the whole scheme would have to be piecemeal. I think it isn't true to call therapy

[14] Keith Johnstone and Bill Bryden.
[15] Wole Soyinka.

any performance in the theatre – under any circumstances we are likely to see for the time being.

If you go on with your plans I think that certainly improvisation can't be prevented from becoming a very popular and stimulating form of entertainment. It could well become a powerhouse for good social ideas – though this has got nothing immediately to do with therapy. They probably have a great future as a sort of political club – the revue sort that have been popular in Germany and France but haven't been attempted in this country.

Onstage the actors must be much more informal. Get rid of that awful row of chairs in the background: it looked like the waiting room of a local national assistance board. Ann should serve coffee: The improvisers should use the bars in the intervals and mix in with the audience.[16] Why not invite some of the audience onstage as spectators, or even sell seats onstage? Unless the audience understand the difference between the factual acting and the fantastic improvising they will be confused. If, therefore, you want your programmes to be partly factual you must ensure that the factual sequences are kept quite separate from the improvisations: it is imperative that if there is any dialogue in them it should be written, rehearsed; if you avoid dialogue – as you did when you dramatized excerpts from the Hola reports – you must still say quite clearly who is responsible for the selection of the facts and the treatment given to them.

[. . .]

Further notes on Hola Improvisations 20 August 1959

The improvisations, then, are not therapeutic. But as long as you don't tell people this you should be able to get them financed by the national health service. You will have to get the psychiatric departments of the larger London hospitals interested (stressing that their interest must be purely fraternal, they mustn't be allowed to interfere). You must also interest places like the Portland Clinic, and you must be ready to badger Whitehall day and night. There's not much public money available for art, but there's plenty for medicine. If you are performing – as a <u>working</u> team – in youth clubs you will of course be financed by one of the large foundations that run full time clubs. The L[ondon] C[ounty] C[ouncil] should help. You needn't feel morally bound not to take money from the L.C.C; when you take money from industry you are already committing the sin that Major Barbara balked at (this puts you

---

[16] Ann Jenkins, the business manager at the Royal Court.

on Shaw's side – Shaw would have shouted for Barrabas every time). This should come some way towards paying for the experiments; the rest of the money can be made up by asking people to endow an actor during the run of the rehearsal period. This is the genius behind the scheme for asking industry to back particular plays – bosses actually see something tangible in return for their money, there is something actual about which they can boast. The daily sketch once offered a man as first prize in a contest – you had to say what would make up a good, readable, intelligent paper, or something. Now if you ask fairly rich people to Endow an Actor for say three months – you have a very marketable project on your hands, they feel they are buying a man, and this crystallizes their aspirations. Unfortunately buying a man for three months will be too cheap for the richer industrialists, but surely this only means that you are broadening the appeal of your scheme? Many not so rich people will be able to prescribe. Naturally they will want to see their man and perhaps ask him to tea: the actor must accept this as part of the conditions in the modern theatre. The scheme could also be extended to writers. The actor will enjoy meeting the people who have bought him. An elementary knowledge of psychology will assure you that the writer will not enjoy meeting the people who have bought him. Nevertheless these people will expect to see something, so they will be introduced to a writer but not to the writer they bought. We writers must be prepared to put in an appearance for each other; the idea that knowing actually what is financing our writer-friends will give us a moral edge over them, is fictitious – writers are not so degenerate as that. This method will enable a book-keeping entry to save the writers' souls, and their self-respect. (Those who can't afford to Endow a Writer for three or four months should be encouraged to buy a few hours of writer's time – always the time of a particular writer, that is the whole gist of the scheme). (The scale of charges should be graded to allow for the value of the activity of the writer, during the time bought.) By suiting the scheme to every pocket in this way you can be sure of extending the facilities of the welfare state. Now that there are projects for workers' shares, workers' cheques, and societies to protect the workers against the exploitation of the trade unions, it is only fair that the workers should be encouraged to become patrons of art. (When I talk about workers I mean those people whose salaries are not so large as the salaries of other people.) The only way to take a pride in art is to invest in it. Of course, the worker will not receive a money return on his art; but we have reached the stage of affluence when the worker can afford to invest his money for other, prestige reasons. He will, of course, expect to be issued with a printed share certificate. This, I am afraid, will have to be gaudy, as it is intended to be framed and hung on the wall between the pictures of the local territorial company and the family on a day trip to Boulogne. It will have to be intricately printed as if in an attempt to frustrate forgery; this will show it has some value.

[. . .]

Activity against the group 24 August 1959

I doubt if I can have such an effect on the group that I can head off the nuclear immolation! Yet this doesn't mean that I must return to the straight-jacket where, in deference to the group's ability to make the worst out of everything I do, I refrain from almost all action. Living is action. I need no longer respect the wrongheadedness of the group.

There are no ethical or social reasons why I should not be a criminal. The drawback is this: if I am a criminal then my criminal acts affect only one or two individuals in the group – they have to bear the brunt of my freedom. But this is true of any action: an action only affects, usually, people I know. At the back of my scruple about criminal activity is a false and unregenerate distinction between right and wrong: I assume that when I commit a criminal act against a person I am doing them a wrong. It is distinctions like this which falsify the social relations.

Before I had criteria for my actions: I was to evade the group as painlessly as I could, and I was to journey towards the experience that attracted Bill Sody.[17] But now I have restated the conditions of freedom, at least the first of these criteria fails to hold. How am I to conduct myself with the group? To start with, the group doesn't have the meaning for me that it has for its members. I see the group as a collection of things. I examine the lines on the crying face without becoming involved in them. I do not feel the pity of my personality, but I understand the crying, because I know that life will make people cry, that we are standing here unable to move, like stagnant water that is turning to green rot. Instead of rejecting the group I retain the group inside me, I take it in with my glance.

It is axiomatic that the free man understands his situation, he knows where he is. In understanding my situation I can't pick and choose, I must look all things squarely in the face: at this rate I am no more at home with the sheer white cliff-face than I am with the smiling face of one of my lovers. Yet the cliff is only important to me because of the space it occupies and the appearance it has (for these remarks I ignore

---

[17] See note 2.

the subjective element in being aware of anything). On the other hand people are more than this, they are emotional, sensing, contriving, ordering beings. The wind may whistle in the trees, but only the mouth can temper the mind to select notes. Now these other phenomena, which people have but cliffs don't have, must become objects to me. My sympathy must not be directed to this bundle of rags selling matches – my sympathy is general, it comes from staring the world in the face. This bundle of rags becomes purely an object for me, a symbol of the condition of the world. All men, all clothes, all buildings, all voices, all gestures, are symbols of the world and its exotic stagnation. That must be our relationship to the human element in society – and the human industry that goes into making and tending things – they are symbols of us. So I may gloat over the bundle of rags selling matches. I note the clothes, the patterns of the grease, dirt, sweat, thread-bareness, and collapse of the clothes. I note how the clothes are held together with wiry string taken from a fruit box. I note the movements of the hands. I note the graining of the stubble on the chin, the scorch marks of sun on the nose and over the eyebrows, and the great dense hollow boots. I note the gesture of the hand and how one boot scrapes along the paving stone. All this is the movement of the clouds, his voice is the colour of the birds, his trailing foot is the stillness of the tree trunks. He represents where he is. A bus ticket falls from under his cap. I watch it drop, and its movement has the force of the distances of the milky way. There is absolute integrity in the man.

I have described a tramp because the tramp conceals less than the clerk, the milkman and the woman hoeing her three rows of peas. But you have only to look at these people – the planes of their jaw bones, the shape of their ankles, the hair spiralling out of the armpit pads of their wooden crutches, their hands as they lift and carry – to know that to tie them down to Mr Jones and Miss Colinton is to utterly falsify what they are. Imagine a great storm at sea. Huge waves are thrown hundreds of feet in the air where the wind slashes at them like the sabres of mad cavalry; and in this sea is a little boat – the Mary Ann. If you fix your eye on the painted name of this little ship you can be unaware of the storm, but at the same time you know nothing about the ship, because this ship isn't the gang-plank and the crew-list – <u>it is the situation</u>. The ship – will the ship get through?

Possibly if you know all about the make of the ship you can say pretty obviously whether or not it stands a chance; but possibly the storm is so bad that no matter how well-made the ship is its arrival in port is a matter of luck.

We imagine that men have built a little shelter of feeling and culture in the chaos of space; but I think that he is only kicking up a din to drown out the wilderness at his door. But which ever is true, human effort is nullified because it stands in direct opposition to its situation. I glance out of my window and see a pigeon standing on one oily black leg against the smooth worked stone of the wall: that is our problem, it denies us. We must not stand out against this pigeon leg and its black coating. We must work alongside the chaos of space, we must take its distances into our mutable awareness. I don't mean that we should work through the spirit of nature. When we eat and fuck we do that; but this isn't living a life of order which triumphs over the chaos of nature. This idea emasculates the laws of nature. Is the rhythm, breathing orderly? It can only be understood as an implacableness; try to stop breathing and it is as if an iron fist is crammed down your throat. If there is order it is because we are shackled into turpitude or at the best submission. When we fuck we rattle our chains. Our submission becomes an object for us, but our relation to it must be syntonic if it is to be free. As intention, however, we obviously can't work in nature, but we can work alongside it.

[. . .]

Guilt and Common Sense 21 September 1959

Guilt is a feeling, but it is impossible to feel guilty without an intellectual idea. One always feels guilty about something, even if the thing that one feels guilty about is known only remotely and cannot be put into words. Guilt is a fact, just as the feeling of burning is a consequence of a physical burn.

But guilt is not always rational. You may feel guilty about something that is in reality insignificant and irrelevant. Nor is guilt just; a man may act atrociously to another man and yet not feel guilty about it. (Some spongers are like that.) Guilt, therefore, has nothing essentially to do with one's group activities – at least in the sense of guilt being a consequence of wrong-doing. Guilt is a dialectic of one's personality. A guilty man feels guilty about his activities, his activities do not make him feel guilty.

Guilt is not simply a relationship between the present and the past. I may feel guilty about what I am doing, and also about what I am going to do. Obviously I cannot feel guilty about having done something when I have not yet done it. This again stresses the isolated character of guilt; and yet guilt is always related to action, or a refraining from action, or a feeling that I have acted or failed to act. Guilt concerns the relationship between the psyche and objective reality. It is a process in which the psyche appropriates objective reality to itself. Before this can happen objective reality must in some way be transmuted, made viable for the personality. But it seems to me that ultimately guilt is derived from failure to do just that, it is a falsification of reality. This is because the conversation of living is carried on within the psyche; but the only healthy conversation is between the psyche and things.

Things appear to us as common sense. They are there, and the relationships between them are known or ascertainable. I know what happens when I strike glass with iron, or bring a flame and a leaf together, or the consequence of light shining on concrete or a distant sea. Guilt is not immediately concerned with the way I move among things, that is with my actions; it is concerned with my attitude towards things.

The conversation of reality – the healthy, sane life – is between my irrationality and things' rationality. By my very nature I controvert common sense; this is because I don't know myself as I know glass and iron. My behaviour is unpredictable. This means that in a way I can never escape guilt – it is a guilt from (not of) being born; it is called anguish. At the back of it there is perhaps the group unconscious. Even if I understand my personal unconscious I am still not objectively stable. The syntonic condition is the awareness of the gap.

I cannot be common sense because I am not objectively real: there is a gap between me and my hand and me and the tiles in the light well. When I touch [a] box I experience sensual pleasure and psychic estrangement. Understanding this fully is the point of the journey.

But the guilty have a different activity, they do not find man's greatness in the size of his desolation – in simply saying the word vast. They defy, break, common sense within the psyche. Their practical common sense tells them the way in which an ideal group could be constructed – society is essentially escatological in theory, although in practise it is all money grubbing and making the most of the spell of fine weather. It is just this fact that explains their guilt: the utopian state is an unreality, and yet it is the objective of their present activity.

[. . .]

9 August 1959[18]

We live in a new age. The voyages to the moon are like the voyages of

---

[18] This entry is dated earlier than the previous entry. It appears at this point in the notebook but is not in date order.

Columbus and da Gama. We need to re-float our economy, radically redesign our towns (by-passing with roads, building for leisure) and fertilize the arts: conservation by its nature can do none of these things. Instead of being willing to put their house in order so that it can function in the new world, the people have patched up the old one and must of necessity pretend they are living in the old world . . .

But we cannot escape the dangers of the future by turning our backs on them. Men must learn to live with leisure. Leisure is wholly incompatible with the struggle concepts of Toryism. The men who cannot enjoy themselves will be the slaves or pets of the machine owners. Big Brother is a capitalist not a socialist. Ten years ago on the South Bank we developed an architectural style and a sort of planning that belonged to its age and even prepared for the future. It had effects in Europe, America and even as far off as India. Today on the same site Shell are erecting buildings that are fifty years behind their times. That is what is happening.

Ten years ago a fascist would not have taken the risk of appearing as a public speaker. In this election Mosley was listened to in silence, if in embarrassment, and collected two thousand votes. Toryism is preparing a fascist seed bed, with race riots, violence, greed, philistinism and economic throat slashings, dictating the expression of our culture.

As his successes mounted up Macmillan talked about this support enabling Britain to play a <u>great</u> role at the summit. He is incapable of understanding that America and Russia must make a deal: at their brightest they can only regard him as an appendage to be placated.

We have stopped short in our tracks and turned about. Now the contraction will go on. How indicative all this talk about 'greatness' is, we are condemned to a myopic mysticism. We have accepted the parochial.

[. . .]

19 October 1959

Plato believed in a rational soul that was distinct from the body. God had created a <u>world</u> soul (in two parts, one undeveloping and unchangeable and the other developing and changeable) and the material world as its counterpart. He also created souls and bodies for the demigods, and they in turn created the human bodies for the human souls which god had also created. But before the souls were embodied in men each soul was allotted a star to which it could return. His myth of the charioteers is beautiful – the souls could attain knowledge of absolute truth, beauty and so on, but if the wilful head-strong black horse led the chariot (and the white horse) astray, then instead of being reincarnated in a higher form, the soul would be reincarnated in a woman or some other lesser form.

The implication of these ideas is that the soul is not 'at home' in the body, because it is destructed and blunted by the data sensed through the senses. The soul, also, is rational, and presumably this is a break with the earlier greek idea of unity between the mind and the emotions. The emotions certainly clog the soul in earth, but possibly Plato thinks that there is also an inferior sort of rationalism, an inferior part of the soul (the black horse) which also can restrain the soul in its flight – Plato compares the soul to a wing (in a rather disgusting physical description).

The soul is, therefore, immortal, and philosophers and creative artists (but not poets, who are imitative artists) can welcome death – as Socrates did; because then the soul is released from its body prison and the false or utterly imperfect data of the senses. This world has very little to offer men: nothing more than a chance of regeneration. But this is necessary only because men are in the world, and this is a mistake that must be put right: men are not in the world to have a chance to obtain something which they could not have obtained if they were not in the world. But this doesn't mean that the way men behave in the world is unimportant: far from that being so, the explanation of their being here makes it all important. To win freedom for the soul in heaven, the soul must overcome the world – and so the man's attitude is not governed by what he can gain from the things of this world, by deliberately exploiting the things of this world so that they give him the utmost of their sorts of satisfaction and pleasure, but on the contrary by reducing the world to something which it is not; namely, a schema for supporting the soul. What becomes important for a man is not his body but his mind. The man looks on his body, and its potentials other than as being a potential tool for the use of the soul, as an encumbrance. This is a very important decision, of course.

But the soul is not a static quality, it must be nourished or it will fail to transcend the body: it cannot be left to its own devices simply by curtailing the enjoyment of the senses. (And, incidentally, although sexual activity was taboo to pederasts like Plato and Socrates, Plato was by no means an unsensual man – as the symposium and parts of other writings make clear.)

[. . .]

Writers and Society 28 October 1959

A writer has two responsibilities: a responsibility to himself, and a responsibility to his society, that is to his readers. The responsibility towards his readers is a subtle one. If the writer is any good his writings are not merely the recording of his fantasies and daydreams, they are an adjunct to action. They may be a programme for future actions, or they may be an attempt to clarify reality so that he himself can see to act more clearly. Writing is not an end in itself because it presupposes a reader. And so what the writer has to say becomes part of the reader's experience. It is in this way that the writer determines culture. Determining culture is not necessarily, therefore, synonymous with laying down a programme of action: and that is why I do not think it is necessary for a writer to solve problems, it may be enough for him to state them clearly: I will go so far as to say that any literary solution of a problem is bound to be arbitrary, because it must use an emotional commitment, and is therefore an attempt to condition readers or spectators to this particular solution, whereas in fact the problem always is, in one form or another, just that – the danger of emotional commitment.

You cannot talk about this in the abstract. I am writing now of the problems of dramatists, but I imagine they closely resemble the problems of other literary writers. The dramatist must resolve the lives of his characters, this is the only way of resolving the problems of his plays. I do not mean, as I said, that he must resolve their problems into programmes of action, the sort that the audience can go out to imitate. He may resolve his characters' problems by killing them, but the deaths (as a convenience for resolving the drama) are unimportant to the spectators, what is important is their knowledge that the deaths are true to the logic of the drama which has been performed. They must recognize that the drama has been an artistic whole. Categories overlap here, but I think it is true to say that what makes an artistic whole does not necessarily also make practical advice to an audience – and an audience can be helped by an artistic whole which is resolved in a way they would find difficult to imitate; and they can be helped in this way even though the problem of the drama concerns them very closely, and the question of their finding a practical solution is one of life and death.

Perhaps this is only possible because the writer falsifies real life. It is quite possible for a mirror to be held up to nature, you have only to train a movie camera on someone, and in theory and almost in practice this someone could be photographed continuously all the time. But obviously this film would not be an artistic whole. The material which the writer uses should be as similar to life as possible. Camera-like authenticity is absolutely essential – but starting from this the writer may either distort it, or else arrange and juxtapose his 'shots', in a way that will bring out his interpretation of life. He must make life real; it isn't real outside a theatre. The writer's solution must therefore be on the plane of reality; the solution which the audience need is on the plane of unreality.

But there is still a further complication, because the writer imitates characters who are or would be in their office, factory, home, cinema etc. acting on the plane of unreality. The writer is a story teller, and this story telling is not quite the same thing as imitating unreality in such a way as to make it real. Presenting reality on the stage does not require a solution: if people could bring reality into their existence they would not have any problems, or at least not problems that had to be solved in terms of a telos.

The import of the story is this. The writer can only imitate unreality by using unreality, and his story represents the unreal. Yet what is his creation of reality – a mere haphazard collation of disconnected things and incidents, such as a man lighting a pipe, a child shutting a door, a girl buying flowers, water spilling over a bucket rim? Or something purposive?

[. . .]

Chapter Two
The Pope's Wedding

Notes for Tramp Play – 17 November 1959

The notes that open this book contain one or two bright ideas. But they don't have the idea of a play in them. After all, a play is an interior dialectic. In a comedy of manners this dialectic is inferred from the appearance, but normally, in a play, the appearance must be inferred from the dialectic. So I have not merely to describe what the tramp does, but say <u>what he is doing</u> and <u>what he is doing</u> it for. My ideas since writing Sody have changed; I am allowing the Sody ideas to be represented by the first production in this theatre evening (that is, 'The Golden Age.') The analysis in 'The Golden Age' isn't so complete or detailed, as in Sody's play, but it will do; and as it doesn't attempt a solution (apart from the hint in the final chorus) it avoids half of the controversial statements in Sody. (Christ! that's wishful thinking).

The Tramp play, then, examines the Sody problem after the finish of the Sody play: but because my analysis has changed, it <u>needn't</u> set out to do what Sody thought was essential. Sody was a success; it is possible that the Tramp will find himself bankrupt. He <u>is</u> a tramp, and at one time I would have thought that was a success in itself. But I must face this as a question.

A. Does the tramp succeed in what he does – is he a Don Juan without the supernatural intervention, or is he a Hamlet, tripped up by his own good?

I ask this because I must say, when a man is free his troubles are only beginning. <u>Oedipus</u>, as a classic example, assumes that there is peace in Colonus: but, in the Tramp play, I do not imagine there could be equilibrium of this sort. There must be something new, something which has only become possible after the revolution in art, the industrial revolution, the two world wars, and the H-bomb. These are developments not only in society, but in spirituality: but I want to take the spiritual revolution further, we must now live modern art. But not as an aesthetic eccentricity or an aesthetic seclusion; we must live it economically and politically. This is necessary because public assumptions have pre-empted personality. Statesmen cover their face with their skirts at the mention of anarchy: this is not merely because they want to defend our gains in medicine, culture, and hygiene, but because they can't imagine any pose other than their own.

I start off with the background to my play. Am I saying, I may not be able to offer an alternative, but I can certainly say that your present way is bloody? But the process of being able to analyse a fault presupposes that one is in possession of a right by which to compare it, or that one is in possession of an exact technique which would in some way have to inculcate a right. What I can say is: the Tramp is the consequence of Sody's action, let us examine this consequence and see what is happening. He was dissatisfied and disgusted, and he was in this condition even at the end of scene six (speech on 'love'), though I hadn't meant him to be. Well, he is now a man who has outlawed himself and has carried his good with him like an open wound. The good that made him sick in society is still with him, it still nags.

Of course, this good could congratulate itself on having brushed off the dust of the city, but I don't imagine that good is an experience as facile as that, good is still his problem, he is still a dirty animal trying to accommodate good. Perhaps good will give him no rest. Sody's experiences of insight are described as the seaside and the flats; I must make sure that the Tramp doesn't merely go over the same ground. The T[ramp] isn't concerned with an analysis of the group, his problem is ontological: not people, at the most people are only an aspect of it; though, as a dramatist, I am glad to say that he will meet people: I must avoid the solution of the cracked cup.

T will be looking at what it means to 'be here' without the assumptions of the group. The group arranges reality in one way, and so falsifies it. It is as if the group took a vertical reading of something essentially horizontal: thus, if you take a column of words from a page you falsify the meaning of the page.

This means that T is examining himself: the problem plays always examine reality as action, as the consequence of motive and reason, with the accent on consequence, on action; the psychological plays examine the same thing, but with the accent on the motive, often with a particular reason as a consequence, which gives the eerie (but absolutely genuine) impression that the ensuing physical action is something grotesquely stuck on, almost an irrelevancy, or an occurrence in another room. My play will examine what it is to have a motive, why it is necessary to act, and in what way action (whatever it is) describes motive or the need to act. Before, writers examined society's problem in handling personality, or the misfit's problem in handling society or even himself, but I shall examine, in this play how a man sees phenomena – trees and earth – as a projection of his own problem, how he is a sort of hopper-bucket which has to drag along loads of phenomenal things and then drop them. The gravel and bark and clouds pass through him: he has a dredger-snout stuck in the mud and sand, it has to snatch out a load and carry it. Where to, where from? These are obvious questions; but I imagine they take this form simply as a rationalization of the experience of being the dredger; it is the experience itself that must be answered by philosophy and examined by art (my plays are philosophy and art). The dredger-hopper similes may be confusing, I used them simply to describe the impact of the work: the hopper hops, it doesn't knit or play cards. I can imagine a derelict hopper-bucket slung in the mud, lying at a tilt, its bottom wedged in dirt, its inside half-filled with brackish water, a twig, and a floating dry leaf. The Tramp, you could say, was in that condition; I would deny this; but, and here the simile breaks down, the hopper would still be working when it is thrown on one side, it would still be 'being there'. Into all experience I want to introduce the conception of being derelict. I suggest that it is not the from-to (the historical and the teleological) which is the object of man's desire, the sucking of a vacuum, but the am, the pure being. It would be objected that the cogito – as Locke pointed out – cannot be introspected apart from its ideas, and so telos is a legitimate interest. I accept that (at long last).

The place. Has he physically fled to the country? This is important. The man is not merely surrounded by things but by actions which must have an import: does he remove all vestige of motive from action and simply concentrate on the physical phenomena; thus, he examines how the water is torn and how it shoots up in a spout between spikes and a bluff, he is not concerned why the stone is thrown, it would be all the same to him if a body had been thrown in the water; he would then examine how the water soaked into the woollen clothes, and how it covered the greasy suit collar with thousands of little bubbles so that it looks like ice. That men with white and black faces had kicked the body down the slope wouldn't be immaterial to him; it would be very attractive, magnetizing, but again he wouldn't be interested in nature but in appearance and physical cause and effect. Perhaps appearances cannot lie, but at the moment I am not looking for moral justification. He could find a reason from an examination of this sort. Perhaps by portioning out blame and praise, and insisting on individual responsibility, we falsify being here. But the problem is important for the play in this way. If I do not let T examine human events, why are the people onstage with him and what are they doing? It would be artistic suicide to make them symbols, because my whole point is that men do not need anything apart from what there is as symbols – things are symbols, they have no other genuine meaning.

The same is true of events. I do not want to produce symbols of symbols; I do not want to dramatize motives and passions, this isn't what I meant by saying the play would be about the T's self.

When I am dealing with appearances, obviously the T is deeply involved: in a way everything on stage is him. If I record events in the play, what sort of events will they be? In this play ONSTAGE IS STRICTLY REALITY; because T is free (as an artist I am now ignoring the audience; I will return to them when I think out the moral work, or consequences, of the play) what is presented is more real than the bogus reality which the audience sees (no doubt their emotionalism will try to obscure even this reality, but I shall deal with this moral work later as a drama-technician). But if I deal with strict reality then my tramp is a tramp and so a large element in the action will be the attitudes that the people onstage take to a tramp. On the other hand, I mustn't let this aspect distort the twist which is necessary if the audience are to see reality. This twist is, of course, the T experiencing himself. I do not want the audience to identify with him, however; people do not identify themselves with a picture – they may perhaps say its so real you could almost be there, or speak to her, but they can't say even that about an abstract. I must, so, aim for an abstract impression; but I don't imagine the tramp is only abstractly involved; on the contrary, I would say that being free from the group gives the tramp a licence to live in 'passion'; but this passion isn't anything like group passion. It is a passion for which only he is responsible, he cannot ever rely on a judge to be cruel to him. Also, I have to remember that seeing a tramp is an emotional experience for people in the group, it is a sort of stifled fright. I should like to be able to say with confidence that for members of the group watching a tramp is an experience of reality, and one which emotionalism couldn't falsify for its own ends; but I don't yet feel justified in saying so. So there is a possibility that objectively a tramp is guilty of creating tension in the group: along the lines of, if you give a baby a tumbler of rum you can't blame it if it is sick. But there are so many kinds of tramps: the black, vengeful, psychopath with a knobby stick, the white-haired old grandad with a baby face and bunches of violets in his cap and every buttonhole down the front of his coat, and the sexless creatures, with pudding-basin haircuts, rolls of sacking, tin mugs, and paper carrier-bags full of chunks of bread, cotton reels, a book and string.

What I could do is examine the relationship between a freeman and a freewoman, the woman could even be young. (In this context does 'examine' mean 'exploit'; I suspect that if you exploit a character (which itself would be morally negative) you exploit the audience).

This T. isn't Bill Sody, and so <u>maybe</u> I should know how he became a tramp; his reasons for becoming a tramp are Sody's reasons, because these reasons are true of human nature, they are not a consequence of a particular personality. Most people would assume that what I say explains only me, but I defend myself as Freud defends himself towards the end of <u>Beyond the Pleasure Principle</u>. My analysis is true of all people or else it is worthless. I am not content with saying that society is wrecked because it incorporates people who are not adjusted to social living (which seems to be true of most judges – as of the present L[or]d mayor of London). Even contented and happily adjusted people are grounded in chaotic emotionalism; adjustment simply means that they have killed themselves and are kept standing because they are wedged up in the crowd; and, this is the main point, adjustment probably isn't a 'mechanism' that retains its equilibrium over all rough ground; it is a mechanism that attains adjustment once, and is then screwed down into that position; so that afterwards, as an equilibrium it falsifies reality. If I said that in any case living is the business of following the contours of the route I would then be accused of arguing the case for emotionalism. But this isn't so. I think that the T. is adjusted. If I imagine a man in society who is a sort of extension of the virile men I have discussed, a sort of superadaptation, then I am imagining a man who <u>is</u> the world, who doesn't have to adjust himself to anything. That isn't living, that is chance. The only men who I know about are men who have to <u>see</u>, and then adapt or understand; that process is important, and it is not thrown away when one is adapted; one doesn't live happily ever after because one has seen the unforgivable or the unforgettable. Is that fascism? No, because it is not a golden age; one incorporates the adaptation in one's life. It is like passing through a door, and not returning. What one has seen is the condition of unadaptation. If you had seen hell could you believe that god is love? You would have to say, there is no god. You certainly can't have both. That is why you can't have men <u>and</u> god.

[. . .]

24 November 1959

So I have to be able to describe things and events as they are in themselves, or for themselves. It seems that at least half of this work is the work of the stage designer; that isn't basically so, although the stage designer comes into it. Obviously I can't alter completely the appearance of things – or, if I can, I want to refrain from doing so until I have more theatre experience – otherwise the audience will not be able to identify where the tramp is. Yet, although I must capture 'the dance of things in themselves', things are only present as perceptions in the mind, and so presumably I will be figuring the things onstage as what they are to the tramp, even though I write of them, here, as what they are to themselves. But here I am up against my description of the pathetic response. Because leaving aside the difficult question of the sequence in time, what happens is this: the tramp's response is to the strangeness of things, he does not create this strangeness, he doesn't create the world. And yet of course this is just what the sanity of delusion is about: it does allow him to take the initiative, even in the vast spaces, but this is a response. The job is to present the subjective onstage: yet the subjectivity of things and events is of a peculiar sort: it is sense data and cognizance, and then in relation to this there is the pathetic response, and this response is the field or occasions for morals and aesthetics. The response comes out of the waiting nothingness which is man, it is not a response that is fabricated from sense data; but this last point is debatable, and I can ignore it just now because I am ignoring the question of time sequence. All I want to stress is that the tramp sees that things and events are strange, and that this knowledge is a personal experience and is not the strangeness of the things and events. In the same way, if one is frightened one must talk about something being frightening; but suppose I look at a giant and see that in relation to the giant I am very small, and I am then afraid: what I feel is different from what the giant feels because he looks at me and sees that in relation to him I am very small, so he feels confident. The kernel of the masochistic relationship is, of course, it obscures this, it becomes <u>mutual</u> titivation, and both halfs of the relationship feel guilt about what goes on between them, because they realize that each is <u>allowing</u> it to happen, each has given permission which means that the masochist had the power to grant permission and the sadist had the weakness to have to ask for it: even if he only asks for, that is – <u>takes</u>, the trussed body.

To talk about the dance of things, or their rhythm or support or structure, is to find how much we <u>have</u> to anthropomorphize things; events as motives or causes <u>must</u> be anthropomorphic, but as I have said the tramp sees things in action simply as things. One must talk about the man <u>creating</u> things; but what he creates is other than himself, it is as if his kisses were lethal. Men move about in a bone yard, they cannot feel themselves responsible for what is there – on the contrary! But they feel blindfolded with appearance. Wherever they look they are being stared out by things. (Vastness is at times a relief from the claustrophobia.) But men feel mated to things. It is curious, but I suppose man's relation to things and events is a thorough-going maso-sadistic relationship; but the only grounds for such a relationship are <u>outside the pathetic response</u>, because it is only outside this <u>pr</u> that men could say they gave permission in order for things and events to be; but, although I acknowledge the anthropomorphic contingency, I want to stress that, in the freeman tramp, things are what they are <u>outside</u> the pathetic response. Without this awareness of the integrity of things and events the whole contention of the freeman tramp would be an abortion.

Now I shall consider the time factor. Disgust is operative in the freeman in the group. Disgust at shit spit vomit profit-motive violence cultural-pretention law greed and treachery. Now motive and reason could hardly be present to this man as things, he himself is in an emotional involvement with the group; does his disgust stem from an emotional revulsion at the excesses and hypocrisy of love and hate, or is it an emotional revulsion because 'Celia shits'? Well, Sody liked human beings when they were dirty animals; I haven't realized before just how completely Sody <u>didn't</u> 'not like sex'. So even in the group filth and dirt were acceptable to him, he loved the animals who hung their washing out on the flat balconies, because the fact that they washed and laundered meant that they were sweaty and dirty. The dirtiness of things is an essential part in their appearance to the freeman tramp. But Sody and Swift seemed to delight and wallow in dirt (also S[amuel]B[eckett] in Molloy); the freeman tramp doesn't do this, he is aware of the almost terror in things; there is no squeamish, coquettish tiptoeing through pastures of ordure.

[. . .]

19 January 1960
Dramatists! There is no truth without commitment.

20 January 1960
Truth is vulgarity. Never pay a woman a compliment later she will turn it into a taunt.

[. . .]

Ibsen 1 February 1960

I can usually get people to agree with me that as a philosopher Ibsen is a muddle-head and a religious crank; but these same people go on to insist that Ibsen is a master of form and should be <u>respected</u> as such!

But Ibsen is not a master of form, he is a master of calculation. He reduces life to squares, triangles and ellipses. He is like Plato's god – always doing geometry; but it is an essential part of dramatic writing for the stage – and here lies its greatest opportunity and its greatest pitfall – <u>that form is always forced from content</u>: the form can never be a living thing, like the character. It can never become part of the character. Think of the greek charioteer, or the classic nude; here form, written in marble, is subtle and multiform, it seduces, it glides like water. But dramatic form, in the way in which Ibsen used it, is never present. It is merely directional – turn left, turn right, close the door. But life, like body, can't get along with calculation; it is stifled by the laboratory conditions. Form in Ibsen is one whole falsification. In Schiller the form is acceptable because, for all its stunts and coincidences, it suggests the manipulations of gods, in Ibsen we merely have a writer saying life is terrible. God doesn't speak through him, and that means man doesn't speak through him; his characters all speak of Ibsen (in the pamphleteering way in which Shaw's characters speak of Shaw). He should have the dynamic appeal of the real new-classicists, such as Racine; but he lacks even that, adventure. (The English counterparts of Racine are Beaumont and Fletcher and Dryden).

3 February 1960

Before writing my new play I want to make my philosophical position clear.[19] Until it is clear I am hindered in writing the play. My philosophical position has changed since I wrote 'The Fiery Tree.'[20] The ideas of 'The Fiery Tree' were a cul-de-sac; <u>very true</u> ideas, but life then seemed hopeless – I didn't make it clear that <u>men can be good</u>, that there is such a thing as goodness. I was too concerned with the social implications of what I thought. Find out the truth, then worry about social implications.

It is usually said that society is a curb on human nature; that civilization is the product of what is best in human beings; and that the tendency is for civilization to civilize men, so that they constantly

---

[19] *The Pope's Wedding* was first performed 3 December 1962. *The Pope's Wedding* is published in *Edward Bond Plays: 1* (London: Methuen, 1977).
[20] 'The Fiery Tree' is unpublished.

develop towards a higher form of life. The mechanism of the process is clear, and in one way or another is obviously true: culture enables us to learn from our predecessors certain things which were problems to them are not problems to us because we are taught their solutions to the problems. The truth here is that of course we cant fight battles that have already been won, we can't invent tools that have already been invented. But whether <u>morally</u> we learn from our predecessors is a more complicated question; our understanding of the moral situation certainly increases – we no longer act as if human sacrifice could placate god – and as a result the way in which we act is changed, but whether our actions are morally 'higher' is dubious.

Freud puts forward a revolutionary thesis in <u>Beyond the Pleasure Principle</u>; it describes a way in which life could have been generated from the action of sun on matter, and how history could then be understood as the desire to return to matter. It seems to him to be a great irony that the more life struggled the more it became self-aware and the further it came from being what it wanted to be – mere matter.

The vital thing to grasp here is the action of truth, the way in which the situation changes. At a stage in its 'development', its struggle, life develops the faculty of awareness and (perhaps before this) it becomes able to organize things so that it can have its own way. An important question is, <u>how</u> do these two things happen; but, by-passing this question for the time being, let us ask what is the effect of this new character of life?

1). Life begins as a struggle to end itself. But consciousness does not have to be conscious of this. I suppose, as far as conduct goes, the important thing is what do primitive men do instinctively? But at least we must accept this paradox as a possibility: because he doesn't understand history man viciously protects his own well-being so that he can carry on the fight against his big enemy – life.

2). The second paradox is that the death-wish may not be suicidal but misanthropic. Man may not attack his life, but LIFE. Now here <u>is</u> the theme for drama, of man who lets himself be the conscious tool of history – who makes it his business to carry out the purpose of life, which is to stamp out as much life as possible. Here is one answer to the question, why dont we commit suicide? Many people cannot <u>be</u> conscious history, and so the proper work for those who can be is to see that the human aim in history is carried out.

So far so good. But there is a slight moral defect in this way of behaving, because it isnt easy to see how I can make it my moral duty to be responsible for the deaths of as many people as possible. Having understood history I should be quite content to blow my own brains out and leave it at that. It seems clear that one of the fundamental, tragic errors in primitive life was the confusion over enemies – my life, and LIFE. To make LIFE the enemy is to be seduced from the straight-forward purpose of my own life, which can only be understood as a complete self-interest – one of the horrors that life faced, when it was fried out of matter, was that of environment, of being somewhere. Now that so much of that environment is oozing, dripping with life, the environment is all the worse.

But this is to misunderstand truth. Poor, ugly life in its struggle for death gave birth to something which is morally superior to life – and that is consideration, the regard for life. Life learnt to pity itself. Self-pity was the most important result of consciousness – it is like the voice of pain. Man has borne so much in his struggle for death!

But again, how do I confuse self-regard with regard for others? Surely this pity is another reason for killing myself; how can I argue that it is a reason for living and getting on with the work of killing others? I can see that this is why I want to avoid suffering in other people, but surely this is no more than another reason for killing them off quickly.

If the purpose of life is death then there can obviously only be one job to do – kill. I suppose one could have a moral duty to kill and preach killing, but it would have to be on a large scale or else limited to suicide. I cant see much excuse for a compromise – running a child down there, pushing an old girl in the river here, slitting a throat there. This sort of thing would be open to misinterpretation – it might be taken as a penchant, a personal idiosyncrasy. We need the really mass-killers – Hitler, Napoleon, Christ, or nothing.

So this regard, which is derived from life, still doesn't solve the problem. There can be no reason for going on living – except that I cannot allow myself the luxury of suicide when so many of my brother men misinterpret life and go on living. I am corrupted by the team spirit; sticking it out with them wont help them, but it may give them the impression they are being helped. The only other explanation of the meaning of regard is unfortunately depressing, but after having seen that the solution to our problems is potentially so easy, it is well to face up to it. Regard may have given me what you could call a liking for life, it may have made me want to go on living. This may be the truth that is understood by my tramps – 'isn't it horrible I don't want to kill myself!' (That is why most intelligent people don't kill themselves, though perhaps some intelligent people have as a reason for not killing themselves a mistaken sense of duty).

This isnt the play as it is drafted; at the moment there is still a lot of social comment – he is hounded out and killed by the group. Socrates. Well, what would happen to a man who told the truth?

Most men show traits of masochism and sadism. But if what I say is true then the point of morality is simple – it is the conversion from sadism to masochism of the raison d'être of humanity. Masochism is the wish to live. Sadism and misanthropy is the wish to die. But the masochist is only going about dying in a peculiarly artistic way: he mustnt be regarded as inferior to the sadist; after all, every masochist is a sadist to himself.

[. . .]

8 February 1960

But I must take up the position that my writing is NEW. It depends a lot on other writers, but only I have understood the dialectic of the group – and even I not fully. And so I must manipulate my style very carefully; without the style the plot would have no meaning, or a false meaning.

The style must be the truth. If I put the truth onstage the audience knows it for what it is; even if they lie and protest and dispute – it doesn't matter, they will know the truth. Of course, one of my ideal freemen would never lie about the truth; but then, I no longer imagine that I can change people in the twinkling of an eye! There are no changes like that – except bad changes. Can the truth be put to the perverted use of the group? I don't think so. It will always ring true to make the group activity seem hollow. And this sense of the hollowness wont be able to be used by them for the pleasure of frustration or self-denigration. It will be more hollow then, and will say 'You're <u>not</u> suffering . . .' And they will start looking for the truth, they will be drawn to it. You must make them see things in new ways. That is, you must contact the true pr in them, not the spurious hysterical emotionalism of the role.

How much of this is wishful thinking? How many people are too dead to help?

[. . .]

15 February 1960

1. If you have a shoal of fishes it is pointless to look for the dry fish.
2. Sometimes I ask myself what we are doing. The only question that

men ask is: where is my enemy. Then the wet moralists say man is his own worst enemy, my dear. I ask myself is it true? It is life that is the enemy. What can you say about life? Ever since the first squids crawled out of the sea, to arm themselves with stings and claws and incisors, you have one story. What can you say about carnivorous plants? Spiders? The animals that break the backs of other animals, and spawn their eggs in there, so that the young can feed on living flesh? Even the pretty colours and patterns you find, are camouflages or decays. And the smells. The only things you can say a good word for are the rain and the light and the wind and rocks. Earth is too like shit to be pleasant.

[. . .]

20 February 1960

An idealist must be prepared to sacrifice his dreams for his ideals; if he cannot do this he may be dangerous; he may also betray his ideals. But this doesn't mean that ideals can never be put into practice.

Note on Dramatic Form 21 February 1960

We need a new dramatic form not simply because we want a bright new package in which to sell what we have to say; or because we want to start a new fashion that will catch the public's eye. We need a new form because the old form falsifies experience. The form of the Ibsenite well-made play, derived from the Greeks via the Renaissance, isn't related to the subject of the play, in the way that a picture-frame is usually related to a picture. This form is not merely a highly pliable instrument which will bring out all the material in the subject; the form itself implies certain 'truths' (which I believe to be 'falsehoods') about human experience. The form is often lazily bundled together with technique, and people assume that because Ibsen was technically strong the form must be a strong weapon capable of bringing out truth. In actual fact I believe that the technique is tainted with the same brush as the form – so there is some excuse for the lazy assumption.

The form assumes that certain events can be pivoted together, and that they have a beginning (often a murky one) and an end (often a fatal one). The assumption is that the events lead to a crisis, an agony, which is resolved; and that the resolution is a development from the agon – wisdom comes through suffering, self-knowledge comes through suffering, etc. It is completely false.

The new dramatic form must be based on these assumptions. There is personal distress – it may emphasize itself in an agon (love affair, family feud, etc) but this agon is an irrelevancy, strictly speaking. It is an attempt by the distress to work itself out; and resolution from the agon is not <u>wisdom,</u> or <u>self-knowledge,</u> or the <u>attainment of peace</u> – it is a self-crippling.

I should add that the idea that heroes and heroines die is the <u>peace</u> or <u>wisdom</u> idea in its most vicious form; because then the audience's herd instinct is appealed to. The audience is approached as policemen. And so we have the idea of the protagonist finding peace, and the idea that the audience is sacrificing a scapegoat . . .

[. . .]

Notes on Tramp Play

People have wanted to go to heaven because that relieved the distress of being here; it was an escape. But there is also a deeper meaning in the wish for heaven.

If you believe in heaven then you are not yet in it. For Christians, to be out of heaven is to be in hell. The idea of a distinct hell creates terror, but strictly speaking it is unnecessary. A belief in hell is now looked on as odd, but Christians still, nominally, believe in heaven. If what I say is true, then a wish for heaven is a device for living in hell here and now. To put it leniently, a belief in heaven is itself evidence that life is hell. But this churchy belief in heaven is a licence to create hell on earth: it isn't easy to tie the argument up in a watertight way, but the trend is this – a belief in heaven is the device with which people create a pseudo-hell here and now to obscure their need to understand the real hell. They would rather not face the real hell.

But human nature can't be satisfied until it has seen hell – until it has seen how bad or meaningless its situation is.

The attempt to create the diversionary hell on earth leads to the immolation. The willingness to go to hell, on the other hand, is the willingness to live. Whatever happens, hell is not avoidable: but what sort of hell can be chosen? The whole dialectic about common sense must be brought in here; because the people who create hell on earth know that they are deceiving themselves, and this knowledge is part of their hell . . .

[. . .]

23 February 1960

I have difficulty in putting into words the different stages of T's character in this play. I know <u>what</u> happens; but these happenings are

themselves partly symbolic; and, apart from this difficulty, I have to
explain what these happenings mean to T, or what effect they have on
him.

Nothing changes, there is only more of it. That is the main idea. I
could compare it to the growth of a business. A man sets up a little shop.
In time he owns many department stores, shops and warehouses; and he
probably owns factories. It is still the same business, but the man is
concerned with more of it.

Another way to describe it is to say this. A man's knowledge is the
connections he can draw between things. At home T only draws
connections between himself, his wife, the foetus and the people in the
streets, and so forth. From 'home' to discovery that 'the child is lame' T
is concerned with the same sort of relationship, though there are more
people and more experiences involved.

In the first stage he is concerned with the relationship between himself
(as a thing) and things; this is childish. After, and before, the birth of the
child, he becomes more of a spectator watching the relationships between
other things. Finally, when the child is thrown into the ditch he makes a
relationship between himself and things. The child in the ditch is a
bridge between himself and the world.

The events are symbolic in the sense that they are emotive (I hope this
is controlled); they describe the extending pathetic response of the T.

[. . .]

28 February 1960

Why is Arthur Miller a reactionary? Because he uses the form of the
well-made play. This form is based on the fallacy that you can record a
series of events and this will give you a meaning in the sense that a set-
up leads to a breakdown. This may be so, but the form incorporates
moral overtones. There is the idea that a misdeed earns a punishment,
and this punishment balances out the misdeed or in some way completes
the episode. The same sort of things may be said about a virtue and its
reward . . .

I suspect peripeteia. Villainy must not be triumphant at the beginning
of the play and defeated at the end of the play. This is trite idealism. The
only idealism which isn't dirty is an idealism which instead of wrenching
facts into the shape of lies, accepts facts, confronts facts. After all, there
is nothing you can do with facts. Facts are death. (I am not writing about
society, which never faces facts.) But just as knowledge of death gives life
a meaning, character and purpose, so should facts give these things. The

form of a play should be this: suspicion of facts – confirmation of facts . . .[21]

29 February 1960

I was out with the army on a mock exercise. The column of jeeps, TCVs and awkward cars was drawn up along the road. Some of the men were strolling down the line for a chat with their mates, or to touch someone for a roll. Others were sitting on top of the vehicles. Some of the local civilians had come out to watch. They strolled along the road and were mixed up with the cars and the men. One of them had no legs and only one arm. His body seemed to be encased in a scaffolding of steel tubes and shining leather straps. He was able to get along – jerkily and slowly, but with a rhythm that came from long practise and showed confidence. His face and hand were completely unscarred. The sight of him wandering in and out among the soldiers and the cars brought out the meaning of what we were doing. We were playing at soldiers – and this man was what the game was about. Some of the boys sucked in their breath as he clanked past them . . .

You are always surrounded by things. Things are always at the end of your senses. But you can never become part of things – or if you did, it would be a meaningless, hollow victory. But you only have a voice if the things speak in you. Anyone can babble inconsequentially; but, the babbling of a brook has a logical meaning, the babbling of people has no meaning. Your voice has meaning – what you <u>say</u> has meaning – only if you are the chair speaking, the cup speaking, the wall speaking, and so forth. What is gained by living with things is clarity . . .

In [scene] 3, T has a pathetic response to all things. This doesn't mean that he is anti-social: he has elevated people to the heroic stance of the leaf and the ocean. People usually diminish themselves to the triviality of patriotism, trade and hobbies. He hasn't turned his back on people. People are like fish swimming in his sea; or, you could say, he looks at things over the heads of people. People's horizons are normally limited to the newspaper headlines and new wallpaper for the hall (so that the milkman is impressed when he knocks on the door); fucking usually gives them an intimation of reality; and so, also, do any personal

[21] In a note to the editor, Edward Bond explains that 'a tragic hero must achieve enlightenment about his situation. Willy Loman [in Miller's *Death of a Salesman*] achieves only personal enlightenment – he learns that his son Biff loves him. So the pretext of the play is untouched – the social set-up of the salesman. Arbitrarily, the problem is left untouched and passed to the mother and her notorious speech ["Attention, attention must finally be paid to such a person". Act One.] This is worse than reaction, it is sentimental. It is a defect that later prevented Arthur Miller from developing as a dramatist.'

relations – because they show them the macabre, erratic impulses which direct life. But apart from that, nothing. And all this is dangerous. You cant contract out of life; and unless you accept the freedom of a tramp (I don't mean those misfits on the roads) you are taking part in the dialectic of destruction – and then you need conflict (which means, the suffering of other people) to keep you sane . . .

As I'm a dramatist I use words. Perhaps it could also be music or dancing or painting and so forth. I'm not so sure about this – particularly music. (I'm a Puritan: I can only excuse – intellectually – music if it is modern, if it makes the noises that we have to hear in the business of living; so I listen to Schoenberg. It also happens that I like Bach, and Mozart and some of Beethoven; my 'reasons' for liking these are more complicated.) These other arts have difficulty in making an exact statement; they <u>can</u> make exact statements, just as pictures can make paradoxical statements, not the sort of paradoxical statements you might find in pre-Raphaelite pictures . . .

3 March 1960

To trust someone is to take a risk.

We are not conscious of life because we hold a meeting, know people, catch buses and keep appointments. All those activities are connected with the past and the future as much as with the present. But at any moment we are faced with things. A green typewriter. Spectacles on the desk. Black scrawling in a work book. These are always present and experienced as two opposed things. These objects that I have listed are like ships under the sea. They rest silently on sandbags. There is no noise and no movement. At the same time hand in hand with this, <u>mated</u> to it – there is the idea of a ship on a voyage: calling at such and such a port tonight, and on a journey to such and such to get rid of its cargo. The human body and the human situation may not be ideally suited for action; but our predicament seems to call for action. If we could derive our actions from 'being' with things, rather than from our instincts and our impulses, that would be all to the good. (No one believes that 'nature' is an evil spirit.)

Perhaps it isnt a question of absolutes, but of tendencies. Most people refrain from being a person; they avoid being individual. One's unreflecting self – the id, one's habits, and so forth – is an amorphous self. The id, I am told, conditions our whole being: it is like the windbag on a bagpipes: it makes no music but it is behind all the music. These are the antipodes: the world of things, and the id. But the ego is not a mere colourless go-between; the ego bears the burden of consciousness and must sustain the moods. Man must live in the ego: the world of the id and the world of things must be summoned into the ego.

Does the ego go mad? You can deny life, refuse to live with the id of things; you can go mad; or you can be a stoic . . .

Aspect of A House. You have the people moving and sitting and lying about the rooms. Coffins are carried out. Visitors call. Apartments change hands. You also have the building. It stands as still as a gravestone. Like a gravestone there is a calligraphy on it. One knows something about the builders and the inhabitants from looking at the building. You cant live without a place. Any moment, however, has a context.

We make certain rooms our own. In those we sit down and relax. We pick our noses. In other rooms our behaviour is formal. We stand. In a strangers room we don't sit until we are asked to sit. But possession is something that is added to a thing. We misinterpret place by respecting things for any reasons apart from those which are inherent in the things themselves. You dont sit on a hot plate. But possession cant be introduced into a thing, as heat can be introduced into iron.

Obviously you cant introduce human moods into things. But our moods are related to things. It is not just a romantic excess to use the landscape to describe emotional states. But, properly understood, the idea is essentially classic; because the medium remains unmoved by the ends to which it is put. Things remain stoical and calm. They are like classic masks.

This either means that certain things are hidden from us; or else that the world of things are able to encompass all tragedy and not break: For most people nature symbolizes the secret, we are afraid. For T nature symbolizes the stoic – it bears everything.

The bare tree outside my window burns like Troy, it is as black and disturbed as the north sea, it is as delicate as a black lacquered escritoire, it is as calm as a sleeping girl, it is as unfeeling as ice, it is as open as a sign, it is as silent as a skeleton.

In the houses across the garden they have switched on the lights. If the wind bends the tree and snaps it off from the trunk – there is no movement. It happens instantaneously, like the travelling of light. There is movement from one moment to the next moment. But there cannot be any movement in the moment.

Someone holds a picture postcard in front of my face. Past and future, this and that, are swimming round the postcard – I can see them out of the corner of my eyes. But the postcard is fixed. It is still and silent.

[. . .]

The good that evil people do. 12 April 1960

I pointed out (earlier in this notebook, I think) that not everything that men do has a sinister end: many things are sinister only because they are done by killers. You have to make a distinction between the act of raising a knife to make a stab, and him checking a laundry list, or knotting a tie so that he can go out and look for a victim.

In the same way, not all the judgements and decisions made by evil men are directly evil. Most people would claim that this is obvious and hardly needs pointing out. But then, they dont understand the way in which these judgements and decisions are evil. Since, in my next play, I want to point out that most really evil actions are performed by people who are usually thought of as good people, this is a point about which I must be clear.

The good actions of evil people are intended to be taken as good because in that way they establish the bona fide of the evil men. Thus, a judge must behave with decorum and authority – otherwise the law will fall into disrepute. But on the other hand, the decorum and authority of judges can give prestige to disreputable laws. This is very much the case in England today. All the major evil actions are performed by governments or societies. A private murderer may kill a dozen or so; states slaughter millions – and they must claim that it is ultimately a good thing that they do so, or at least that it is inevitable.

The argument of inevitability is unusually weak, even as an excuse for the behaviour of governments (that is, the people – with piddling exceptions). It is inevitable only because the alternative – slavery – is rejected out of hand. It is good that slavery is dishonorable; but this seems suspiciously like the argument of a potential slave owner.

I think, therefore, that notions like equity and honour, are used simply to give face to predation and violence. They are used not merely to deceive the have-nots – who, surprisingly, often see their leaders as incarnations of their ideals – but also the haves; though I think they feel very guilty about these 'self-deceptions' – because it is a case of closing one eye only.

Guilt has no meaning without the notion of a standard that one has failed to live up to; there must not only be such a standard, but there must also be the idea that one ought to live up to it, or that it would be to one's advantage if one did live up to it. I think that those men – who we would normally call good – have a guilty relationship to themselves. This was my contention in 'The Golden Age.'[22] This guilt would

[22] Bond refers to an early unpublished play.

probably be based on relationships with other people, but it need not be; one can have the feeling that one is letting oneself down and I don't see that this has to be based on a misunderstanding.

If, in my new play, the good man is very rational, he must also feel guilty – unless he could think that his good (evil) was brought into being by necessity – that he had no alternative but to do such and such. But necessity in human affairs (I mean economic and not psychic necessity) only has meaning in eras of need and work. When our needs are met without work, it is no longer economically necessary for a man to do anything to another man. The other prop of good (evil) is idealism; but ideals are myths, they are concretizations of wishes. That is why men see their leaders as incorporation of their ideals – there is a psychic disposition to do so. And so the solving of economic questions doesnt solve the questions of culture.

Human notions of good are based on common observations – such as it is good to have food when you are hungry. They have no ingredient that could be called guilt. One need not feel guilty at snatching food from the plate of someone else who is also hungry, if all one has to consider is one's own hunger. Guilt is the idea that to do oneself good is to do someone else harm; conscience is the idea that in some way this is doing oneself harm. So masochists do good (give sadists their pleasure) in order to harm themselves; or they harm themselves in order to do themselves good. Do we refrain from snatching other people's food only because they might hurt us or our conscience might trouble us?

Our morals belong to an age when we had necessity as an excuse – though primitive man is unlikely to trouble about excuses. In the Christian era it was never intended that we should be good on earth; angels belonged to heaven. Whether this was a frank appraisal of human fallibility, or a comfortable licence, is unclear; a bit of both, I suppose. But necessity is a very good excuse indeed. In an era of necessity guilt is out of place. In human terms evil is never really necessary, but it gives freedom to one's disposition. In an era of freedom, without necessity, such as our own, many things must be considered when we try to assess human conduct . . .

[. . .]

28 July 1960
    The first thing to say about my philosophy is that it makes ethics an ultimate reality. This aligns it as a philosophy with the thoughts of Spinoza and Freud. I have not examined the meaning of logic (in its academic sense), nor have I tried to create a metaphysical ontology – if

there is one it is almost a by-product. I was concerned with the power of human psychology. I started with an examination of people, and only from that did I go on to examine things; and even so I've always considered things only in relation to people. When I talked about the purity/isolation and factness of things, I am only emphasizing their relation to people; because it is the shock of their disconnectedness from people that caught my imagination. My philosophy is a human philosophy; and it is also a philosophy of a time of crisis. It was formed at a definite point in the crisis; I said such and such has occurred, and in the light of this we can understand our present behaviour and know what its future consequences are likely to be. Quite simply people when they are young develop an emotional complexity which is essentially destructive because it wishes to experience, to fulfil itself in emotional crises; I gave this emotionalization a particular characteristic; you could liken it to a piece of elastic. If you stretched the elastic and held it at a particular extension for a long time, then this extension becomes its normal proportions, and so to stretch the elastic one would have to stretch it even further. The same is true of emotionalism: one becomes emotionally blasé and spiritually void; and because we are stupid enough to live in the moment, each moment demands utmost priority; and the result is escalation. One is always driven to extremes; the ultimate extreme is death.

(I'm not saying this accounts for an inherent death wish. Freud's question 'why do people grow old?' hadn't yet begun to concern me then.)

I wanted to explain human activity. My argument was historical, I had to explain our historical degeneration. The final immolation wouldnt be experienced by everybody; it was enough to see it approach and hand on the curse to the children. Perhaps part of our anguish is that we may not share in the final catastrophe – we may have to be content with individual deaths. It was enough to leave the world worse off than one found it – one could then say one had lived with purpose.

But what about forms of melancholia, where people just dont want to live; this may be carried on into suicide. This seems to be an individual death, a turning away from the purpose inherent in society. This is the old problem of the particular and the general. Certainly people may take control of their own lives, and end them in this way – ignoring the perhaps more imposing opportunities offered by society. But the suicide always acts with an audience in mind; suicide is a way of drawing attention to oneself. If the suicide kills himself in order to add to the general misery of mankind, then his suicide may be said to be idealistic, or a martyrdom. I dont think a free man would kill himself – and so all suicide must be devoted to the common purpose. Suicide is not a private act, it is a public act.

The increase in social consciousness has gone hand in hand with an appalling increase in our destructiveness. It isnt enough to say that we are more destructive only because we have more powerful weapons in our hands; fascism is a mental phenomenon, it has nothing (ontologically) to do with the armament laboratories.

Social institutions are there only to create and extend crisis. But these institutions enshrine the common ambivalence; and this is something which I will now try to state very clearly. In all crises there is a polarity – one pole represents the degree of danger and degradation into which one has got, the other is one's standards of good and peacefulness. This explanation sounds like a put-up job – or at best an 'as if' explanation. Does a man hanging over a cliff think of the joys of terra firma as well as the horrors of falling? (He doesn't think at all, he feels.) All human activity has this notion of polarity – so, considered from the point of view of purpose, all human activities are hollow. They are meant to revolve round this central ambivalence. This was the role I cast for good; it wasnt something in its own right that was out to conquer evil – the two worked for a common purpose, and considering the final goal one could say that the moral purpose was very evil.

[. . .]

Divarications I 26 January 1961

The black streets and the trees rearing up in horror. Charred pillars supporting nothing. But no debris left by the Huns and Turks. This desolation is caused by the stare of time. I am nailed, but my arms don't stretch out like the wings of a bird.

What do I want? A cunt? A drink? A fag? A square meal?

I am walking on empty tables. Whatever it is, it's under lock and key.

In that big empty day, which opened like an operation and was stitched up by a miser; in that broken feast, when the wind made the food cold; in that big sea, when they came to take him in a police car, I said: I did not kill the child, I did not eat his flesh. I did not burn down Buckingham Palace, I did not lay waste cities and build Treblinka, I did not look when the coffin passed.

Then where are the leaves from the trees? Why is the street empty when I step into it? Give me back my fingerprints. A murder hunt for a lost scrap of paper or sixpence? O yes.

II

Dig deep and burn the earth
Dig long and narrow and deep
Swing the body down with ropes and planks
And cover
Use the ropes often tomorrow
Board up spaces with the planks
The earth will slide off my coffin
During the slow breathing of ages
And new earth will take its place
During the slow breathing of ages
But I must put up with it
Take the weight
For sixpence lost
A handkerchief torn
During the slow breathing of ages
My arms cramped
Not with the grasping eagerness
of the rack

III

Still talking to myself
Without enough life left
To make the effort to die
Looking down down down
Knowing nothing
Except I dont know the answers
But, then, I am the examiner

27 January 1961
I

So I have killed him
He lies under the table
His head in the cat's saucer
Half his jaw on the other side of the room
The char found it

His blood smelt
But I didn't eat him
Or drink anything
When they took him away

I didnt feel angry or afraid
I didnt feel anything
Except the cold half-empty cup
In my hand
I didn't say anything
Except: watch the step

I must insist
I didn't eat him
I cleared up after me
Removed the mess

You will want to know about it
I have nothing to say
I can only describe it
I dont know what you mean
No, no one <u>deserves</u> to die!
I shan't erect a monument
That's just something else to keep clean
And get in the way of traffic

II

How did I kill him?
I went down a long lane
And over a hill
I passed workmen in a hut
By a hole
I pushed my way
Through the low branches of trees
I hummed
But every so often I stopped humming
Then the silence began to make me stumble
So I started to hum
He heard me coming
And crawled out into the bush
I followed his noisy breathing
And scolded him
For running away
I dragged him back by an ankle
The night was clear
Some of the birds were still awake

Many times he kicked free
And writhed at my feet
Like a snake with a broken back
When I got him home
I smashed his head with a stool
And pushed him under the table
He left no message
A few scraps of child's property
In a way difficult to dispose of

I cant say I'm willing to suffer for what I did
It's so long ago and far away
And it pulled out my nerves
As if they were stitches in a coat
And I fell to pieces
Though no one saw this
Because the pockets were empty
But I will put myself into your hands
In the meantime I must sing

III

It didn't happen like that
He was alone at a bus stop
Pirates came
And hauled him off

4 February 1961
The reeds in the shallows are still
Listening for a voice that has passed
The clear eddies across the mud
Are full of clouds and winds
High over the hills
A tin gapes up from the water
And boys have dragged a dead black branch to the edge
If I could shout to it and tell it my name!
If I could give a name to the place
That would run like blood through its body
The violent rejection of creation
Has nailed it fast
Dead and waiting

At night it is sealed up
And lies like a trap for the day
If I could teach it its name!
The earth makes me angry
Who would baptize with this idiot water?
The light has shrivelled up
Like an old brow
It smells
And geography and history fly like bats from the trees

Notes for Hermit Play – 12 February 1961

(Taken from tapes made over last three weeks.)

1. In my previous plays I have relied strongly on verbal revelation (e.g. man on bank in 'He Jumped' etc). In this play the final words will be trivial, the revelation will be in the implication: young man, wife, body of old man, unopened tins of food. The wife has long harangue, longest in play. 10/12 lines – Blistering rage – but simple, narrow, nagging, questions – not transcendental answers; but about major questions, not who put out the cat. Y[oung] M[an] says nothing. Sits with hands dangling between knees. Pause, then he says. . . . 'what?'

2. No good play can be written without iron technique, even when as in this play the plot is simple. Subtle enough to seem uncontrived.

3. Meaning of play. No graspable sequences of cause and effect. Dobson or Hogarth's series 'you do such and such, such and such will follow, and such and such from that' etc. This view is necessarily concerned with naive moral distinctions (Cf. 2 practices). Anyway, directed at innocent and therefore has no appropriate audience. A fleet of ships in convoy. No visible chains connecting them, but they sail together.

4. The H[ermit] may have killed someone. But don't treat this like a thriller: it is the possibility that is my subject. May or may not be so as fact, but another fact is that men can murder, we do think of them as possible murderers. So we live in an atmosphere of bad crime.

5. Traditional tragedy is concerned with passion (when it stops being strength and becomes weakness), failure of will, delusions etc. Basically, man's control over himself (and his 'destiny'). Relationship between action and the society etc (theatre) against which one has to act.

6. The only possible subject for modern tragedy is disease. Treblinka. Future Hiroshimas.

7. Rain has stopped play. D/S talking, sun out (said not seen). Back on [cricket] pitch. Out 3rd ball. Could this match develop into gang warfare? Men in white on black stage. No ball; mime.

8. <u>Cause of death</u>. Build general tension. <u>No</u> ten. Will. Storms, however. Other woman? Catapult has two fork prongs. One is the H. The other the YM's other concerns. YM not fucking wife? Ruinous. He is taking the food up to H.

9. Scene of death. Why does wife send girlfriend off to police. Her social sense stronger than his animal passions, alas. Or afraid. She sends the girl automatically, but when she understands goes to call her back, but then changes her mind and refuses. Argue.

10. Shakespeare – Man, irascible temper, preyed on by vicious evil man. Becomes wrongly convinced of wife's jealousy, and <u>because</u> of that murders her and then himself. <u>Because</u>. Hamlet, a young man who cant carry out his vow of vengeance, until in a moment of anger he kills the man <u>because</u> anger has given him facility. Dobson again.

My play = such and such happens, then such and such, a marriage, a murder, a wife sending for police. But no suggestion of <u>because</u>. Only a record. Because is not only absent, if it were in it would falsify what I want to do.

11. The YM could be a big hero of the cricket match. There could be confusion about result, <u>not</u> an argument. One group talks as if X won, the other group as if Y won, and I leave it like that.

12. Scythes. Grass on verge of pitch to be cut. 5/6 young men with scythes. (Hung in trees to rust the iron out of them, etc).

13. Describe effect and not cause. Stone falls on man's head. He feels flash of pain. Falls, goes out. Comes round later. You could say the stone was dislodged from ledge by bird, fell at such a speed, glanced off head at such an angle, etc: describe man's conscious experience. Tells nothing about pain – Western social scientific and analytic and descriptions of this sort must always give structure to art, but they don't describe the

pain. Drama, however, can evoke the effect. This doesnt mean (necessarily) empathy. How it is done is another question, but this is what has to be done.

14. 'Explanations not enough'. Explanations themselves can be good or bad, however. Ibsen, his explanations predate his facts. He glues his medievalism onto modern framework. Scientific hieroglyphics written on ancient parchment. Brecht (3d Opera)[23] Dialectical approach. Even truer of Mother Courage. But on top of this you have a certain feeling or quality, which (I claim) has nothing to do with the dialectical approach or rather it does not have the same content as that of the dialectical approach.

15. In this play I say one is puzzled, one doesn't know. Explanations dont inform one though they can help us to understand the future.

[. . .]

14 February 1961

Morals are divided into ends and means. When there is a moral end – such as personal happiness or public welfare – there are certain skills that enable you to proceed towards achieving that end.

Is the evidence we require to find the right ends the same sort of evidence we require to find the right means?

Many of the ends, for example happiness, seem to have no substance outside of means, because happiness is achieved through doing something, or possessing something, the question is to find what makes us happy.

But if one asked 'what ought to make us happy?' – one is talking about a happiness that would be a duty. Outside instances of pure coincidence ('I happen to like what I should like') this sort of happiness is purely an end. A philosophy of this sort is not utilitarian because it is not a philosophy of happiness, it is a philosophy of duty: it is my duty to behave in such a way that finally I derive happiness from doing or having certain things. Such a philosophy would not be unlike the philosophy of X[Christ]ianity.

But I imagine that most people, when they think about moral ends, don't have in mind a teleology: the means, for them, are means to maintain certain things in existence, though I imagine that most people

---

[23] *Threepenny Opera.*

would readily agree that in order to maintain an institution in being it is necessary to reform it from time to time. In these cases, note that the end is probably as utilitarian as in the philosophy of an end of dutiful happiness, since presumably the justification for the institution is that it contributes to the general wellbeing. (The justification could be, however, that the institution is a means for approaching an end of the first sort, in which case it is best to consider it as a means.)

The important point to note is that although a moral theory should be all of a piece (this seems to be a general characteristic of morality) the behaviour appropriate to an end and a means may be different. That this is common knowledge is expressed in the general acceptance of sayings such as 'I must be cruel only to be kind'. (Note the secondary sense of 'only', as limiting the means to that one end.)

But we must be on our guard. The paradox lies in that morality and is naturally concerned with idealism; but as it has also to be a guide to practise, conduct, it must involve itself in an un-ideal, sordid world, where often 'the good' is only distinguished almost imperceptively from 'the bad' (the dilemma is sometimes particularly acute when choices have to be made), and when good is simply creating opportunities for the bad, though being 'good' in this sense is very sentimental. That is why it must be strongly insisted that moral conduct is rational conduct and that the ends should be implied in the means. The only allowable difference between ends and means is the difference between the ideal and the practical: the 'ideal' is the state in which the means we use in practice have complete prevalence. Heaven as commonly understood is therefore immoral.

Morality cannot be postponed. Ideally the 'means' should be the 'ends' (when it comes to acting). Realpolitik should be considered a science and therefore governed by the implicit duty to tell the truth; it is, therefore, a separate heading under morality (a sub-component) and, because of the duty to tell the truth, must always justify its actions with psychological explanations, and these must then be judged from the moral standpoint; and, if proper attention is made to the correct relationship between ends and means, this judging will be severe.

In general, rational conduct must take human psychology into account; and this is obviously important in considering what means are appropriate in a certain case. But to me it does not seem so clear that human psychology is necessarily involved in defining moral ends, and I am not sure that morality can be derived from human nature. (Hobbes' statement that natural law can be derived from human nature is

acceptable as long as it is not supposed that this <u>justifies</u> natural law or
tells us what moral ends should be.)

3 March 1961
A Love Poem
You declared your love for me
In words and actions
But why did I expect
You were not lying?
It was foolish to think that love
Would calm the seas
And give me memories
Of dignity that came through lust
And not through stunted segregation

Naturally all grocers tend to steal
Naturally all politicians tend to lie
Naturally all priests tend to pervert
Naturally all armies tend to loot
Naturally all lovers tend to deceive
And all love tends to worship infidelity

So why did I think you were not lying?
After all, I know my own lies
But I started to walk in anger and surprise
And met a mad Irishman
Who talked of the moon
The back of the brains
Cars drink whores
And touched me for half a crown

He jumped and pointed and argued
But he was half dead
Not through sickness
But because it was dark and he was mad
I thought of the dead in your lies
And the sweet gentleness of death
When little Ernie was dying
And there was no gauntness or whiteness or pain
But death plumped him up
Till he was like a little round

Sugar-plum cake
A mellow sugar victim

But remembering
The eaten bellies
The smashed limbs
The choked lungs
The torn entrails
You should have been faithful in your love
I lie on your breasts again
But it would have been better
Far better
If you had remembered your responsibility to the world
And loved me.

4 March 1961
A possible scheme for the cricket match. Rain has stopped play. Talk by
home team. YM takes stand when rain stops. Opponents fielders round
him. As he increasingly hits out the fielders draw away. The captain (off)
can reposition some of them. Finally H bats alone onstage. Pit pat pit pat
etc. No commentary at this stage, but early the voices (off) of the home
team describing their surprise at the progress of the game.

   The striking becomes monstrous: watching it is like watching a
gigantic machine at work. Finally the lights dim down quickly (but dont
[?]), and the next scene starts with drunken singing of For he's a jolly
good fellow.

   When the scene has become unnatural (justified because this is the
climax of the first part of the play [what does the match mean to him
afterwards]) naturalism could break in once or twice in well-defined
episodes, with precise beginnings and endings.

6 March 1961
   O[ld] M[an]: I'm not a hermit, it's just that no one comes to see me.
   Actually, the OM wouldn't say this, but it about sums it up.
Obliquely he may say that after not seeing people for some time (perhaps
he was ill) the thought of facing them again horrified him.

   YM could extract one of the old man's teeth. This could be the
physical reality for the psychic reality of murder. OM could explain how
previously he drew his own teeth.

   Activities for OM – cooking. He could prepare meal and YM be
unable to eat it. Just sit in front of plate. Dim out.

[. . .]

Notes For Hermit Play – 20 March 1961

Cut out final bit about 'I strangled him' etc. This indicates bewilderment. My intention at this point is to demonstrate something more mystical: knowledge. The YM is in the condition of history. He is 'at home' for the first time, but the home is a great palace.

The H doesnt have this knowledge – he is always ignorant.

The sort of knowledge = imagine a man who has just completed a jigsaw puzzle. He sits on one side doing nothing. He isn't 'knowing that the jigsaw puzzle is finished.' He sits in a state of accomplishment. It is, however, passive relaxation. It is active insight – I'd almost like to call it 'in-being'.

Not knowledge in the form of knowing that something is the case . . . but knowledge analogous to seeing X, without the physical events (I'm not talking of visions).

Not a state of being possessed, but a state of possessing he is finally 'all right'.

[. . .]

25 March 1961

H's place = hell (from 'He jumped'). H's place: only a few sticks onstage, and these all huddled together (for illusion of being cramped, without having to use much scenery), actors to use the whole stage (up to the corrugated iron).

1st scene: someone asks if there's a paper. No answer. Then they all row about some pointless triviality. All take sides.

Wife: (sometime after marriage) tells you she's 'past her time'. She has mild hysteria (no other <u>dramatic</u> symptoms, but a bit naggish) goes to bed for a few days? (Although she's now 'on') then YM gives her short money (because he's been having time out at h).

W taking up with former boyfriend (ref. tape recording), but they may not actually be fucking. No very overt references to him. He just appears at their house once or twice, is seen once alone with her.

Row over h[ire] p[urchase]? Perhaps YM does try to repair some household gadget and fucks it up.

31 March 1961

'Kant insists that moral goodness exists in the will, utilitarianism in the consequences of the action. <u>Can</u> these views be reconciled?' Statements:

K, what matters is why you do it. Util[itarian], what matters is what you do, all the consequences relevant.

No necessary connection between K's claim that moral truths are a priori (true, but what does it mean?) and his claim that only a good will can be absolutely good.

Consider 'good actions done on spur of moment' or a prolonged bout of heroism, when there is no time to think? These are especially selected (by society as being 'good actions'. This stresses good as the public criteria.)

In what degree is deliberation necessary to g[oo]d will? It seems I need not be aware of my personal maxims (principles): they may just be descriptions of the way I always act in certain cases. Presumably only true of empirical ways, not the a-priori ways (such as duty-doing).

Reverence for moral law (m[oral]/l[aw] acceptable to perfectly rational beings.)

The theory is internally consistent, but it is not <u>necessary</u>. It is descriptive, but not of actual things. It is prescriptive because it says what ought to count is the motive; I consider this a religious ethic. But it of course in no way ignores the social function of ethics.

A disordered heap of things. These are sorted out into some order, and this enables one to see what there is. But the order is given by the sorter, there is no other special order. Yet the order does clarify, and not only because it shows what there is (a posteriori) but how they function (a priori).

[. . .]

23 March 1962
Usually easy to understand the political and economic and social meanings of <u>free</u>.

But there is a further use of <u>free</u> that is interesting. This usage describes the condition under which a person habitually acts. It describes the possibility of action, not the intention. For example, I may say that I am free to lift this cup. I am free from the hindrances t[ha]t would prevent me from lifting the cup. Clearly there are a multitude of possible hindrances, and I could not describe them all. The full content of this class of things – the hindrances that could stop me lifting this cup – are not known by me and are unknowable by me.

Freedom, per se, is absence from all restraint. Lifting a cup is not a freedom, it is an action. Freedom, per se, is not definable. If, as I think right, it should be defined by its negatives, and all habitual actions are related to it, the general bearing (rather than the specific instances) of the things in the class of hindrance is no doubt common to all habitual actions. This consideration is the germ in Sartrian existentialism, which is not so much an assertion of free will as an assertion of the possibility of free action. (It is not so much a philosophy of human nature as an aesthetic philosophy concerned with human action taking it into a drama; especially human drama in habitual actions. Schopenhauer is its paradigm hero). The implications of the idea are stressed if I say that I have to plan to lift up the cup (with the obvious innuendo that plans go astray). It may be objected that it is nonsense to talk in this way. That is partly true, but only in so far as it is nonsense to talk of such things philosophically. Because this is to subject them to a closer scrutiny than they usually receive. The difference is that my argument does not illuminate in the way that classical philosophy illuminates (or has the overt intention of illumination), it merely describes.

The notion of free will, as it results in actions, has two enemies: on the one hand determinism, and on the other hand the fact that people cannot prophesy they can only guess (I guess that I will be able to use the cup). The word freedom has a grammatical function, but no specific function since it can only be described by its content (which is not specific).

We are not concerned merely with the members of the class of hindrances, but the likelihood or the unlikelihood that they have of becoming actual hindrances. There is a possibility that something will hinder me. It is this possibility that something will that we compare with freedom, rather than the whole phantasmagoria of possible things. Actual freedom is never more than contingent. This is an immensely banal idea and has no doubt been epigrammatized by Omar Khayyam.[24]

But the trouble is that a thing cant be contingent on negatives, and freedom must therefore describe something actual.

It seems, then, that free is an impossible word. It describes something actual but can only be described by a class of things that is
a) unknowable
b) limitless
c) phantasmagoric

It is therefore not possible for me to say that I am free to lift the cup. In fact, I must say that I am not free to lift the cup, since it is not merely difficult to say that I am free to do so, it is impossible to say that I am free to do so.

[. . .]

---

[24] Omar Khayyam was a Persian poet of the eleventh and twelfth century.

Chapter Three

Saved, Early Morning and Censorship

Public Garden[25]
There are no lovers on the grass
The boats have not been hired out
Sounds from the streets are barely heard
There are no kids to play and shout
And ask old men the time

I stand on the deserted bridge
I lean over its empty eye
The distant trees are like black clouds
Too dense to float into the sky
And break over my head
I turn. I walk past empty cars
Pass the white notice at the gate
For a short while I am too dazed
To think of things to love and hate
I face the traffic's roar

11 November 1963
    To begin with, it is necessary to make a play out of nothing – though something dramatic may come of it. It comes by breaking through. For a long time one sees shapes of moving figures bulging behind a canvas, and then a hand, a whole arm, a shoulder and even a head, break through. Dramatic discourse must be avoided.

    <u>Dramatic confrontation</u> must be nearly eliminated. Drama comes from facts side by side, only a spurious drama can largely depend on facts confronting facts.

    A long scene (not of 'nothing happening,' which is a modern fad) of

[25] c. 1963. Bond is undoubtedly thinking of *Saved*. It was presented by English Stage Society at the Royal Court Theatre, London, on 3 November 1965. *Saved* is published in *Edward Bond Plays: 1* (London: Methuen, 1977).

<u>intention</u> in meaningful and plot movement, with two or three isolated words dropped in.

Y[oung]M[an] lying on floor with knife as if dead – start scene – pause – half raises himself, scoops out more dust from crack between floorboards – puts ear back to crack.

The big woman makes him darn her stocking. One of two longish holes at the top inside the thigh.

Some ideas[26] – 18 November 1963

The boy befriends the lonely girl downstairs (the one he's eavesdropped on). A scene with them is in a rowing boat. In the end the r[owing]/ b[oat] attendant (young blond in semi-nautical cap) calls them in 'Number Four, time up etc'.

Later he (the r/b at.) takes girl out. B jealous – but r/b leaves g abruptly (for someone else) – g just tells b. this – no preparation.

M's girlfriend is, like M, in St John's ambulance brig[ade]. M and g/f are going to a rally for the chronically limbless. Gruesome. The g/f is always giving lurid descriptions. B parodies this with a head on little wheels using tongue as propeller and brake (something like boat).

Play leads up to tragedy. M by implication seducing B, H finding B darning the top of her stockings while she wears them. (B and H have their night scene. H doesn't have to have an excuse for coming. He might say distantly 'I just come' – but <u>they both</u> accept it and expect it and H realizes B has this understanding and hence doesn't offer any excuse other than the barest formal excuse.)

But it doesn't fall into tragedy. Everything – or everybody – becomes insulated – and there is no <u>reaction</u>. There could be a scene carefully observed, but with (in common usage) no dramatic revelations or actions, except a reference to some distant revolution in the newspaper. People cutting hamsters in half with scissors are just accepted. 'It didn't scream.' 'Too surprised.' – but it <u>mustn't be someone's pet</u> – as this would only make a sentimental point.

In other words, people who should be at each other's throats just come together – and the 'action' disappears behind the dream(??).

The curtain comes down halfway through a sentence, cutting it off. Normally, a scene must be rounded off very patly – as if one was saying 'The End'.

24 November 1963

My play ends where others start. Critics have made great play with

[26] Ideas for *Saved*.

the notion that good dramatists know the strategic point at which to start (the end is consequential and falls into place). But this is dramatising actuality – or giving it dramatic shape, which is the imposition of illusion, and the glib proffering of specious explanations. A dramatist should describe and not impose – and he can only solve by being irrelevant.

26 November 1963
The old man (in white) finds YM lying on floor (as described). He tells him about violence in the war. 'A nasty incident 'e didn't scream. I never heard no one scream. During. The only screaming I 'eard was when peace come. Fell down like a coat fallen off a hanger.'

Old man hurt head falling down stairs. W tried to save him but in the confined space her effort came out as a push.

There could have been a drowning (or murder) in the pond. Then it has just been dragged when YM and G are there.

SC[ene] **Sequence** 9 December 1963
Meeting
Pond
Family
Desertion – YM and W.
Two early (Night scene.) A family scene. Perhaps W finding YM with ear to floor.
husband finds W and YM
Park scene and child murder.
?
Night scene.
G bickering H O/M will kill Y/M. G doesn't want anymore trouble had more than enough. Final scene.

Why do people sit around saying nothing or talking about very trivial things?
Because they have nothing to say.
Because they are afraid of what they will say.

Taking the farce situation of suburban small talk and indicating its tragic contents.

17 December 1963

Use unfinished sentences – especially in last scene – and then I could also exploit an unfinished anecdote.

The earlier scenes must have a Dostoevskian passion and intensity.

18 December 1963

Teddy boys stone one of their gang to death in the park.

[. . .]

Christmas 1963

The clockmaker is as much a machine as his clock. His motions etc are movements in the brain, and <u>these</u> movements cause the clock to strike as well as the movements of the gear-wheels – all are equal as efficient causes.

[. . .]

Freedom and Liberty

Freedom and liberty are words only to be applied to bodies, as water in a jug isn't free to run away. Of men, liberty is freedom to move; a man is free if 'in those things, which by his strength and wit he is able to do, he is not hindered to do what he has a will to do'. What isn't subject to motion isn't subject to impediment, and so cant be said to be not free.

Fear and liberty are consistent; as a man, through fear, may will to throw his goods over board in a storm – he is free not to, should he choose.

Liberty and necessity are also consistent; unjugged water is free but must of necessity run down; so voluntary actions are all <u>caused</u>, and are therefore necessary.

[. . .]

3 January 1964

The young boatman could be the pram burner. As climax to Act I the local housewives could stone him to death after he comes out of the court, with a sack over his head, between two policewomen. As the housewives shout, Y/W screams.

Act II (final act) begins with her and her girlfriend in a scene to show her anti-social pessimism – she does something mean, rather worse than 'a nasty little theft' – and her fears that there are 'worse to come' are conveyed.

Scene with women waiting and talking about him. Earlier, although he'd left her y/w tries to help him (waiting at local court?) – he could either be eager, or remote.

Then a scene suggesting new climax: the night scene. Then possibly a scene in which violence is low comedy (rag-day) then final scene.

[. . .]

The child killing 19 January 1964

YM finds BM beating the pram. BM claims that he was only beating out the flames. (YM does the same beating actions as BM.) There could be a final scene with BM dying on stretcher (BM and YW have been estranged for some time) and YW.

There could be a form-filling scene in II. Questions (by YM or OM? or OW?). Married or unmarried. YW: unmarried. Parent or childless. YW: childless.

Also a weird row in which YW and YM argue about the killing and at the same time about something unimportant such as a tin of sardines. Accusations about the killing and about the tin of sardines being screamed at the same time (and both switch about in this way – not YM about killing and YW about sardines and vice versa).

[. . .]

Pram S[cene][27]

BM wheels baby on. Says 'stop crying your mum's only gone to spend a penny.'

Ted comes on. Says 'O 'e loves it!' They burst a big blue sausage balloon, tied onto corner of head. Why? What's 'e done? etc. Dare him to hit it. He does. Pull its hair. He does. It's screaming. Make it bleed. Go on. Cut its fingers. Makes it bleed. Baby sobs – hiccups. Throw this at it. What? No. You. Me? Go on. The other Ted throws a stone. Several then stone it. Laughs and mad scream. Baby has been silent for some time.

YW comes on. Moans about everything being left to her. Oo burst your balloon? Wheels pram off.

YM and YW could wait for BM to come out of prison (YW of course wants YM to leave her alone – she still wants BM) – but YM comes with her. BM doesn't want anything to do with them. YW blames this on YM.

28 January 1964

After BM rejects YW there is an 'after prison' scene. YM makes some gesture of pleading with YW that they order their lives differently – that they find 'some common ground on which to build'.

[27] From an entry in Bond's notebook dated 27 January 1964.

31 January 1964
Notes on II

YM could be sewing a button onto his shirt. OW tells him about the hole in her stocking – 'Darn it!'. He drops the needle between her legs and has to grovel for it. She could sing in contralto while YM does the darning – a principle-boy song – she would either have to explain that she once played P-boy, or be dressing for the part in a Red Cross panto[mime].

OM comes in. Pause. Takes something. Goes out. Bit more business. Cut.

Next scene – OM and OW have a sudden row – the first time they talk in the play. YW is afraid that it all means more trouble – this gives her the opportunity for an outburst.

Then the night scene – which deflects the arguments. 'There won't be any more rows'.

Then an intermediary scene. Then the final scene.

OW is of a higher social class than OM.

[. . .]

A Play[28] – 10 January 1965

Siamese twins first born of Monarch. Fight for crown?

At end one dies, and the other has to drag him round the stage? A final horror-scene where he is shown attached to a skeleton? Always wanted to kill him, but didn't because shared blood system.

From time to time they kill someone [they say] to sustain audience's flagging interest.[29] Act I ends with a garroting. Something for them to remember. The audience – the bored intellectual, those lonely people on their own, carrying books or a superior magazine. Never mind, it was a lovely meal. In Chelsea. Ever so nice.

Garroting – Siamese twins ideally suited for this. 'Every deformity can be turned to an advantage, as the social worker says.' The whole play is punctuated by deaths – 'to keep the interest going.'

Talk: Shakespeare's knowledge of how to get on with the audience. The gift of direct humanity. This play's equivalent to be direct violence, and insulting taking into consideration their true feelings.

Intellectuals like all those corpses in Hamlet. But that is typical

[28] Background notes for *Early Morning*, first staged at the Royal Court Theatre, 31 March 1968. The dialogue here is the characters'. *Early Morning* is published in *Edward Bond Plays: 1* (London: Methuen, 1977).

[29] Bond comments, in a note to the editor, that 'the characters either spoke to the theatre audience – or there was to be "a stage audience" '.

intellectual whimsy. Working class audiences are realistic enough to make do with a punch up, or a good kicking, and a little unfaithfulness.

During the gathering 'I believe theatre should be entertainment'.

[. . .]

A Comic Play 18 February 1965

I have usually allowed my characters to indulge in a little self-analysis at the end of a play. Len does this in <u>Saved</u>, at the beginning of the scene with the old man. This ought to be replaced with an intimating incident – he gets cross with his case, and bangs or kicks it because he can't shut it – he might even stomp – or be cross because he can't find his keys.

In the new play explanations <u>should</u> be given – but by incidents, and verbal tendencies or emphases – not by verbal ideas.

Work – 19 March 1965

Mr. Simpson pulled his front door behind him and started to walk towards his gate. He saw Mr Gordon coming on to the street two doors up, and knew that Mr. Gordon had seen him. He could not turn back. Mr. Gordon himself wondered if he could fail to notice Mr. Simpson and hurry past or cross over, but as they were friendly together he realized he could not.

As he walked Mr. Simpson glanced down at his flowerless patch of rubble and for the attention of Mr. Gordon he did the elaborate gesture of his head, neck and shoulders – so that their meeting and greetings were led up to gradually and comfortably.

As he approached Mr. Simpson's gate Mr. Gordon realized that he would have to walk slower, or he would over-shoot the meeting awkwardly. He managed to get to the gate as Mr. Simpson closed it behind him.

'Nice day'.

'Not raining'.

'Hope it stays like it.'

'The farmers'll need it.'

Mr. Gordon said 'Yes'. The early morning light and the damp made the pavements and air glow like snow. Mr. Gordon liked to walk to work on the other side of the road, but he wouldn't mention this to Mr. Simpson. There might be misunderstandings. Really, Mr. Simpson ought to have known that. Mr. Gordon thought 'like him not to'.

At the corner they came across a cat. The back legs and pelvis had been crushed and the tail severed. It had dragged itself to the side of the road. A dog had just found it. The brute had its jaw flat to the road, the flesh pulled back from its teeth, and the teeth grinning. Then it lifted its head over the cat and yelped. It shook its head with excitement, and Mr. Gordon thought of a dog bringing a bone from a pond.

Then it bit the cat's rear, and blinked and dropped it when it found its mouth full of blood. The cat hissed. The men chased the dog off. It slunk down the road, twisting from side to side like a water snake, craftily turning its head from side to side to catch glimpses behind, without taking the risk of turning or stopping. Then it shrank away, worried by the taste in its mouth.

Mr. Simpson lifted his boot over the cat's head. The cat turned its head sideways. The teeth were broken. The lorry seemed to have pressed all the life forwards till it was jammed into the eyes. Mr. Gordon stamped down and caught the end of the jaw awkwardly. The teeth buried deeper in the flesh.

Mr. Simpson bent forward and wondered if he could save the cat. The front of the face was shredded and wet. But the eyes and brow and ears were crisp and glistening.

Mr. Simpson came back from the hedge with a flat chunk of cement. Mr. Simpson awkwardly clutched Mr. Gordon's mac. It creased, and the four buttons, with the white whorls in them, were dragged towards Mr. Simpson's fist.

Mr. Gordon said 'Eh?'

Mr. Simpson stared at Mr. Gordon's eyes and then looked down at the cat. He saw the glisten go out of the eyes and the brow. The fur creased, and looked dusty. Then the eyelids shut, and the eyes were almost completely closed. It was dead, except for the breathing.

Mr. Simpson said 'I know what's best for it' and brained it with the cement stone.

Mr. Gordon said 'Yes'. He felt relieved and helped to move it into the gutter with his foot. The drops of transparent fluid, and the smear of blood, on his boots did not worry him much. He felt he had done the best.

Mr. Simpson was a bit late for work. He cleared a few parcels left over from the night before, and then he unscrewed his flask and poured himself a mug of tea. He sat on an upturned case, with the steaming mug in one hand, and a luncheon meat sandwich in the other and chewed. His head was stuck a little forward and his eyes were empty. He chewed and did not think.

Mr. Gordon did not get the job he was applying for. Before going into the office he had cleaned his boots and trouser bottoms with his crumpled handkerchief. [From] waist-high up the walls were glass, and through the glass he could see the girls drinking tea. The woman in the office had pushed a cup of tea towards him and said something. He had drunk half.

Both men were beginning their old age.

A Legend – 22 March 1965

Many years ago a queen gave birth to two eldest sons, joined at the shoulder. One son put the other into subjection and was crowned king. He could not kill his brother without killing himself. This brother was always the centre of dissatisfaction in the kingdom, and the king longed to be rid of him. Finally his brother died and the king was stricken with remorse. He refused to have his brother cut away. He became a skeleton, and the king carried him everywhere. Finally his brother's ghost came and took his bones, and a little later the king died.

They occasionally both begin the same sentence at the same time. This is exasperating in a crisis.

There are obviously many possibilities for the cause of the trouble. Does A want to get rid of B, or do A and B equally want to get rid of each other? Why? Because there isn't enough (of everything) to go round or because they just don't like sharing? Or don't trust each other?

In one scene they finally hit each other in exasperation – and shout in pain as they hit, not as they are hit.

The Relationship with the audience. Just as they can't get up a good relationship between themselves, they can't get a deep sustained relationship with the audience.[30]

One of them consults an anarchist, who sits by, always unmoving, watching his grave – his last major action was to dig it. When asked why he does this (hoping for illumination or help) he replies that there is nothing else to do – certainly nothing to hope in. (After they ask the question they have to wait a long while for him to find his voice.) But he sits on the pile of earth – and they shan't take that!!

Perhaps his attendant could say that's all he can remember. He came here for the greater glory of God – but that's all he can remember.

Perhaps the surviving twin could go back to this grave later (at night) and throw himself in it.

Play 24 March 1965

Possibilities. Each twin has a different idea of how this country should be run. If the Neolithic Revolution – one could believe in order/ regimentation. One shouldn't be bad and the other good: both bad,

[30] See the previous note.

though one can be worse than the other. The anchorite could be the (abdicated) father – or a general they have defeated. (Originally he had crawled once or twice round his grave, for exercise.) He could give a speech on hands – these hands will one day be dead. The audience's hands, lying on their bodies, or sticking stupidly in the air – making artistic gestures in the interval (he's got lovely hands, lovely) will be dead – like a pair of salted claws.

The difference between A and B: this can be given an objective correlate – political, economic ETC – but must also be psychological in themselves. Just being bound to someone is enough to make you hate them: you'd either have to hate them or love them.

25 March 1965

Possibly A could talk B into joining him to defeat the present king. After they had done that either A (or better, B) could turn on the other, and take the dominant role. Anyway, at one point A (or B) stabs or insults someone, while B (or A) tries to prevent him.

5 April 1965

Abdicate – one could want to abdicate, but the other wants to carry on the fight.

Or – A forces B to abdicate. A then reigns. But B has some effect on A. And in the end – when A fails and B is dead – A wont be parted from B.

Who is the rightful heir? Good/evil. Libido/Super Ego?

Could the repressed one be the one who makes all the effective decisions – that is, the one forced into abdication? The apparently forceful one is always 'being in charge' of massacres and putsches etc. The mild one is at the end seen as the really ferocious one – but with an awareness of culpability and guilt.

The skeleton. It could be said that the living one must batten on the other one even in death. Even then it can't leave it in peace.

6 April 1965

There are snaps and photographs. Photographs can often tell the truth about a face – but only snaps can tell the truth about people and places – about life, in fact. Plays should be made of snaps. (The great fault of television is that it is almost always 'photography' – a great TV artist would have to take snaps.) 'Snaps' is probably a good title for the play. An element I haven't touched on is the gaining of experience – a child's exploration. Children have the sense of touch, adults have the sense of

Braille. That is the experience of growing, or aging, or losing – and it ought to be an integral part of the play.

Another useful analogy is Marvel's The Garden – but this is the experience in reverse. But it ties up with the first image (the adult – the man reading tombstones in braille) and envisions a mental recreation of data from the other five senses, in both there is progression in the sense of getting to know an environment and becoming aware of all one's emotions – this doesn't mean deepening or intensifying one's emotions, at least in a crude sense.

21 April 1965

Primitive man would have known only a few men, and known them only dimly. His knowledge of space and time were restricted to his own limited experience, and a few retold memories. Danger was constant, and risk could not be eliminated. Even then, men were seized by their society, and a man could only escape into forest and death. From the beginning men were totally involved in defences.

Order, and therefore aggression and coercive power, were available to neolithic men; otherwise they could not have made such large buildings. No doubt the hierarchy was supported on the surplus value earned by the community.

Primitive men used surplus value to impress, placate, aggress, and defend. More advanced civilizations were able to support if only incidentally the creators of beauty (as in Egypt) and finally, in Greece, philosophers and scientists also. These last began to classify and analyse.

The Greek cities were unable to organize proper defence. The Republic was meant to fulfil an ideal norm of the perfect organic society; but this is a rationalization for the impregnable society; a society without internal discords. But the question of its foreign policy is avoided.

Rome had the organization lacking in Athens and even Sparta (which was far too isolationist for an expanding world). But it was centrally weak. The Roman workers could not sell their work because it was cheaper to plunder the Empire. They were taught loyalty to the state and Caesar, but not humanity to their fellow man; had they been taught this they would not have been such effective conquerors. They were idle, and therefore capable of mischief. To amuse them the games were inaugurated; and to feed them bread was given away. Really they recreated the life of the savage, because no man was sure of his life. He developed a mental defensiveness, a cringe. Surely, he could not get out of his mind what he had seen at the games. Crimes seemed arbitrary and capricious and punishment was terrible.

Sexually he was effete and over-replete. Naturally he turned to xianity, especially the puritanical, pauline version. It must have been the chastity and the brotherly love that made the immediate appeal, rather than the Christ-myth. That myth probably referred to primordial events; it claimed that the primordial war in the family was at an end. The father had won, but the son had not really been beaten: father and son were one. This sense of synthesis and stasis had a great attraction during the dissolution and the dark ages. Men, of course, still felt personal guilt, and they still had to earn their share in the divine amnesty – they were still one removed from the elect. But at least the meaning and form of salvation were undisputed; the possibility of release had been granted once and for all on the cross.

Hell helped to relieve aggression and to keep men up to the mark.

In the middle ages there was further development. The cult of the virgin and child shows the new interest in sex – Christian chastity and rigour had caricatured itself, under the compelling neurosis of individual men, and a reaction resulted. Also, the monasteries had become wealthy and powerful, and supported by this the popes started to exercise temporal power. Cynicism resulted at the worst, indifference and laissez-faire at the best. Indulgences could be sold for either reason.

As society accumulated more wealth it explored further. New wealth, new, valuable, storable foods were discovered, and men were free to indulge in more varied and strenuous activities.

The Protestant protest was complicated. It involved the implacability of God (Calvin) and the powerlessness of the church and its sacraments (Luther). This seriously affected the doctrinal stasis that was the base of medieval life. Both Luther and Calvin affected the self-knowledge of man. Luther tended to abolish the divine pact, he made each man a Christ again; salvation still had to be sweated for (though not in the way that Christians had sweated for it on the x[cross]). Calvin went to the other extreme, but the effect on men was much the same. There had to be a rigorous denial, in a man's mind and conduct, of anything that suggested he was not elected. Both Calvin and Luther abolished the society-and-church that donated indulgence and salvation (the law could punish and the church excommunicate) and placed the emphasis on individual awareness and effort.

Men were more themselves and less members of societies. Each man therefore sought his own salvation, and the idea of duty towards other men became to be lost (if it had ever existed). In any case, it was found to be absent when it was most needed.

The machine uses men. If men can't farm and grow for themselves they must sell themselves as servants and attendants to machines.

The Reformation took away the church's coercive power (and its vested interest in preaching morals) and obscured brotherly love. Enclosure and enticement removed peasants and farmers from their land. Men found themselves in cities, and were exploited by factory owners. These men felt free to pursue their own interests; and they even reversed completely the medieval idea of society as a corporation able to grant salvation to all those who truly asked for it, and thought that society was there to defend their own depredations. Society now became truly coercive, and real class enmity developed.

Men now had no 'basis' in their lives, nothing that would attract their attention and beliefs. Social injustice became, at the same time, very evident. It was necessary for practical and now, ideological reasons, to correct injustice here and now. The old estates were also reactionary in their dotage. Against these things there were protests and finally rebellions. Politically there were revolutions, and aesthetically there was romanticism, in which the son/father conflict again became raw and bleeding.

Protest cannot, of course, be itself a basis for continuing life – but it must always be granted that protest is often necessary and best.

Nationalism was probably an effort to create some basis, some corporate identity and security, which at the same time would allow opportunities for pride and aggression.

Materialism, and the romantic protest against materialism, seemed to have combined in our own age in fascism. Men have behaved badly because there are no corporate restraints and no brotherly loyalty. Men have become national and partisan. Grudges and resentments must be indulged here and now – there is no conception of a total order or balance.

Men have discovered that without a god in society everything is possible.

Although men's knowledge is vastly extended, really men live in a much smaller world than that of medieval man; men feel that they must solve all their own problems, and they solve them in the light of their immediate promptings and appetites. Medieval men, of course, felt that their problems were solved in society, which was balanced.

Scientific power and the absence of human restraint have, of course, reduced men to the condition of primitive men: they live in continual fear.

[. . .]

Siamese Twin Play[31] 29 June 1965

It is a play about freedom. A wishes to be free from Z. You cant have very much that is more basic than that. Perhaps Z is a half-wit – his brain was damaged at birth.

Part of the final scene will be when A and Z (? Z dead) meet 3 Siamese twins (who have heard legends of 5 or 8 joined Siamese twins). Would it be too cheap if the play were modelled on a journey, A seeking someone or something – and this is what he finds?

If Z is halfwitted, could he be the first-born and legal heir?

The danger of the 3 twins is that they ought to be the subject of the play (since they are in a worse condition [leaving aside the question of their attitude] than A/Z) – and they cant be brought in to solve something. It is a bad dramatic argument to say that there's always someone worse off than you are.

30 June 1965

One of the twins could be a woman: but that is almost a perversion.

The story could be told of the woman alone on the desert island who thought she was the last person alive. She is dying. She is pregnant. There are wolves on the Island. She gives herself a Caesarean section with the lid of a tin: a) because her instinct tells her to produce the child b) because although the wolves would savage her, they would suckle the child.

The final scene could be A (wearing crown) with skeleton of B attached to him, in conversation with the 3 twins. They could tell one of two stories, such as the one of the woman on the Island. But I think I would prefer a final scene of him on his own – perhaps the skeleton would have rotted to a few sticks, or have been removed.

One of them could lose his girl because of the other. (When they were children one could have masturbated when the other wanted to sleep.)

I am approaching the twins through the particularities of their lives: I want to find the basic confrontation, the fundamental agon.

If one committed a crime he could not be punished (in some ways) for it without also punishing the innocent twin: he couldn't be hanged or imprisoned . . . .

They are caught in a flood at one stage: presumably they must cooperate if they swim.

I am reluctant to conclude the roles of A and Z because I dont want to make them personifications of a theory; A as super-ego, Z as id, etc. This

---

[31] All of Bond's notes in this section refer to *Early Morning*.

is because I want them to personify psychological theories, but at the same time economic, philosophical, political etc theories. Because characters in a play must always be in a situation. 'A' may want to murder his brother, but lightning may strike 'A' before he can. This has nothing to do with a psychological examination of the play. Bad Freudian dramatists simply use characters to exemplify theatrical (and no doubt actual) types. The proper dramatist is concerned with a philosophical account of the whole of life, knowing that human beings are only one part of this, and that chance (which in the aggregate may be called fate) cannot be explained in psychological terms.

1 July 1965

They could sit down together when quite young and complain of their situation: one real natural flaw and there's nothing you can do about it etc. There really is no physical remedy. They must resign themselves. Adaptation.

When A wants to sit Z wants to stand. That is quite natural. But they must always arrive at a compromise.

2 July 1965

... It would be subtler to give Z fits rather than make him mentally retarded.

What is the conflict? Is just the struggle for adaptation and freedom sufficient? Or must A or Z fight to control the other? Or help the other? Or even for the other's rights?

Never to be alone – except for the death scene (and subsequently) when A (? Z) is alone for the first time?

Could the silly, 'fit' one survive? Having killed off the good one? So that the final circular journey with the crown is a mad, foolish triumph. A could have become reconciled to Z, and even started to nurse him? – after fighting him at first, and terrifying him by saying that he will have him cut off, and Z is too weak and silly to survive on his own? Then, the foolish character would triumph. Ideals and aspirations would have been washed away, or burnt out, and only the stupid, empty shell would survive. If this happens, A/Z must meet the 3 T's earlier, when A is reconciled, and nursing Z.

4 July 1965

I would prefer that the intelligent one survived. Then he has to endure the consequences – not merely that the audience has to feel them.

It also opens up the opportunity for a Blake-like comment on human situation – since, awareness is the essence of this (and Z would be unaware).

The inheritance: if A (say) could gain intellectual ascendancy (or emotional ascendancy) he would be free and single.

Having A survive is more complex and dense and can include a consciousness of the other ending. A never really makes contact with Z anyway.

If A 'nurses' Z, this mustn't be sentimentalized. And when Z dies A isn't grief-stricken. Z is a retarding (but unavoidable) burden to A. (Why doesnt A rejoice when Z dies, then?)

5 July 1965

I dont want to have a strong A and a weak Z – both must have human failings, and Z mustn't be sub-human. Could A have a bad temper?

The kingdom could declare itself a republic at the end of I – because they're tired of the internecine war. In II A and Z are in exile.

A could have a sarcastic scene when someone reports to him the various incidents of the revolution, which are not, of course, seen by the audience. 'What a sight! – that must have been worth seeing! – what a spectacle etc'.

A and Z are both born very intelligent – but Z gets shot at in the wars (bullet meant for A?) and gets a permanent brain injury, which makes him slow and a bit childish. In I they fight for the throne with great ferocity, in II they suffer the consequences of their ferocity.

In II there must be a great feeling of the consequential. Certainly one is freed and, existentially, able to choose – but one must bear the consequence of one's choice. (If existentialism claims anything more than this, it is as fatuous as Christian Science.) I see the movement (not necessarily the scenes) as short fragments – almost shaped like deductive mathematics.

The search for an explanation or some mental scheme of resolution, accompanies the drama: it is voiced in a dialogue that accompanies – and is partly shaped by, the action. Thus, one must arrive at the resolution while listening to the roar of the furnaces at Auschwitz, not in tranquil recollection years later. Then, at any rate, the dramatist (at least) would have to make you tortured by nightmares.

26 July 1965

If I had to describe the main psychological characteristic of the age I would describe it – not as the Century of Sex, or Violence – but as The Age of Faith. People will believe almost anything. They no longer require the authority of a pope or army, only a slip pushed through the door. The origin of the slip is almost anonymous. The limit of their belief is only defined by the natural contradiction of the various things they are asked to believe, and even this limit is not rigorously observed.

You might say that housewives do not believe that X is whiter, and the fact that they accept the free spoon that goes with X isn't proof that they do. But I think they do, and their reward for believing it is the spoon. Psychologically their critical acumen is killed by their education. No firm says 'X doesn't wash whiter than Y – but we give you a spoon with X'. Not many housewives would have the courage to take X and the spoon – not many housewives would want to.

[. . .]

Comedy is concerned with the humanity of men: it isnt concerned with man as artist, fabricator – architect or mechanic – or spaceman, except when men are being unsuccessful at these things. It isnt concerned with human enterprise and achievement.

Comedy is concerned with death. Of course, I am not saying that death is the subject of comedy. But it defines comedy. In a technical and scientific age comedy is obviously very potent because it is a sort of anti-faith, admitting truth into an area controlled by propaganda and national prestige.

The Lord Chamberlain 1 August 1965

I would do almost anything to prevent my play being banned except alter one comma at the request of the Lord Chamberlain.

If the director asked me to change a word or alter a scene, I would do so, because he would be trying to improve the clarity, or truth, or theatrical force of the play. But the Lord Chamberlain is not helping, he is interfering. His aim is extra-theatrical.

The play is about sex and violence, but it is also about other things: humour, dignity, suffering and hope. Sex and violence are in the play not for the effect that they will have on the audience but for the effect they might have on the characters in the play. It is the indignity and suffering that is affected in the characters that I hope will affect the audience. I hope, that is, that at the end of the play, the audience will have achieved a balanced, sympathetic conclusion about the characters. It is this final conclusion, and the impressions on which it is based, that is definitive: their horror and revulsion should be transitory.

Sex and violence are at the moment obsessive preoccupations. Many people have died and suffered through humanly inflicted violence in the last few years. The men in my play kill a baby. In the audience at any showing of the play there will no doubt be people who fought in one or more of the recent wars: some of them will have killed. Probably one or two of them were war airmen. They may very well have dropped incendiary bombs that burnt a baby to death – a man who has done that may very well be present in the audience. In one respect I would claim that the men in my play are more moral than him – at least they urinate on the baby to put out the flames. To the child this would be a blessing. Of course, the pilot or bomber would justify his conduct with rational arguments and claim that in some ways he had no alternative. I accept that, so far as it goes. But it leaves open the questions of will, and freedom, and duty and excuse, and motive: and these questions are not susceptible to the easy answers of the Lord Chamberlain. And in any case, I am not concerned with the apologetics of violence, or even the sufferings of the victims; I am concerned with the consequences to the agent.

It is always puzzling how (quite apart from the matter of nature) a man can let himself become an habitual killer. If we realize that the killer just doesn't think about what he's done, the puzzlement is partly removed (although only to be replaced by bewilderment about human nature). It is the job of the serious, moral dramatist to open the subject of violence, and make thoughts about it possible and, because of the impetus generated by drama, necessary and alluring. And naturally a serious, moral dramatist is drawn towards the most pressing problems he knows – and at present this is the problem of violence.

If the dramatist is going to pursue this aim effectively – it is not enough for him to talk about violence – he must demonstrate it. This is the essential requirement of the theatre: demonstration of the problem. No good, effective theatre can avoid this. If I want a good, ultimately effective, viable theatre, then it must have this freedom to demonstrate directly. The alternatives are a novelettish, talking theatre, or a theatre that is essentially second-rate and trivial because it cannot demonstrate the most pressing moral problems of the times; and even the first alternative of the 'novel' theatre, is second rate, because it is merely a bad book, or a cumbersome lecture ('. . . of course, you could understand what I mean if only I could just show you x, but let me try to describe it as . . .'). You cannot have the present censorship, and a culturally virile theatre. The censorship is an aesthetic obstacle. It is far too crude a method to be morally helpful in any aesthetic problem that is at all complicated (and most aesthetic problems are fiendishly complicated); on the other hand, it is thoroughly ineffective even in the most naive, policing-moral matters, since you may exhibit almost any pornographic, suggestive obscenity you like, provided you call the place where you do it a club. Why do we retain the censor?

[. . .]

Play 26 August 1965

Masks. These could be worn by characters in I to represent social activities. They could all pick out of a basket their Statesmen masks, their judges masks, their army/war masks etc for appropriate occasions. A could at one stage throw off his mask in a fury. He could later try to remove his mother's mask, so as to make contact with her, but she can't/ won't take it off. In II the sympathetic characters don't wear masks – although the chain of men at the end could wear saint or tragic masks.

The boys' father could be dead – killed, actually, when he was a boy (they say) because his mother tried to murder him and he didn't really get over this. The queen marries the old mustachioed general. Perhaps the boys fight him – or by following him they become involved in internecine struggle (this is better).

In (2) B is shown in advance decomposition – a sort of bluish mummy with a featureless head hanging down.

Then in II the General could come and try to force A to return – the dual monarchy problem, also, is solved by then – 2 being dead.

The Garroting Chamber. Straying queen. Only A (and A attached to B (2)) is left, to perform justice, so: – A's argument. Perhaps the general could have been in the army and killed father. Or, better, general could have forced the father into waging a war – and have killed him indirectly in this way.

Drama is the basis of theatre. This play isn't a drama, but it is good for a writer to occasionally write something outside the drama. Naturally, he wants to return to the drama. When he does so he should have stronger powers in his control.

I am afraid of my plays becoming agglomerations. One wants to reduce things to create simplicities. (But beware of over-simplifications, and vulgar simplifications.)

Scenes in II. Weed scene (a host of golden X – the name of a yellow weed). The chain of war scene. The male/female twin scene. The grave scene. B (2's) death. etc.

The play could be called The Yellow————.

This play isn't dramatic; because it is a final play – following the shape of the burial service. It sums up a dead society. It is the internment of Hamlet. And it is not dramatic, because, although a funeral can be very dramatic, it is <u>not</u> dramatic for the corpse. It closes the door on a society and an era.

Perhaps the chain of men could be the general's sons (especially if A has killed the general) – but this is so explicit that the audience might find it confusing.

The Censorship

Most of the remarks I have to make apply equally well to the censorship of novels, films, paintings, etc., as they do to the theatre.

But first I should like to indicate some of the peculiarities of the present censorship that are specific to the theatre. The obscenity of a book must be judged on the whole book, and not on isolated passages removed from their context. Isolated passages and even isolated words may be forbidden by the theatre censors; yet there is less justification for treating a play in this way than there is a novel. Someone might perhaps buy what he considered was an obscene book, and skim through it reading only what he considered were obscene passages. But surely no one could go to the theatre and watch only the scenes he considered were obscene and spend the other times at the bar? The audience of a play is forced to experience the whole of the play, and for this reason the play as a whole should be considered when it is judged for obscenity. (This presupposes that the censorship is concerned with the moral well-being of the individuals in the audience, and not with 'the tone of society' – which I deal with later.)

The obscenity of a novel or picture is discussed in court under the rules of evidence, and expert witness is heard on the moral and aesthetic value of the work. The censor of the theatre works in private – and there seems no established method of appeal.

The censor of a play may say it is potentially demoralizing – but allows it to be seen by club members. One may be demoralized provided one is willing and able to pay for the privilege. (The equivalent for the novel would be legal obscene book clubs.)

<u>In general.</u>

An obscene novel must be capable of depraving a reader. But life is far more corrupting than art. If someone is of such a nature that he can be corrupted by what he reads in a book, he will certainly be corrupted by what he sees or hears in his daily life. Banning certain words or scenes from a book or play will not save him.

A play <u>may</u> corrupt someone, but a good play (and I will deal with bad plays later) has morally desirable effects. If someone will be corrupted anyway, one ought to risk corrupting him by a play if it is shown that other people benefit morally from the play. (Freedom of expression is in any case morally good in itself.) This might sound like justifying the ends by the means, and I agree that the moral state of the argument is ambiguous. But it is sound common sense. The moral good that the play does outweighs its moral harm, and in any case the moral harm would be done by other means.

The censor is a colonel – trained to bayonet and shoot with the rest of them. He has probably killed someone. But he feels that violence must be restrained (it must) but at the same time it must be conserved – and unleashed when the government chooses. This argument is the enemy of art. Art wishes to take the structure of violence to pieces and find out how it works and how it can be disposed of: it is at least as able to do this as science is.

The present censorship has an effect that is opposite to the intended effect. It stops one dealing with violence analytically and seriously – and so lessening the amount of violence perpetrated. One can deal with violence only in a shoddy way – as in the sunday papers.

And our attitude to sex is clearly old-maidish and worse – nasty. You can't go naked on the beach, but for a small fee you may look lecherously at nakedness in strip joints, where the human body is degraded by its surroundings. It receives a sort of respectability there because money is made out of it.

We ought to have nakedness on beaches and in athletic meetings (what effects would this have on the records?).

Censorship should go, but there should be the restraints I have indicated above, until we are morally enough mature to do without them.

2 August 1965

. . . We have now domesticated all the animals that usually dwell in our cities or houses; only man remains undomesticated. Men have domesticated their pets, but they have not domesticated themselves.

16 November 1965

I have been comparing your drama critic's first review of my play Saved with the remarks printed in 'The Times.'

In his review of my play Saved of 4/11 [4 November] your critic explicitly accused me – that I had used violence to appeal 'to no emotions beyond those aroused by the act itself.' But in The Times of 15 November he writes 'On one thing everyone is agreed: Mr. Bond (cannot) be accused of exploiting violence for its own sake.' This surprising volte-face has been made without any explanation or apology. I am wondering how much of his original review your drama critic now wishes he could surreptitiously withdraw. Certainly his original attitude of hysterical attack has been changed into a facetious defensiveness. Now I am at fault because I have now pointed out some of the subjects dealt with in the play. But I have had to do this, only because your critic, and certain others, failed to see these things.

He is especially facetious because I have pointed out some of the subjects dealt with in the play. But I could do this only because your critic failed to do his job. Your critic has not only <u>denied</u> any of the play's specific subjects. What I have mentioned are to be found in the play. Will he deny the Oedipus relationship, for example, in the face of all the evidence? Will he deny that the play is built round a liberal humanist's struggle with himself and his environment? This was a betrayal of his critical obligation.

He also further accuses me of being muddled because I said that <u>Saved</u> ends hopefully although it deals with a hopeless situation. There is no muddle here: to the people in the play their situation appears completely without hope, but as an observer I did not give up all hope.

The most curious of your critic's latest remarks is that 'morally the production offers a blank cheque to the audience's imagination'. I must again surprise your critic: the moral involvement of the play is stressed, especially in the last three scenes, almost until it is over-stressed. In this respect the final seven minutes of silence speak volumes.

[. . .]

New Play 14 December 1965

Possible beginning. Male character wearing the garter: – In 1873, at the advanced age of 53 (for this sort of thing) Queen Victoria gave birth. She had been a widow for ten years. The peculiarities leading up to this birth, and the extraordinary consequences of it, so shocked and dismayed the British public at large, that every inhabitant of these islands took a formal vow that they would not tell their children about these events. A few hundred idealists, and a few thousand cranks, who would not take this vow had to be disposed of at a centre on the Isle of Wight. History books, almanacs, and newspaper record copies of these events were rewritten. A fictitious past was substituted for the actual past. The Empire co-operated.

Foreigners were a problem. Some were disposed of. Others were bribed. Many in fact did not understand what they had seen – they thought it was part of the British eccentricity. They were frequently told it was part of the ritual of cricket.

Florence Nightingale with red lamp. She is very fond of privates. Has a lesbian affair with Queen Victoria. She tends the soldiers in the Civil War. Private Stoat, Corporal Weasel, Sergeant Fox fight over who she is sleeping with next. My turn t'night, m'am. F/N could have been the fiancée of the twin that gets killed.

'Victoria – the private life of a mother.'

John Bull is a woman. F/N is jealous of her, that is why she sulks in bed for —— years. (She also receives men.)

'The gooseberry bush.' Victoria must clout someone over the head with her sceptre.

'Sixty glorious Peers' – (all had by V.)

20 December 1965

Kill someone (intentionally?) by bursting a balloon behind them, or some other practical joke.

The idiot twin could appear free (dead) towards the end. This could perhaps anger A (he could partly have still been trying to control B (2) by not having cut him free). Perhaps B (2) could also show traces of intelligence at this stage. A could try to kill B (2) again – but of course, he can't do that!

Death doesn't happen suddenly. It intertwines in our lives. At some moments we are deader than at others.

Some entrances could be made down a chute – at one stage perhaps someone could try (unsuccessfully) to escape up it – perhaps A, or a cornered victim A intends to shoot – all other exits closed by troops.

The first, and only woman hangman – well, we are fighting for our equality.

[...]

The essence of the play is ENERGY
[...]

23 December 1965

John Bull will be Flo Nightingale in disguise – so that she can be kept at court.

[...]

27 December 1965

All my main (good) characters have done only things of which I
approved, or made mistakes (through comparative weakness) at which I
could sympathize. But A is to do something 'wicked' – not in 1 – there
he is bad for other reasons. But also in 2., when he is a sympathetic
character, because he is coming to self-knowledge, often being shocked at
his behaviour in 1. But this self-knowledge will contain some deception,
that must (at the time) be corrected by my and the audience's
judgement.

[. . .]

General

It seems that the greater the play the less the message. For example,
what is the message of Lear? Of course a lot can be learnt from it, but
nothing of what is meant when people talk about a play's message.

Most of Brecht's plays aren't specifically or even especially communist. Christians can subscribe to most of them. The Caucasian Circle
could have been a Christian parable.

But his plays are certainly not Christian. Official Christianity is of
course far more ascetic than Brecht – but I like to think that X[Christ]
had a mistress.

[. . .]

Repentance 18 January 1966

Perhaps this is the main subject of the play. The nurse becomes a
hangwoman and then repents and becomes a whore-nurse. G and V also
have repentance. They turn away from what they are to what socially
they should be. A's repentance is different, because he definitely wishes
to be himself, and find repentance without disowning himself, or
criminously accomodating himself to society (and its dual nature).

The others are so horrified by their violence and bloodshed, especially
when it is brought home to them, that they decide to build a better
world. N(ightingale), for example, takes up nursing so that if ever she is
ill or hurt, A's attitude to her whoring would be that she's doing good –
because she's making the men happy. But perhaps she could insist on
seducing someone who is dangerously ill? Perhaps she has the pox. A
would like the pox to be fatal. In fact the ideal life would be like a fatal
pox – annihilation to thorough enjoyment, or enjoyment morally
justified through annihilation.

Clinging to B (2) is like clinging to his dual, destructive nature.

[. . .]

The Tragedy (in the Comedy) 6 March 1967[32]

I am having difficulty in choosing the right way for A to betray his own army and trick V's. At the moment, I have used 'H-bombs and Cornwall' and the 'valley and dam.' Don't like H-bombs too much like a conventional tract. Must be dramatically exciting to look at as well as symbolize within the teaching: the attack on life and not lives . . .

Notes on Comedy 19 March 1967

The resurrection end seems stuck on. This should develop out of the play, especially the last act. From the moment he sees what they eat, he announces that he wants to get out of heaven – and that he <u>will</u> get out . . .

The Political Argument

If V[ictoria] states one case and Al[bert] another, I have to decide between them, or at least develop their arguments dramatically. At the moment this doesn't happen, because A's catastrophy is a 'plague on both your houses.'

---

[32] Although dated March 1967, these three entries are from Bond's previous notebook. I have put the extracts from the notebook here to provide the reader with the overall structure of *Early Morning*.

Chapter Four

Lear, *Passion* and *The Sea*[33]

3 June 1970

The renaissance artist was also a scientist and a rationalist. His art was concerned with understanding and portraying the world. This led to oversimplification and the romantics reacted against it. Their art was concerned with the hidden, with what could not be understood by immediate observation, with <u>motives</u>. At the end of the 19th century, science became interested in the irrational; it extended its scope to the hidden, to explanations rather than real 'understanding.' Now, it is not only possible for the artist to be rational again, to be a scientist – since this now covers also the irrational – he can't be a good artist if he isn't; and by good in this context, I mean the artist who is concerned with the safety and happiness of his species.

Lear's Reality

He runs a kingdom surrounded by two alien kingdoms. Are they stronger-weaker than he is? Lear builds a defensive wall, but he is also an aggressor?

Do the neighbouring kings attack him because they are afraid he is going to attack them out of greed or similar motives?

Is his country richer than the two enemy countries?

Lear's old, the two enemy rulers are young (?). Because they marry Lear's daughters (but one of them could be an <u>older</u> Lear!). What were Lear's relations with the two rulers' fathers?

Why does Lear build the wall? Is his kingdom prosperous, and are its citizens more or less happy?

What's the relationship between the two rulers
at the start of the play?
Later?

[33] *Lear*, *Passion* and *The Sea* are published in *Edward Bond Plays: 2* (London: Methuen, 1978).

Our sense of morality has been corrupted by a sense of guilt. But there isn't real morality until the sense of guilt is atrophied or removed.

5 June 1970

Living is made phoney, pretentious and cynical, sarcastic, competitive, illusory, a performance, a put on. Art can be simple, direct, and have value. This isn't turning away from the ugliness and difficulty of life to the romantic daydreaming and useless fulfilment of art. The art I mean has its origins and roots in life, and also creates living.

Lear, why does he go blind? Does he get his sight back?
The formal structures mustn't weigh the play down: the passionate woman in white. Cordelia starts as a country girl but becomes efficient but still 'rural' like a female Castro.
Lear blinded with a sword slash.
Mother and child: a mother murdering her child.
Poetry should be like bread in the mouth.
An owl perched on a can.

[. . .]

13 June 1970

Lear's anger to his 'daughters' is the aggression put into him by his education and upbringing, for political power.
Lear meets G[rave] D[iggers] B[oy]. They talk. GDB takes Lear home. Lear meets Cordelia and her child. They live together. Perhaps a visit from the court. More talk. Then the home is surrounded. GDB killed and Lear taken into captivity. They won't put him on trial because he now has public sympathy (?). His daughters would like to do so to demonstrate their impartiality and they're risking nothing because they will decide the verdict! Lear condemned to life imprisonment.
Escapes.
Cord[elia] has turned revolutionary. She overthrows daughters and somehow Lear brought to her. He is, of course, an enemy of the people. But she won't condemn him. She pensions him off. (Note: Cord was passionately and maturely devoted to GDB.) So her initial relationship to Lear is complex – she's afraid he's dangerous and thinks her husband-lover shouldn't get mixed up.
At one stage Lear hides in a grave and then climbs up out of it.

First play: 'Lear'.
Second play: 'Lear later on,' or perhaps 'Lear afterwards.'

[. . .]

14 June 1970
When the man points his bloody gun at me
I end his fate with his tears
A woman like heaps of rags rises in
Fright while I come from trees
Her hands!
This wet is the blood of snow
For stones weep when we walk on them
I will not close my eyes to this echo of blood
It is shed and each sound in the clock is the drop of it
A clock is a grave
And at each clock a gun is pointed
That is the city walls and the keep
I am a live target
When blood drips from the ends of guns
I do not run to kill it

Lear: Myth and Reality 15 June 1970

Perhaps the two are interfused and reflect and alter each other. After all, if we are mythic and act mythically and see myths, that is the way we will see and react to reality.
So it wouldn't be true to say
daughters = reality
Lear = myths
because Lear must become aware that he makes his daughters. That is, reality is a projection of myth.
Perhaps there are some hard facts of reality which impose themselves on mythical man – such as a drought or a good harvest. But these facts don't <u>have</u> to be good or <u>have</u> to be bad – there are some good and others bad. But the myth <u>can</u> be completely bad (or its effect completely bad). If a man's attitude to life and events is good and he sees them in a good light, is this because he is free of myth, or because he has a good myth? Must a myth always be bad? Or is it in practice usually bad, especially in politicians?
If Lear feels (or I know for Lear) that he is blinded by his childhood, and can never see straight, never see clear and unblinkered, he must certainly feel that his myth is bad. So his search for an heir is the search for his past. And children are born while we still sleep in our mother's arms: this is true of mythical man.

16 June 1970
Lear. End of scene 1. After shooting 3rd worker Lear shoots into air once or twice.

[. . .]

Feeding Lear in a highchair and a straightjacket so that he's fit to stand trial. He finds in Cordelia what he lost in GDB. He dies in her arms.

[. . .]

At the start of the Father Deputy Destruction Bonanza, G or Bodice sends her husband out 'because he's squeamish' or 'shut the windows. The guards are squeamish'.[34] The FD is brutalized into a thing and sent wandering about. Finally he is put out of his misery as an act almost of decency, except that it's casual. Further Deputy killing scene. Two daughters knit. They use their knitting needles to mutilate FD – by 'shutting off all his senses.' We should see one of them with her child.

[. . .]

A[35]	The air is bruised
	Look he has cut the air and it bleeds
B	Flowers, my Lord
A	And when she speaks she bites the air
	Why can't you hear it shrieking in her mouth?
B	Yes, my Lord
A	Do not wear a sword
	You cut the air when you parade with it
	She cuts the air when she points
Fool	Oh he has a crutch
	And that clubs you to death
A	I have been a long time in the grave
	From time to time I stick my head out
	And frighten the parson
	Like a dog smelling of fish

17 June 1970
Angel
The angels passed over the fields at night
Wounded wings

---

[34] Bond refers to Warrington.
[35] 'A' is Lear.

Touching the ears of corn with blood
More deaths sit in trees
More pelts and bones in the grass
More skulls on nests
Like a swan frightened to land or cry she dies in flight and falls down like
    stone

19 June 1970
The World
I am held to the world by a ball of fire
Perhaps it will go out
And I will die

It will die out in time
And you will die that way
You feel all death now
And live your death
Before you die
Be offered up dead
From the grave of your life
                    [. . .]

The value remains, the price is marked down

Shopping
Old woman in supermarket
Looking at price of marked down goods
                    [. . .]

20 June 1970
Blake inherited money from his father

21 June 1970
The king was killed by the Thanksgiving service for his recovery from an
    earlier illness.

I'm always putting my foot down, as the prisoner said on the treadmill.

I am buried in the desert under the sea
Who reaches me must drown in the desert sand
                    [. . .]

My sister has a mind like mine. I must not trust her.
Lear wandering on the wall. Or finds it when old.
Perhaps one of his daughters could go blind.
Perhaps officer isn't blinded – they want him to keep his sight so that he
    can see to wander and find Lear. Keep the blindness for Lear.
They have kept their cynicism and because this lets them make some sort of
    judgement they think they have kept their soul.

Cord says they feed officer otherwise he steals it. Better have the credit of
    giving what is going to be taken anyway.
Like madman digging pits in air
Their cause is a dream
The effect reality
The wound eats the knife
The pain cuts
A cry!
The next day a man falls on the street
And a cloud – bruised net – descends
They are buried in desert under the sea
Drowned in sand

[. . .]

Scene Arrival at GDB's house. Cordelia's sceptical.
Make the atrocity scene completely and in detail, and symbolic of the
cultural malaise.

The O[ld] C[ouncillor] is used later as witness against Lear when two
daughters hold a trial of him. OC always fits in with everyone – but not
cynically, he thinks it's for the best and whoever is in power is the best.
He's finally killed in an accident. He spent all his life looking where he
was putting his feet and was killed by a slate falling on his head.

If Lear dies in Cordelia's arms is he consoled, or is there still some
irreconcilable – perhaps something that GDB knew. Presumably
Cordelia has a new husband/lover (after her miscarriage).

GDB at wall when soldiers come. At one point say that Bodice is
opening a car factory.

[. . .]

24 June 1970
    Could the pigs run wild when Lear looks after them and go over a

cliff? They could be very proud of the pigs, because the herd is large for someone in their station.

The daughters attack Lear for all he's taken from them, all he's deprived them of. But they put all this in the abstract – not that Lear took their pocket money! Or treated them unnaturally because they were princesses.

Roasted, or at any rate <u>stuck</u>, pig.
Important: the two daughters as accusers, furies.

Last part of the play: wind.
Windswept, grey, cold. Cordelia by Lear as he dies.

The earth sucks breath from the roots.
<u>Note</u>: GDB tells Lear that officer is like a (lost) dog looking for its master. This contrasts with officer's actual attack on Lear in the night scene.

Violence scene: To think – we carry everyone of them in our body! Everyone of them has been folded in us – grown out of us, it's part of us! 'Royalty' must be broken down from Lear. 'Royalty' is what makes him destructive.

[. . .]

I mend chairs[36]
I sharpen knives
I draw pictures of your loved ones
So you see them when they're dead
I can make a cradle for a child

30 June 1970
When Lear does befriend officer they keep hacking bits off officer and finally give him back to Lear dead.

They haven't got a leg to stand on. This won't stop them standing on their heads, as they've often done in the past.

---

[36] Bond refers to the carpenter.

Plays: a particular truth can only be told in one way; a general truth can be told in many ways.

In the past evolution has developed through a biological method. It has <u>collected</u> purpose out of chance, design out of accident. A creative thing (any animal) has sustained its life by biological processes. More significant species have maintained and developed themselves by means of these processes. That is, what is possible for the species is possible only because it is possible for the individual. Change and development comes through the individual – which is leading a biological existence. The species pattern is derived from the biological processes of the individual and not the other way around. So all development has been a posteriori (only the <u>possibilities</u> being a priori.) So that there hasn't been a technological impulse; the means have been strictly limited to the needs of the individual – its survival. The survival of the individual and not the species. And this has given the activity of animals its distinctive characteristic. Its existence has been strictly limited to its own experience. Or it has had to live emotionally and physically all the effects of its existence. Or, its experience has been limited to itself. It has to live immediately the consequences of all its actions. It has no alternatives to acting. (It lives in a timeless world. Its sense of time is limited to elementary rhythms.) It can't move (do anything) except through the consequences of what it does – it has to live itself, it can't move for anything else – of course it can do things for them – hen and chicks for example. It is always present at the consequences of its acts, which it therefore has to experience and live, and these all become part of the evolutionary record, and are the process of evolutionary change.

Change is always tested by survival. It's piecemeal and is part of the living process. So that the nature of change is conditioned by the nature of existence. And this guaranteed a certain practicality of existence and change – though of course in time species can be destroyed. But this is through an inability to adapt. A natural rigidity is slower than the changing environment.

But these things aren't true of human beings. They can act as species (and not only as individuals.) Accept ideological conditions and manipulate change in ways that are divorced from the actual living processes. They can speculate and experiment with individuals – that is, the species can experiment on the individual. And then the aims of the species can be taken as superior to the aims of the individual. So emotion is no longer an individual process, with each individual surviving through its own experience. It becomes a species undertaking. So the events that have in the past always checked and guided evolution no longer work and there is no biological reason (as opposed to an environmental reason, which is why species have disappeared in the past). We are unprotected from the consequences of our actions in a unique way.

If the methods of change are (for us) radically different, so will be the consequences – even if we don't survive. The biological need to test one's environment may be reduced or completely cut-out. An animal must <u>feel</u> (have emotions) in order to survive. It must respect the individuality of the members of its own species – there <u>is</u> some destructive aggression within a species but not much, it isn't on a human scale. This attitude may not exist for much longer in [human] individuals. We assume that with increasing intelligence and cleverness we will get increasing sensibility. But technology may bring about a decrease in sensibility – because sensibility is part of the living processes and is worked out in the process of one's life, even as a species-characteristic this is true. The increased sensibility of homo sapiens is the result of his living like an animal. Technologically living like a man may be something different – and nastier for the individual.

You don't have to look for a single cause of why human beings behave badly. They have an instinctive defensive ability which takes the form of aggression; this is so with all the higher animals. This defensiveness becomes aggressive if fear and stress are constant and severe. Aggression of this sort then becomes self-perpetuating – because it provokes counter-aggression in others and this in turn reinforces our own aggression. So unless there can be a radical change – an environmental removal of stress (this would have to come before a political removal of stress) – aggression must always escalate. There are, it seems to me, no 'rational' safeguards against it. The one thing aggression (in this stage of society) cannot be is defensive. Because defensiveness (given our technology) implies an undiminishing threat.

If one <u>hates</u> the enemy (as the Europeans hated each other at the time of the 1914 war) there can be no escape. If we suspect them, or consider them opportunists then we haven't yet completely surrendered to our own defensiveness. In other words, in modern times the enemy is always oneself. This isn't true of the natural jungle.

(Although primitive men sometimes live in little-populated places – if their enemy is implacable and cruel (characteristics which might have come from earlier times of extreme want) the process of escalating defensiveness can still begin.)

Russia is a very religious country, it is Russia (as readers of Dostoyevsky's Grand Inquisitor would expect) that has crucified communism. The 20th century has to learn (if there is to be a future for us) that religion is about man and not God. God is interested in the body, the devil is interested in the soul. Soul is the hell in which bodies are burned.

Man creates God as the better part of himself. He must then learn to live with him and not be afraid of him – because God is frightened by fear caused by men with a dagger in the raw waters of God.

1 July 1970

　Lear horrified when Cordelia marries D[ark] M[an] – because he thinks GDB is still alive. (Cordelia: He's dead! Dead! And his child died when the army raped me!) Lear takes GDB as his son: he is the innocence that he destroyed in Bodice and Goneril. So he is even more horrified when Cordelia insists that he in effect killed GDB!
Lear learns: the ruler destroys. It's a law of politics.

2 July 1970
Lear: Part 2
Lear has now come into the jaws of reality (from the dream of the myth.) Why don't the jaws snap shut and crush him, why isn't he killed after the trial?

The cause is a dream, the effect reality
They cry and then they feel the pain.

I can only enter into my life through art.

Revolution – so when Cordelia pardons Lear.
And they argue over GDB and DM
Lear and the fountain episode – before or after the row with Cordelia. Strictly the problem should be posed before and the solution should come after, forced on him by Cordelia and the second death of GDB, the death of the ghost.
Dramatize the defeat of daughters and sons-in-law.
Autopsies on daughters.
Attack from a third party. Perhaps Bodice could be in League with the third party.
Lear escapes: wanders away with ghost.

Returns to the old GDB's house which is now derelict.

It is now almost full to the top and the water is red. Cordelia's army comes for him. Lear is blind at very end – but there is a miracle because he is guided everywhere by a ghost (or is the ghost dead? No, Lear finally kills him, and then he has no one else to guide him. Lear has to kill the ghost violently).

Lear: I am an old man. I have learned many things but I am too old to use what I know. I have no illusions. I am waiting for death.

In a capitalist society, crime makes an honest man of you.

Part 2. Or Cordelia could <u>have</u> to send Lear back to prison (of a sort) and he dies there, and not at the house.

Remember, the blood fountain symbol (and the other symbols) are alright, but Lear (and the others) must accurately report (not describe, but report in the sense of the sound of an explosion or an echo) and recreate the experience that the symbol represents.

[. . .]

Part II

Lear has escaped or been released by one of the sisters. He returns to GDB's house which has been knocked-about.

Lear goes inside. Comes out.

There is blood on the floor. They've broken the doors, the windows.

GDB Are we going to stay here? The fountain's full. The water's red

Are you going to stay here? They killed her, I suppose.

It's strange they didn't burn the house.

Lear Why is the water red?

GDB They dropped the bodies in.

Lear O

GDB They'll come and look for you here.

Lear arrives at GDB's house blind. His radical preaching attracts attention. Cordelia sends a messenger to warn him. He tells her 'a revolution must also reform.' He kills the ghost because he is a pre-human member of a food-chain! He then goes to the wall and though he is blind he starts to dig it out. This last scene is Lear with soldiers and underlings. He is guided to the wall by a peasant who's horrified when he starts to dig the wall. People gather. A soldier warns them. He is shot. He is wounded. He speaks some more. Is shot again. Slithers dead down the wall.

The men who shoot Lear don't know who he is – no one in the
final scene knows who he is. But don't make a Victorian-pathos
thing out of this – they just don't happen to know who he is.

4 July 1970
Creation
The divine must become human
The artist must write words with blood and blot it out with blood
The light must shine like a shadow
Its blind fingers feeling each speck of dust
Breathe in the furnished air and breathe it out
Crucified on a cripple's stick
Tears must be shed
Dry, become green with age
And nothing is washed away
The hand grows like a tree in a tin can
And nothing is touched
All this
And still the clock's hands will not scrape out the figures of time
The divine becomes human by becoming inhuman

He writes with blood – other people's!

Lear 20 July 1970
My father
Is a path of dust
That leads to a desolate place
On the side of a mountain

Below a tarn
Where a bird falls
Rakes the water with claws
And rises with flakes of light
The boulders are bodies covered from disaster
His groans and the nightjar mixed
I watched:
He is mad
The waterfall rustles
He searches the empty papers
Always for nothing, nothing
And drops them
Searching and weeping

But this is the place where he lived
Made thin corn grow from dust
This is the stone where he killed
He called it the killing stone
This is the path he made with his feet

He shouted and stoned birds in the morning
Wore rags of wool and hair
Was drunk with water
He walked as if following a coffin looking at dust
He danced like an enemy

And his children played at his skeleton
Whistling his bones while he worked
Too old to be born

This is the place where he fell
Blood on his own field
If they had buried him then!
But they hoisted him through the streets
They pulped his hair for paper
They covered their feet with his skin
His bones are rods and his teeth are dice
They eat what they can and use the rest

This is the place where you sit
You cannot wait when nothing will come

Lear 7 August 1970
Starts with short or no beard. Then later appears with long beard
(Darwin, Vinci) – but after a pause in his appearance on stage, because
beard to be 'actual' and not like Arthur's beard in <u>Early Morning</u>, Act
Three.
Story. Could be started and left unfinished in Lear and GDB talk, and
not completed.
GDB to be much more desperate and clinging – like a cold little starving
child from Dickens or Blake – before Lear kills him 2nd time.
'Innocence must be killed twice.'

Reality is a duty
You can only overcome your limitations by accepting them
Don't fight your faults

Lear: In the scene where GDB is killed the soldiers also kill the pigs and
their screaming is heard during Lear's speech attacking the soldiers.
Tolstoy without guilt.
After trial scene. Lear goes back to cell very disturbed: the ghost of GDB
appears to comfort him.

Autopsist's joke
'I was a boy scout. The idea came to me from a pocket knife we had with
a gadget for removing stones from horses hooves.'

Are you married? I thought you were a child. I'm old enough.

I want her smelling of pigs' blood.
                                    [. . .]

Middle section
Trial
cell: 2nd trial/death of daughters/Lear blind
soldiers come in from time to time (as weeks go by). At one appearance
they talk obliquely about the revolt, whether they'll change sides. When
1st daughter caught she offers to collaborate against her sister and tell
them her plans etc.

Act III GDB cries and rolls on floor 'Tell her I'm here! Tell her I'm
here!' Cries for a long time: Lear and Cordelia talk. This changes use of
GDB: at moments Lear's pleading with her to recognize GDB, as if
pleading to her to recognize her humanity. Lear can't tell Cordelia GDB
is there, or can't effect a reunion between them, because GDB is a ghost
and can't have sex with Cordelia. So the dialectic is now between Lear
and GDB – their relationship is concerned, not GDB and Cordelia or
GDB – Cordelia – Lear.

After fountain story: GDB laughs gleefully 'what fool told you that':
Lear then says something short and functional (like a pass-the-salt) and
then says 'Yes, fool.'
                                    [. . .]

Lear's thoughts on seeing his father's body
I saw him
He died long after his death

Bones under
A white shroud: a fallen tent
He lies – his stupid skull
Grinning and not
On the morning
Tank track

Those going
To die
Walk past him
Children holding
Old women's hands
Step round him
Their journey:
Rubber sheet
Straight jacket
And shroud

Song
O has she sent death to visit me?
Is that death's car rattling on the street?

Is this death that comes in
Raises its veil and removes its gloves
Sharpens its knife on my arm?
Is this death pulling my teeth
Counting my toes to see nothing escapes?
Is this death that visits me?

Each bone is numbered for reassembly
The skin is preserved as far as possible
An impression of teeth is taken
She must find somewhere clean for the killing
Meet death, she says
And gives him a cup of tea
She has told death to call on me
And when I am dead

They will put me together
And no one will know
Death has visited me

<u>Lies and Truth</u> 1 September 1970
Lies throw
Jewels
Fur
Gold
Your
Truth is an old man
With an empty bowl
Lies
Throw jewels and gold
At you

Truth is
An old man
And an empty bowl
2nd soldier to stare up at heavens must be a soldier he deals with earlier
You are the king.
You can't call me that. I have no power now.
The young men have always fought and died for the old men. This time the
old men must die for the young men.

The stars can't see me and I can't see them.
Let me live
But you're a ghost.
But I live in a way. When I'm with you. Let me stay with you.
I'm so frightened when I go away.
Then you're dead. You don't
                    know anything.
Yes, but I want to live
I wish you were dead
No, let me live
I wish you were dead
No, no, please: let me live
No, I wish you were dead.

One has to admit all the suffering in evolution – predator-prey and accidental
sickness and suffering for the inefficiency of age.

You'll never get anywhere with her. It's like buying rings for an octopus.

You never get anywhere with him: it's like trying to shake hands with an octopus.

No Poem 25 December 1970
No poem this winter
I am too busy
Looking at the clock
Moving between places
To know where to go
Or listen to the silence
Between tick
                    and tock
Or see the blood
Trickling
From the clock

Does happiness
Always have
A shadow
A flock of birds
Choking
In an old bake-house

                    [. . .]

Daughters
Trial
Cell (ghost) scene
Rebels hide-out scene
Chain gang scene
Last scene plotting wall and secretly distrusting and threatening each other

Possibilities: They get rid of their husbands and take over the army –
    because the war is going badly.

Draft of New Scene 11
Procession. Coffin. Bodice follows it. She wears deep elaborate mourning. She kneels by the coffin.

Bodice: Leave me.
They all go. She stands.

Bodice: God has been good to me! He has answered all my prayers. My husband is dead. I poisoned him myself. It's no good leaving these things to everyone else. It must be kept in the family. The war is going well and the rebels will soon be cowed. The greatest army in the history of our nation is in my hands – and I should lead it! God has blessed me!

Cordelia (Fontanelle) comes in. A soldier follows her.

Soldier: No! – (to B) She dodged behind us.

B   Let her stay (Soldier goes)

F   You can gloat. Everything has gone your way. But now there is trouble. My husband has fled. He has gone back to his own country. He was afraid to stay.

B   How did you let him go. Can't you look after anything. I gave you the tablets to give him. You can see they worked with mine!

F   I didn't know he was going to do it. He deceived me. What can I do now?

B   My spies were watching him. When he left I gave an order that he was to be stopped at the frontier and his head chopped off.

F   But how do you know they will do it. He might dodge them.

B   I have his head at home.

F   . . . What will we do now?

B   Win this war. (Spreads out a map on the coffin.) Your husband's troops may not be reliable. I must speak to them. In view of this you can hardly expect to share the command with me. But as you're my sister, you shall have the second in command. (points). You will take this section and I shall go forward on the main front.

F   (Aside) I must do what she says. She has been lucky and I have been unlucky. But my luck will turn.

B   Go and leave me alone with him for 2 minutes. People will expect it.

F   (goes)

B   She is expendable. The army she commands is unreliable, and she will always envy me my good fortune. I shall get rid of those all at once. I shall wait till they're fighting and then

I shall see that her ammunition doesn't get through to her. Besides, I shall need it myself. I shall have a lot to do. And now to church. Soldiers!

The soldiers come on and start to carry out the coffin. She takes out a handkerchief and follows.

Advice 15 January 1971

1. Sacrifice your own character to become yourself.
2. Any act done because it is a duty results in a feeling of guilt. Political justice is putting this guilt onto an innocent man. The condemned is always a victim. Why must political justice always victimize the innocent? Because that is the only way to avoid the tyranny of duty. It creates the pseudo-freedom which is called 'liberty'.
3. The foundation of marriage is usually a batch of lies: therefore, divorce is made in heaven.
4. People who prophesy doom are usually those most able to bring it about.
5. Scar tissue is stronger than ordinary flesh, but it has less feeling.
6. On the gates of paradise there is a carving of a father holding his son by the hand.
7. Internal tears!
8. At the entrance to hell Satan has built a copy of the gates of paradise.
9. The ant walking in the dust towards his prison gate does not hear himself sigh.
10. Armour keeps the enemy out and the prisoner in.
11. Father Christmas is Satan. Santa Claus is Satan Claws.

Primitive men worship animals as gods. They saw themselves as part of nature, and even felt inferior and vulnerable in it. When they ate meat they ate their god, and were let into the coherence and strength of nature, which was superhuman and divine. It contained heaven – and celestial phenomena such as storms and lightning – as well as earth. The animal was closer to nature, more intimate with it, than man, and so nearer heaven (and all its violent strength, and beneficence) than man. Animals were inarticulate but they were wiser. Perhaps a madman's ravings were their silence articulated.

January 1971

Boy doesn't believe Lear's story about being an officer. Thinks he was poor old refugee of some sort – and that Old Councillor was the same.

Lear says odd things while he's eating his soup and other times. Odd disconnected things from the Lear song. So Cordelia is angry that Boy has brought a crazy man to the house while she's pregnant – but Boy is all the more insistent that he won't abandon him.

Lear's blind story could be direct to audience.

Lear wakes and says my daughters are cutting off my head!
Lear says to GDB   Have you daughters?
        GDB   None.
        Lear   O, not so loud! Where is the sanctuary?

My stomach's shrivelled and the hair's turned white.
[. . .]

Advice
1. The tyrant squeezes human blood from a stone.
2. Whoever hits a child slaps God in the face.
[. . .]

3 February 1971
   In Act I Lear to plan a future with GDB. We'll settle down and be at peace here, and I will learn how to live. ETC.
Lear says the cut's gone!
GDB (or Cord) It wasn't deep. There's something wrong with his hands. He can't hold a knife.
Lear It's almost healed in a night.
[. . .]

4 February 1971
   My daughters empty the prisons at night and feed the men to the dogs. Hup, Rover! Hup, boy! Tricks for human flesh. The foxes slink out. And night stands by the gate with my daughters' keys in its hands. When old men become revolutionaries the world will be saved.

Possible new end.
Lear and Cordelia
Cordelia goes
Brief exchange between Lear and Boy
Lear 'my life is like a tree'.
Sounds off.

Boy runs back – dies
Lear calls Thomas! Susan!
They come on. Explain that the pigs went mad. Running wild
Lear insists on talking about his plans.
Leave them. They will come back. Listen; I must talk to you.

Lear: Everything passes even the waste
The fools will be silent
We won't chain ourselves to the dead
Or send our children to school in a grave yard
The torturing ministers and priests
Will lose their office
And we walk past each other in the streets without shuddering
[. . .]

Lear cut prison 4 episode – add to bodice: clock chimes rapidly.
Opening of Act III Lear sits rigidly, as though listening expectantly.
Repeats. She should have answered! Why hasn't she? Why? Why?

4 February 1971
The crucified pig: a little CND play[37]

Amplified sound of pig screaming

The men who walked on the moon are
                              nameless
As the men who dropped the bomb on Nagasaki
They did what they were told
They would have done more
They offered to do anything

Pressing button. Which one is it?
O dear, I'm such a silly! (Gets finger stuck) As she talks (Yakety
yak, Yahoo ho-ho-ho-boo-hoo, etc)

For CND play 19 February 1971
I did what I was told to do to others
who did to me what they were told to do
when I saw the blood running out of my arms
        I cried

[37] Bond demonstrates here that he was working on *Passion* and *Lear* at the same time.

I lie in my grave while the bird sings
My tanks set fire to the corn
My bullets stripped the trees bare
I made where I was a grave
I walked and laughed in it
Once when it was quiet
I heard a bird singing
Building a nest
In the cardboard boxes we put the bodies in

My flares were brighter than stars at night
My guns louder than thunder
I ravaged more than the locusts
My bayonet was sharp
I kept it whetted in blood and the cries of pitiful men
I crippled to make men happy
The simpleton drools in the bath chair
I am the father of millions of orphans
I am dead
The birds sang as the blood
      ran from my arms
I lie in my grave and it sings still
It has the sky and I have the earth
If I could rise now on wings and fly
I would sing
I would sing
I would sing
     'Pity poor man!
     He is mad
     He is lost.'

21 February 1971
We are gods
Only mortals are ill
Therefore I will never be ill again!

Peace, madmen!
The dust on my wings shines – the sun
You who bend iron but are frightened of grass

Peace!
Peace!
Sing in winter!
Snow is your childrens' tears
Peace
Peace
Peace
madmen, peace!
The dust on my wings shines in the sun
You who bend iron but are frightened of grass
Peace!
Peace!
Peace!
I have learned to sing in winter
Inwardly I dance in my shroud
Madmen this is not your world
You have no right to destroy it

25 February 1971
(Scene before the autopsy)
Ghost: Look how thin I am. Feel my arms. Are you afraid to touch me.
Lear: No. (Feels his arm) Yes, thin.

Ghost to keep drawing attention to himself in this way. It's affecting my
back, my head, there's something wrong with my head.
Ghost watches Lear being blinded.

Now I know what I must do.

It's strange that you should have me killed, Cordelia, but it's obvious you
would. How simple!
So old it doesn't matter what he does.
But he's concerned not with the effect of his life but with the political effect,
with the effect in life (as a mechanism of life).
Well would he have done the same thing if he was young. (Ghost for
example, dug wall up when young.)
Lear: Why did the man I shot dig the wall up? Why did the GDB dig the
wall up?
Lear (in this speech) doesn't give a programme – he explains what it's like to
be in his position when he comes to know what he will do.
You're like my daughters, but worse than they were.

How simple! I see law does more harm than crime. Morality is a cover for violence, truth is a word concept people play with, power is given to the weak, and the future is looked after by madmen, and I see that when crime is law the innocent become victims.
That is why you destroy the innocent.

4 March 1971
Don't let me speak at all when I should be silent
Don't let me kill the snake because it is long and its belly is speckled.
Don't let me whisper in rhetoric
Let me whisper quietly to myself
Don't let the gold teeth of
Living men

Don't Let Me

Don't let me whisper in rhetoric
Let me whisper quietly to myself alone
Don't let me speak at all when I should be silent
Don't let me kill the snake because its
        long and its belly is speckled
Its eyes open at day break
Its forked tongue breaks water
It sloughs an old skin in spring
Don't let me weigh the gold teeth of living men
Don't let me pass the basement railings
Without releasing a thousand prisoners
Don't let me sit with judges among bones of innocent men
Or polish chains for governments
Don't let vanity, pride or indifference
Corrupt my bones
So that my flesh leaves me in horror
Like birds flying at gunshot
And I am left a naked skeleton
With gold tongue and white stick
And a shadow like broken ladders
Let me talk to the men I make Lepers
Put water in a jug and dust on a path
Let me beg at the feast I lay

8 March 1971
    I have 'faith' in human nature. I think that a minority of people will

always <u>not</u> side with power, but will want to be kind, generous and merciful – so that the humanitarian trend which does run through history will continue. Also, a minority will be creative, and a minority will want justice – want it creatively, not only as a result of a particular injustice they've suffered, but want it as a general condition of society. But I have no 'faith' in technology. I think it did provide easy solutions to difficult problems which in the long run could be much worse than the original problems. Overcrowding, minority pressures against governments, increased criminality in dense, alienated cities – all this could result in, in effect, technology to be used to change human nature. I think so far we've seen this only at one remove. Technology has certainly changed society! If this New Society <u>is</u> one. If people can't be free and happy, technology could be used on people to make them <u>fit in</u>. This could be done in a 'scientific-humanitarian' way – for example by identifying future non-conformists while they're still at school, and 'tinkering' with them so they can and will conform. But it might also take a different direction. That is, governments might use the negative traits in human nature – aggressiveness, anger, jealousy, covetousness, insularity – to create, in effect, a society of terror – in which nonconformity is terrorized, and reward for conformity is the heresy of aggression and the assurance of personal safety.

10 March 1971
Power is impotence.

11 March 1971
The pig is a form of lamb.

31 March 1971[38]
   Man on seashore. Drowned body washed up, he died while trying to pull his jumper off over his head, presumably so that when it's off he could swim better.
The body is the clue.
The man is trapped by the mystery (in the crime or in some other sense) and the body leads to an answer.

Does the man work on the shore or is he just walking?

Although the man is much younger it's as if he's a Lear who lived. But

[38] Bond's notes demonstrate here that he was working on *Lear* and *The Sea* at the same time.

Lear died because he had to – because there wasn't anything else to do. He killed himself when he knew he was going to be killed.

Cordelia presented him with an answer, and so did extreme age. Yet he himself discounted the age part, he wanted (and was willing) to live longer. It's as if death was the only meaningful act he could make with his life. The actual digging in the wall is significant, the hole could be filled in in 30 seconds. But it would be difficult to ignore the fact that he died on the wall while destroying it.

You can't escape by saying the solution (death) was only valid for him. The problem is a general one, and we need answers that have general validity.

Poem in a Wood 22 April 1971
Be easy simple direct
Be the tune on the unstrung harp
The iron flute makes no noise
Only the echo of stifled cries
But the stringless harp sings!
When dry grass rustles like stealthy feet
The leaves flutter like stalked birds
And in the ravine of a ditch
The fox's carcass
Lies like discarded clothes never worn
Then the unstrung harp is a mirror

A writer's greatest gift is his sanity
And the blind watch taps a path on the floor of the sea

The Puppet Magician 4 May 1971
Blinded by his own tears
His eyes burn with the venom they wept
Deafened by his own voice
Vomits blood in his own stomach
His flesh is cold
When the bones poke him
Like sticks poking for water
He is seduced by his own lies
To smile at his own questions
Knowing society is possible
Only through courtesy

Ocean 10 May 1971
The ocean always asleep
Murmuring in sleep
Shouting and raving
Covering and uncovering graves
In a dream
Like a dream of earth
Where history is a conjuror
Blowing out footprints in the water
And saying Look
In this grave I have 3 centuries
And 10 in this
Sea is the natural soil of time
And the Old fathers
Run ocean through shaking fingers, washing their hair and mouths
The iron is spray
Beat by wind
They say
This soil is my kingdom
And all my sons have bled here
Their blood has made
This sea loose
And my wings were broken
When I was a bird
But I am free to roam this water

10 May 1971
He had a mouth like barbed wire, and he was always trying to catch you.

There was a young man. He lived in a city. He was discontented. So he took time off from his work and went to the country. He now spent his days walking. One day there was a storm. The sea seemed to boil. The mountains split and threw huge rocks in the air and they landed on the shore with terrible thuds. The wind seemed to strike the land again and again. The young man sheltered in a cage. There he saw an old man sitting on the stone floor and doing woman's work. He was pounding something in a hollowed out stone. The old man asked the young man to buy some bread. The young man didn't want to be put out into the storm. He bought the bread, ate it and went to sleep. He dreamed about the storm. Sometime he woke up and heard the storm outside. Then he went to sleep again, and dreamed about it.

In the morning he felt very ill. He said 'The bread was bad.' He looked around for the old man – he was gone, but his grinding stone was lying on the floor.

The young man could hear that the storm had stopped. He went out. The sky was overcast and the sea was grey. It was rocking backwards and forwards like a wounded man hugging himself.

The wind made the sweat on the young man's brow as cold as ice. He lent over some rocks and was sick. Then he felt a little better – but empty and tired. He lay down behind some other rocks and went to sleep.

12 May 1971
W[omb]A[nd]D[raper]?[39]
This story is more terrible than tragedy.

The modern writer has to reveal a world deeper and profounder than the world of tragedy. Tragedy attempts to make meaningless things and events have meaning. A modern writer has to show that what has meaning has been made meaningless by human stupidity, fear and pride. Pride may seem an old fashioned sin. But it isn't. It is a form of mental cruelty, and modern people are experts at it.

Fisherman: I am not religious. When I was young I asked God to send me a good catch. My wife became ill and we had no money in the house. The catch was so great it broke my net and all the fish swam away. I couldn't buy the ropes to make a new net and we almost starved. Since then I've learned the greatest calamity that can befall a man is having his prayers answered.

He pulled off a bird's wings to see what made it fly. But then the bird didn't fly and he said he was mistaken and so he'd stop trying to find out what made it fly.
Could the shells be from a sea gun-range: protecting bad-weather firing? . . .

In one scene waves pound on the shore all the time and gulls cry etc. In a later scene the sea rustles, and then only occasionally and there are no (?) gulls or other birds (?)

---

[39] WAD refers to *The Sea*. The letters might have stood for 'Womb and Death' or 'Woman and Draper'. Edward Bond does not clearly remember.

23 May 1971
<u>WAD?</u>

A direct, factual style. The play tells what's already known. Like a Mystery Cycle Play. Ornamentation of a <u>very</u> bare bones. Keep the scaffolding <u>very</u> simple – like a solid foundation of truth. The structure built on this in a way 'winks' at the audience. And yet this structure must also be responsible for these facts.

In modern times all men live in ruins – emotional and intellectual. Even intellectual (facts are the ideas in which we believe.) A fountain and a storm. A fountain that goes mad and sprays jets on passers-by.

At this stage don't worry too much about the continuity between the sections. Instead, there should be a sense of comparisons.
I storm
II draper/insanity
III Y[oung] M[an] and D[raper']s attack on drowned sailor
IV O[ther] O[ld] M[an]
I Storm. YM bumps into OOM. Shines Torch. OOM appears in beach as fantastic ancient ghost. OOM talking to himself. Drunk. No.
Or: YM was in a boat with dead sailor. Boat sinks in a storm. YM comes on shore, then finds OOM who is lit up by lightning. The guns start. YM didn't know gun range was so near.
II Her dress? Parasol. Summer gloves button at wrist. Patent leather shoes. Her speech? D complains she's always altering the curtains. She comes back a 2nd time and changes her mind. Goes. He cuts the cloth – she's trapped. He orders stuff from town and then has to send it back. They don't trust him – he can't get things for his <u>good</u> customers. He'll starve. She returns, as she was passing on way back from bank – has changed her mind. Refuses to take the material.

Does D stab her?
YM says somewhere that coming to this place is like going back 30 years.

I did begin with OOM wandering about saying an analogue of Was Anything Done?
Could the murdered 'Duchess' have a daughter – whom YM takes up. Last scene could be between YM, D's daughter (DD) and OOM – he sort of gives them a blessing: YM + DD = OOM

24 May 1971
   Attitude of D and D[uchess's] D[aughter] to OOM[40]

The reality of myth and the myth of Reality. How to escape. Reality in fact ought to be living a balance of this myth and the practical.

Duchess isn't to be a theatrical Grande Dame. Must resist this temptation. She's more elevated than this. Wears a straw hat.

Draper's shop. This is a violent clash of the practical and the mythical where nothing is sorted out into its proper place. Other customers come in? It is the place where everything goes wrong because the sufferer (Draper) makes them go wrong – whereas the accidental is the real. The door to Draper's shop is low – you have to duck to get in. (TL = the lady) TL doesn't like this, I don't feel a need for any humour in this play! Instead there has to be chaos, stillness, silence, and beauty.
In III we have The Attack in which the chase of II reaches out and threatens YM. In IV we shall have to have the reconciliation.
IV YM is trying to go away and is in fact leaving, perhaps without any conscious effort. The inquest has found the dead seaman is dead by drowning so YM is now free to leave. Relationship between YM and DSM was presumably close and friendly. D kills himself.
The sign of a good writer is that he's got through to the world of fact. This creates his style. It is intricate, profound, 'plastic' but before all the other things it is <u>simple</u> because it doesn't evade.

The writer must still tell lies like a liar, if the character is needed – but the untruth is commented on by the director's or the writer's observation, his style scrutinizes the false witness!

30 May 1971
   What is YMs emotional relationship to D's attack on the dead sailor? Is YM 'free from' the Draper by that time, or is it like a concealed attack on himself: is he then free, or is Draper his vicarious self as a victim?

1 June 1971
   It seems to be like a recapping, retrospective play not a modern play like <u>Lear</u>. But this isn't completely true.
                              [. . .]

---

[40] Bond refers to the Duchess, or T[he] L[ady], meaning Rafi; D[uchess's] D[aughter] meaning Rose; D[ead] S[ea] M[an] or D[ead] S[ailor] meaning Colin; and O[ther] O[ld] M[an] referring to Evens.

Revolution

Any change must be willed by those concerned – change can never be imposed because it provokes resistance, and any relevant change is always so substantial it can't be imposed un-noticed.

In final OOM/YM gun to fire in distance – this time in full day time – at regular intervals – say 15 shots in all not marked in the text at definite places. Because this is a modern play and so the threat must sound through this illumination.

[. . .]

2 July 1971

Could D be an ex-colonial. Or a retired soldier, or an airman? Could D have a daughter? While he waits in the town feeling some guilt about DS (though this isn't his only motive, or even his main one) he gets drunk – on a prolonged quite high level of drink for several days. He isn't shown suddenly singing.

[. . .]

Perhaps final scene should still have the guns sounding in it. Should suggest peaceful resolution. Under the mask isn't the face of resignation.

Could D[drunk] be a pyromaniac, and set fire to the Great Hall (G[rande] D[ame]'s home)?

YM's 'bad' behaviour isn't just from guilt because DS is drowned. He has this defect (if he has it) before and thinks (perhaps rightly, but what really hangs on what he thinks anyway?) that's why DS is drowned.

Perhaps D is the victim of an attack, he was burgled and his life earnings were stolen during it. Perhaps his wife died after being hit – his own mind is affected and he's always looking for whoever did this to him? (Better than if someone stole a patent of his and he's permanently embittered.)

Don't let the myth swamp, or even infringe upon, the immediate identity of the thing in reality. This identifying is important to my play. You must see the man and only afterwards be aware of the sort of light you see him by.

Perhaps D could be drowned.

The arts council is the sort of institution that would think of appointing Hitler as a Rabbi.

24 August 1971
Truth without power is impotent, but power corrupts truth. Why?
How can ideals become reality? How can hope become practice?
Society is negative and reactionary. Social institutions resist change, with violence if necessary. Therefore change, if it is to occur, is <u>forced</u> onto them. This means that change has to use the methods of reaction.

Both these methods have a logic and dynamic of their own. You cannot use violence and contain it (without the use of more violence and so on and so on, until those associated with it are exhausted, disgusted or dead – and this takes time, and in the end events are probably back at the place where they started. Napoleon and Stalin). Violence creates an atmosphere of violence. Violence is a biological function. If a living organism is threatened it reacts violently in defence. All aggression is, at base, originally, self-defence. A firing squad creates a society of fear and counter aggression. Friend becomes enemy. Trust is betrayed. In an enclosed system, such as a country going through a revolution, the violence escalates. Violence in a revolution is like a light in a powder keg. In this way violence perverts the aims of a revolution, and the ideals are lost. The classic method of revolution has obvious advantages – but it must always destroy the r[evolution.]
What we want is an effective way of revolutionizing society.

Individual action. Leave the university or factory. Alright but ineffective if the individuals doing this are isolated. Must be a fairly massive movement. How do authoritarian societies operate by consent? Why do people embrace the things that are most dangerous to them. Hitler. Why do they seem to insist on the things that threaten them most! H-bombs. We can't understand a society that can build its houses on the slope of a volcano (Pompeii) – but we build ours inside a volcano. Don't people know this? There is a refusal to see it, and an inability to imagine any other alternative? The other side do it, don't they?

Reactionary politicians <u>not</u> conspirators. Heath, Nixon, etc, haven't the minds or the emotional stability to understand what's going on. (Chastity is a rape of the personality.)

The idea of a leadership of the elect is a revolution. Lenin was a stalinist.

We don't have a revolutionary situation, except amongst some of the young.

In 1917 the Russian army left the front, and there were bread riots in the cities. There was a revolutionary situation – it occurred, wasn't made. Lenin thought the revolution wouldn't come in his lifetime. He couldn't make a revolution, he moved in on it when it was already going.

There was conscious mass suffering.

In our present time most people are content in the sense that capitalism provides them with cheap drugs: cars, records, TV. In many ways these have lowered the quality of life, made places less pleasant to live in; but they have also removed obvious dangers from our sight and removed the hunger, malnutrition and cold from most people.

They don't want a revolution. The suffering is elsewhere – the environment is being poisoned and made ugly, but that doesn't immediately concern them. They have still never had it so good.

Why should they change anything?

Here it seems an elite will have to start a revolution, before the question of it leading a revolution could arise.

The reason for a revolution:

1. Prosperity founded on the suffering of others (Vietnam).

2. Prosperity entails suffering at home and limitation of real happiness. So factory slaves become angry and trivial. This makes society angry and trivial – America is now a dangerous place to live. Our present situation demoralizes people.

3. There are long term dangers in our technology. Thus, prosperity depends on working and using cars. These cars then destroy our environment. In a real sense, our 'prosperity' impoverishes our lives.

4. The military danger. Our social aggressiveness makes us unable to control our technology. We are now in a position to destroy ourselves, and our society is the sort of society that eventually destroys itself. We haven't the will to live, to act in a way that would ensure our survival. We are consumed by petty aggressions. The fascist mentality would drop an H-bomb to kill a fly.

So there is a need for change.

We need:

1. A society in which people can function naturally. Their work and their pleasure will fully use, develop and realize their biological structures.

2. A society in which dangerous weapons (H-Bombs and germ weapons) are not made and no one is prepared to make them, or at least the people who are sufficiently intelligent to make them are not willing to do so.

3. A society in which there is real scope for political initiative. This means smaller political units for many functions.

4. A sane commercial and economic society. We must not make things like cars, and TV sets, which we only need because the work of making them makes our lives so unbearable. We make ourselves ill in order to afford the cure!

How?

You either force people to stop doing something, which harms them and you, because they don't want to or can't stop doing it. Or, you make these people want to stop doing it, or you make it impossible for them to go on doing it.

If they want to do it enough you have to use strong crude force. As argued above this counter-produces and converts you into them.

How do you carry out the alternative?

[. . .]

10 November 1971
Sea Play
Sea as symbol of space (which is itself the very symbol of what the sea has always symbolized. But do it this way to 'colour' the space symbol. Idea all space contained in sea.) What existed before anything? Nothing. Why? Because there would be no space to put it in. But what space is space in? All space is in the sea.
Leonardo gazing out over the sea.

Pearlmaker
Experience is
A wound inside
(It feels like grit in an eye)

Men cry the wailing sounds
To which they dance their dance of joy
The grit is bathed in tears
And the pearl is made
Opening and closing doors
In many mazes
The pearl maker works
And the pearl is made
In dark sea

What cannot be made into pearl
Is splinters under the nail
These become claws
Hands have only a few skills
And one tongue
But the claws of madmen have all
The tongues of Babylon

Sounds
What is making this loud noise?
The feet of moving soldiers
What noise is drowning the noise
The sound of the prisoners shaking their bars

November 1971

The Japanese avoid systematic philosophies (unlike say the Chinese) which may be why they are so receptive to outside influence.

There is an element of fascism in Zen. The Japanese military cast is closely connected to it because it teaches – indifference to pain. Yukio Mishima, who was a belletrist in jackboots, also interested in Zen ideas (in 'steel and sun') and he glorifies the army in exactly the way Enoch Powell does.

Violence can destroy anything.
It can only build prisons and castles.

The lessons of the commune and the October Revolution contradict each other.
Note: Lenin as a realist. The realism relates to his own epoch. If he were living now it doesn't mean that his realism would lead him to hold the same ideas and opinions. When we say 'what would Lenin do now' we usually mean 'what would Lenin, holding the same opinions and ideas, do now?' This is not only living in the past, it is solving the problems of the past! In this way realism gives birth to naturalism.

Canute told the sea to go away
Men can't be caged
Neither can the wind
A chain is as strong as its weakest link

A mob is as strong as its biggest fist
– that is our great misfortune
Brecht s[ai]d: Lies can be written in blood
The truth can only be written in ink
He is like a Pilate washing ink stains from his fingers

November 1971
He was conceived on a cold, windy, wet night
On a seat of a car
On _____ heath
His parents got deep
satisfaction from the occasion
Birth is
the blind meeting the blind
In the dark
The last landowners left
When the mob goes
After the riot
Coroners, police, country litter
Tired ambulance men
Empty packets
And birth

Misery is a thin sheet of ice over happiness
That is all
Nothing but that
Still in the cold
Broken ice mends

You mend
Pieces of cups and glass
Ice mends itself
Overnight

13 January 1972
WAD play
At end. OOM sits. YM stands opposite and to one side. Talk. YM
explains how his house has been destroyed. Short answer from OOM.
He has an open book on his lap. Then he says something longer; and he
could finish by reading something from book. During this girl calls (off)

YM's name. He is going to her – but there is no need for either YM or OOM to show a response to her.

Scene: when draper cuts cloth. Cut immediately to body on beach. Draper heard calling (off) like mad seagull.
YM and OOM walk on.
Hide when draper stumbles on – rigidly, as though his ankles tied together by short rope.

Drowned man was to have married daughter of the 'Lady' – an obvious but not stated relationship between the YM and the daughter.
Lady's rival is a middle-aged spinster.

2 years ago
Passing the abattoir
I saw pigs going to death
They left the lorry
Their faces were wrinkled with curiosity
Their ears hung forward
They walked so delicately down the ramp
It was late afternoon
Getting dark
At least I have survived to this afternoon
At least they had lives till that day
This is the poem I am unable to write
                    [. . .]

D[uchess] decides to take nothing after all, at end of scene
D taps on window and calls YM in – she already knows everything.
OOM says body will be washed up at X on 13th or 16th and at Y etc. Doesn't have many chances

Dead man to have been friend of OOM. That is why old man comes to his funeral. (But his friend can't – isn't he more the 'George' half of the pair. <u>Consider this!</u>)[41]

6 May 1972
Girl: (when talking to YM) How calm the sea is today. There's no wind only a breeze.

[41] An allusion to *Early Morning*.

The immaculate hands and feet of dead emperor
The authoritarian clown.

The desert rose blooms
A tongue in the sand
Lying before
The brick sphinx
The heat like salt
Crossing the petals
I will come over
With the dog
Paddle, spitting out
The water like this
Vicar: I was admiring your bibliographical splendours.
Finish a sentence with etc. Ha. (or Ah).
The Marxists are always building the last barricades and the capitalists are
    always hiding in the last ditch. I sometimes think the 2 will never meet
    head on

[. . .]

10 June 1972
Why is time dangling on a crucifix?
Warring blunts action
The unchastened act is a sound ringing a bell
The action that learns!
The action that learns!
The crossroad is always the one chosen by the enemy

Not for one moment
Of time
Have men escaped
From the knot
Of fate
Where the past and the future meet
In furious collision
We throw our knot into the air
And call it the banner of freedom
And what is painted on the banner
When it lies on the desk on the platform
Is lost
When we throw the knot into the air

And the mask appears
Like the gaps in a skeleton

To teach children to work they give them a stick
To teach them to run they give them watches
To teach them to speak they fill their mouth with cries
To teach them to hear a wolf grows their ears
To teach them to see they strike matches on their eyes
To teach them to feel they make scalding tears
To teach them to remember they bind their hands blindfold their eyes and
beat a drum

[. . .]

The distinction between town and country is going.
We are becoming like a community of technological peasants.
The nearest you get to a peasantry in England is in the suburbs of
great cities.
People living in these technological villages lack the political will and
energy usually associated with cities.

[. . .]

A great weakness of communism is that it has a built-in apology for its
own mistakes. This is part of the theory of alienation. In a way you could
call the theory of alienation the aesthetic side of Marxism and the
economic theory the other side. But it isn't an option or escapist form of
alienation, of course. It is integrated into the experience of living under
capitalism, or living under any political form which denies freedom of
choice. Alienation isn't just existence in limbo. It is itself an active state.
It can be a very active state and it has 2 potential characteristics. They
are potential because they are only fully active in moments of crises. The
passionate state of alienation is itself functionally dangerous because it is
the condition of miserable acquiescence that enables capitalism to quietly
flourish, or rather proliferate. The 2 potential characteristics are
capitalism's answer to communism. They are very effective answers:
they are fascism and madness.

   The danger of this is that at the moment, in or out of crises, popular
criticism and disengagement from communism (as at the moment) can
be ascribed to popular alienation – of course so and so would say or do
that, because he is the victim of capitalistic education, and so on. The
danger that this is only partly true. But those are the circumstances in
which we have to work – there are no others and when we fail to break

this barrier: we have failed. We do fail almost all the time – and I do not think we need to fail.

But to break that barrier of ideas is probably the only road to communism in a western democracy. I want to insist on this point. Classical Marxism states that capitalism is pregnant with its own destruction and that it must give birth to communism. Had I lived in the 19th century, I would have believed this. But it is clear that man didn't foresee the false trend and adaptability of capitalism – along with its ability to adapt workers to its needs. So we can see that communists are always preparing to mount the last barricade while capitalists are always hiding safely in the last ditch. Now as capitalism is always pregnant with fascism and madness and as it is totally armed – by technology – communism does not become inevitable. It does not, and that is a fact we must live and work with if we are to produce a communist society. Because rather than give way to that capitalism will destroy us all. Not because it chooses to do so – no sane man would choose that. But because in its crisis it is mad and fascist and it will destroy us and itself just as madmen and fascists do. And for the same reason.

So we have to breach alienation, we can't wait for the golden apple to fall into our laps.

The Sea in Germany 10 April 1974[42]

The critics wanted to understand the metaphor of The Sea. They interpreted it in this way. The Sea showed a cyclical image of the world, as history. Each tide was very like another. It washed the shore clean, sweeping everything away. And so there was no object, no point in human endurance. No aim could ever be reached, and if it was it would soon be washed away. Everything periodically returned to the formlessness, the meaninglessness of the sea. Political action was a waste of time, human suffering and happiness were finally meaningless. The wheel turned and the gods laughed at human effort. Really life was a sort of dream. So why act, why do anything.

Curiously, this interpretation could only be made against what the play specifically says. The play specifically decries such an interpretation in the last scene. I would regard such views as naive and reactionary. So 1. why did many German critics make this false interpretation and 2. what did I intend the play to mean?

The play is a comedy. This means it has to be taken seriously but understood, interpreted, with subtlety and irony. Possibly irony doesn't

---

[42] Although these notes are not chronological, they are sequentially correct.

translate well. Before he produced Early Morning Peter Stein asked me how I could write a speech in praise of Hitler and Nihilism.[43] It had not occurred to me that the speech could have been interpreted literally. The character who says it is, at that moment, mad, and the author was therefore using him to say something to which the author's own attitude was ironic. Do you usually go to madmen for advice? I've also had letters from German students asking me to explain jokes as if they were statements of dogma.

I once wrote: Like everyone else I am an optimist by nature but a pessimist by experience. But I will go on being true to my nature. It would be a mistake to learn from experience. German student: But Mr. Bond, how can you say that our experience mustn't . . . etc. And so The Sea has to be a dogmatic statement, it must stand for something precise, it has to be concrete. The Germans like to say the truth is concrete. What does that mean? A tree is concrete, so is a mist. Both are being 'true to their nature.' But when you think in that way there is a danger. There is no alternative between elation and despair. You are like a tightrope walker. You are either high up in the air, or you have fallen right down to the ground.

I'm not talking about the nature of things but the psychological attitudes to thought. Its interesting that Hegel became obsessed with the reality of opposites, the contrasting of opposite things, so as to arrive at a synthesis.

There is a tendency in German people to regard every statement as if it was a summing up, a final judgement. This can only be the accumulation of errors. Look at Brecht. Consider the enormous contrasts as he jumps from one isolated position to another. The extreme reactionism of Drums in the Night – the extreme humanism of the Lehrstücke, where he deliberately sets up an unreal situation to force out of it an unreal and violent truth by which real people are then meant to live. Neither of these alternatives can be a pattern for practical living. And what is the final position? An attack on the party he had insisted it was everyone's duty to follow implicitly. So what use were all his plays? We are told, in effect, by Brecht that we should interpret them in a way he had not intended. Now all that is naivety, but because Brecht was prepared to make dogmatic statements he is seen as a realist! And because I insist on describing the complications of an issue I am called naive.

---

[43] Bond refers to a production of *Early Morning* at the Schauspielhaus, Zürich, 2 October 1969.

The danger of admitting complexities is that you refrain from acting. True, and that danger has to be avoided. The danger of simplifying is that you then act but make mistakes. That also ought to be avoidable. Brecht of course understood this. He even, in the theatre, insisted on the use of irony. I am arguing only about what he did practically.

So what did I intend the image of The Sea to be? I began from two points. On the 19th century saying, I believe it was Dostoyevsky's, that as god was dead everything was possible. That is a good description of the theatre of the Absurd. I've never been able to understand it. Even if there was a god, he would only be a god because my moral sense credited him with being a god. Its irrelevant to say I got my moral sense from him because a moral sense has to be autonomous. So god would only be good so long as he acted in accordance with my moral nature. This is really pointless. So the moral responsibility for the world is given back to, or over to, men. My moral sense doesn't die with god, I reach moral maturity – though alas not political maturity. One knows what is right but not how to get it. But I am responsible for the world – and therefore I will make errors.

So this brings me to my second point. It is useless, meaningless, to swing from exaltation to despair. We can only progress by making mistakes. If you live in a century of very great mistakes then you have to be very careful about this. Beckett lived through the time when the Germans were gassing Jews. Auden said that all the left-wing poetry of the thirties didn't save one Jew from the gas chamber. And in the concentration camp you learned, so I've been told, that only the strong survived. Or, as Brecht would say, the tree can bend in the storm but not crack. But its then too late to learn the lesson.

I've lived in a time, at least until recently, when Europe was disillusioned. It followed from the collapse of civilization in two world wars – the first characterized, perhaps, more by stupidity and the 2nd, perhaps, by barbarism. I am by nature and intellectual conviction, incapable of being disillusioned. One constantly gains. Our species constantly learns more about itself and how it has to relate to the conditions of its existence. But I have seen many people despair, whole communities lose conviction in the possibility of effective action. And I also know people now, who call for action, who will end in despair and disillusion. They are unrealistic, they are not enough concerned with the mechanics of change. For example, it is sometimes necessary to use force. But force by itself changes nothing. The only things that change social, and therefore political, relationships, are ideas and skills. (I mean practical techniques in economics and sciences.)

So The Sea is an image for constant opportunity, new chances, and all change may, perhaps, produce some good. Because you have witnessed a failure, that doesn't mean that life, the world is a failure. And when I personally make mistakes I don't assume that I have been betrayed by The World Spirit!

The Old Man in The Sea describes, to the young world, a universe of constant change. That isn't a metaphysical statement. I based that on statements by English, American, Russian astronomers or physicists. That is just the total background of human action. A scientific description of the universe and our form of life. What it says is the universe creates rationalism, or enables rationalism to create itself. So it isn't a doomed work, like the world of the absurd, or an evil world, like the world of some metaphysics and religions. It is a theatre, a stage, where rationality and sanity may perform. Now you may think that is irrelevant. Well, its relevant to me and I think to other people. Just as Dostoyevsky had to state what seemed to him to be the nature of the whole world, so do other people: because only then can they understand their own behavior. I don't see the world as absurd or evil, and so there's no reason for my own actions to be. When the German critics stated, against the text, that The Sea was a metaphysical image, and that it made human action meaningless, or ultimately doomed to failure, that was wrong. I understand it as an image, as a description of the nature of the world, as being a place where we are not destroyed by failures or mistakes, where disillusion is irrelevant, and where there is always a new generation who are innocent of our failures, and so as a species we are always given new chances. We tend to see ourselves too narrowly, we are obsessed with solving our own, immediate problems. Of course, we have to solve them. But we should see them in the context of a universe that creates rationality, otherwise we despair and call ourselves Absurd. I think the misunderstanding was this: the German critics thought I was suggesting the image of The Sea as a solution to our problems. That our struggles didn't matter because the sea would one day sweep us away, the wheel would turn, the universe would contract and expand, and new worlds would be created, to go wandering through the same meaningless maze of history. I didn't see The Sea as a solution, but only as guaranteeing the possibility of solutions. It creates the opportunities for rationalism as against evil or absurdity. [We are not condemned, we are invited.] And so the old man says to the young man I have told you these things so that you will not despair – but you must still go and act. The Sea, then, is only a distant background to action – but it is like the distant sun which throws light so that we can see what we're doing. It is not itself a substitute or negation of action. And this should have been clear to the German critics. After all, if you ignored what the old man tells the young man, and interpret it in this way, what is the most you could accuse me of? Mr. Bond says we have only a few hundred million years left and therefore anything we do today doesn't matter. I would say we have at least a few hundred million years left and what we do today matters very much. And if our species is destroyed it wont be because the sea has washed us away, or the sun gone out, but because we've destroyed ourselves. I don't see that's an irrelevant warning to give to a time that's still too cynical and nihilistic and fascist. And I certainly can't agree that it should be seen as a pessimistic thing to say. As I told the German student, I'm a pessimist by experience and an optimist by nature – but then, I had to explain that joke, just as I have to explain this comedy. Oh, and the 'rut' the old man talks about is also ironic, especially when its directed to many people in present day audiences.

Chapter Five
On Art

18 July 1973

Would there be any point in composing music like Beethoven's if you knew it would only ever be played in a steel works, where not a note would be heard? Or if not only Beethoven were deaf, but everyone had been deafened by the government, and no one except you knew how to sight-read music?

It doesn't matter how great an artist is, his art has no meaning until it is placed in a social context. Didn't it have meaning just for Beethoven? The difference between pure water and drinking water. We need pure water to make it impure by drinking. We need ideals to make them impure in our living. But morals have to retain their purity or they are meaningless, and useless. Art has to retain its moral purity, be identified with it, but it will be used in situations of compromise. Art shouldn't compromise with the use that will be made of it.

Art is ideal work that must be put to practical uses. But it mustn't become merely practical – pursue a practical aim as propaganda for a finite objective; or, to avoid misunderstanding, an aim that is chosen from outside the activity of art. And yet the context has to be considered. Art is always socially objective. I don't discount the importance dreams have in people's lives. But they have to incorporate their dream experiences and lessons into their lives, or fall under a train.

Art has a political value. Politics is the unending attempt to cope with the human crisis. The solution becomes more and more imperative as we create the means to produce the solution but have neither the will, nor really the knowledge how to make the solution. Art always gravitates towards the human crisis. The point where people despair, and when their happiness and strength are most revealed. In a sense that is when they are most vulnerable; when the bird of bright plumage leaves its cover it is shot. I don't say this out of pessimism. Just that we become reminded of vulnerability. But there is a contradiction in this. We're reminded of the fragility and impermanence of individual men and women. This doesn't mean that their society likes to be impermanent, fragile and inhuman. Every life is partly a tragedy, and probably we need to experience this tragedy, take it as our lesson, so that we become more deeply human. When we have a sense of tragedy we are less vulnerable, we despair less easily – or certainly we do not become reactionary. It is the sense of tragedy that stops us from being trivial or reactionary.

But it is the aim of politics to prevent tragedy. Obviously it has to be. Or else politics are reactionary. Reactionary politicians rely on the inherent tragedy of life in this sense: life is cruel and competitive, and this serves some higher purpose, the elimination of the weak and so on. Their tragedy is in the <u>strength</u> of people – not in (as it should be) their vulnerability and 'weakness.' Reactionary politics <u>use</u> tragedy for political ends. As political reaction is inherently tragic it always associates itself with a divine redemption. Finally, its politics will be unable to create a happy society.

Reactionary politics in democratic society have a peculiar problem. The modern welfare state cushions its members against financial hardship. But financial hardship is an important incentive in the <u>reactionary</u> social structure, so it <u>creates</u> a group of 'work-shy' people who exist on public assistance. This creates social disturbance. The people who do work (and some of these are necessary) object to those who don't. They demand that the government in some way punishes or penalizes those people who don't work. So, apart from an influence executed by its basic theories <u>reactionary</u> politics create a situation in which they soon will be attacked and regarded as social outcasts and misfits.

19 July 1973

Art and non-reactionary politics share, certainly in many ways, common ends. Politics can't subordinate itself totally to art – because it has a wider activity that includes the <u>implementation</u> of practical aims. But can art subordinate itself totally to politics? The question centres on the 'practical' activity. Does the practical activity of politics involve certain compromises which are destructive in art? Politics has to make situations, plans and so on, work. Ideally it optimizes the possible. It creates the best possible circumstances for people to live in. This is a utilitarian aim. I mean that in certain situations the few are sacrificed for the many. Are there situations in which the many are sacrificed for the few? In all probable political situations this would probably be reactionary. But it isn't the crude question of giving precedence to the talented – that is an artistic <u>and</u> political problem. You could give precedence to Rembrandt <u>and</u> to the ship's captain in a storm. The question goes deeper into real problems about 'values.'

Take, for example, a situation of good politics. The politics function well, for the good of the community. But the politicians are not all wise; indeed, it may be a very practical question – that <u>in fact</u> politicians, in the process of getting power and influence, become a certain sort of person, with certain limitations – of sympathy or vision. Now it would be alright for the artist – whose progress to becoming an artist is different from the politician's progress to becoming a politician – to criticize the practical consequences of the politician's limitations.

The politician (who incidentally probably controls the artist's income, and in this, and in various other ways, his ability to make art) would have a practical objection to this. He might even concede the truth of the artist's criticisms but say that they have no practical application. The politician could criticize himself (if the political process hadn't been too restricting) but then he'd stop being a practical problem-solver.

So is the artist just a sort of conscience standing over the politician and the practical man, like a saint in the church-window pointing at heaven? So that the politician is left to do the best he can, keeping one eye on heaven but his feet on the ground? This seems to be a banal role for the artist. Is that <u>all</u> the criticism and consolation we get from a Rembrandt portrait?

Shouldn't the artist be concerned with the practical application of the ideal, stressing its priority?

[. . .]

July 1973

If the future was inevitably determined, if you could say that after a certain amount of misery and effort – the amount depending on human will and understanding – a free, reformed, happy, democratic society would exist: then the role of the artists would be clear. If the future could not be indefinitely forfeited by politicians, but their activities were a sometimes wayward but in the end successful movement towards the future – then the role of artists would be simply to minimize mistakes and any strayings from the direct paths. But politicians could probably themselves act as a corrective or the popular democratic will would act as a corrective. The whole process of constant watching and adjusting could be a political process. The values needed for this could come out of the ordinary processes of day to day living. Why art? – when politics are inherently democratic in this way. Is art a purely individual reaction to life, which doesn't teach anyone anything – except in so far as a way of pain 'teaches' others to avoid sickness and accidents? But there is no 'knowledge' in such a cry, no guide, except the negative one of avoiding certain things.

Suppose the values of art can be learned through the ordinary processes of day to day living. Would they still operate with imperative force? Day to day living is a mixed process. One must eat, keep warm, protect one's family, and so on. These are limitations on altruism. They also limit activities to specific local areas. Why should one want to relieve the misery or destitution of people say thousands of miles away? On purely pragmatic grounds, as insurance against one's future destitution and so on? But all this is likening art to analytical moral theory – what is the nature of moral judgements, and perhaps moral feelings? But art isn't simply another name for morality. So that if one could understand why people act morally, feed starving Asians – one would know what art is! But could one <u>ever even suspect</u> that art was a prudential activity, to guard one against future destitution; a way of saying, look I am like <u>this</u>, this is my degree of sensitivity, my capacity for suffering, so protect me when I am in need? Art as fear?

It depends on what <u>your</u> pain is! If other people's pain is genuinely your pain, <u>why</u> it is your pain doesn't really matter – you will only be free from pain when the others are. Even your selfishness (if that's what it was) would have to operate like altruism. But of course by selfishness is meant indifference to other's feelings. The question becomes political again, because indifference to others – class or national enemies – is an often used political method. This indifference isn't merely not incompatible with political activity – such as winning an international or class war – it is often an important part of the activity. One must hate the enemy; or at least their leaders and act towards those who are led as if they were hateful. This is a pragmatically justifiable attitude in the day-to-day world of politics. And artists have certainly described evil. But what is the nature of that evil? Does it normally reside in political institutions and their accomplices – or elsewhere? The politician would, of course, say that it depends on the institution. If the political cause is good, then it is justified in adopting certain non-universal moral values, ie., class moral values. Moral conduct, as a day-to-day activity, isn't then universifiable. It is restricted in operation in order to achieve a final state of universal morality – or the nearest to it that human beings can get.

Art, I suppose, wants to universalize morality. Politics must insist on certain practical restrictions. And this is assuming that the politician has goodwill! Politicians therefore have to create details of immorality – however moral their overall scheme may be. Can they do this and stay morally sane? Once you practice details of immorality what is your moral guide? Perhaps that final moral objective is so passionate, so desired, that the immoral <u>don't</u> destroy or tarnish that passion. But that depends not on the strength of your vision, but on the weight of the practical problems – how intractable and incorrigible they are. Perhaps one unjust death would be justified if it redeemed – in a practical way – the rest of life on earth. But can you really isolate a few dangers? Doesn't your activity become a political style? Doesn't it create certain expectations? This is a practical psychology question. If you lock people up, frighten them, and give them no practical experience of free choice – what do you expect them to do when you let them out? This is a crude example and not immediately transferable to political situations, but it makes the danger clear. To justify immoral details even practically, you have to show clear moral advance that couldn't have been achieved without the immoral details.

Writers have usually been in opposition to their government or the prevailing political feeling. Tolstoy, Solzhenitsyn, Rabelais, Voltaire, Molière. When they haven't – Goethe – there seems to be a compromise in art, and one is fobbed off. Shakespeare is a special problem. He certainly criticized contemporary political feeling – but he offered a reconciliation. Was this based on a political compromise – did he, as a practical bourgeois opt for a limitation on morality, and then decorate this with poetry? The answer is no, because the last works are genuine art, genuine questioning. They don't really reconcile one to present conditions at all!

So I think that art isn't just knowledge – permanent and pure idealism – to be contrasted with the compromises and dirt of politics. Art must also be a practical activity concerned with the details of living – just as Rembrandt is concerned with the wrinkles on his old people's faces. Certainly art should be committed. But should it become propaganda – following out political directives implicitly and faithfully? The statue of justice over the low court is always figuratively more impartial than the judge. But this still leaves the 2 worlds unbridged: politics and art. Should art finally judge political activity when it becomes morally restricted?

July 1973

The connection between art and politics is always intimate. It has always been. Art reflects prevailing social attitudes and the social conditions on which they're based. It isn't always direct propaganda for these, nor does it show formal, hollow, respect for the propertied classes who pay for art and who arbitrate on what good taste is. A lot of art has always been critical, of course.

But it can never escape into a dream or a world of the ideal – except as a criticism of the contemporary and real. This is true of romanticism – though romanticism often incorporates an explicit political protest which it parodies from real political activities, and in so doing it incorporates an element of reaction; because these political activities were themselves a dream deluding itself that it was real. That is the influence of Neoplatonism in art. Dream-solutions are essentially part of political reaction. Art must always avoid dreaming in the sense of 'make-believe.'

But art can't escape from politics because society is the problem, the subject, of art. This is only to say that art can't exist in a vacuum – in an ideal – and that it can't exist for itself – because it has no existence in itself. It is a criticism incorporating and expressing – and proving – certain standards. Art is a sort of proof.

Art is never the subject-matter of art. A hen may be an egg's way of making another egg – but an artist is not a picture's way of making another picture. A value intervenes in the merely mechanical activity! Art is an aspect of the everyday. But it can't be fulfilled by the everyday. It can't be satisfied by ambition; it doesn't have, it doesn't express the desire to be satisfied in this way. It can't ever be satisfied by political success – that is, by changes in the political society which it mirrors.

Whether any one piece of art is eternal doesn't matter. No culture is concerned with a sufficient long span of time for this question to be posed, let alone answered. To want art to be eternal (or to want it to be anything else) is sentimental – it is like caging a bird to make it sing.

Could you say that human nature was compartmentalized? That these various compartments – such as relating capitalism to the physical world, and utilizing the physical world to get a living, and creating art – are all isolated? That human beings are a collection of disparate, self-sustaining faculties. In this case art would relate to the whole man – as an inspiration or relaxation – but it would remain pure – something men could turn to when they need it. But then what would its private history be? Why and how was it created? Would it be compatible with a biological, physiological explanation of the world and its origin? Could it represent some earlier, perhaps initial, energy or rhythm – the energy that propels man, pushes him forward into development? That art reflects or embodies this, and not a relationship between a man and his society?

Perhaps. But this doesn't give it any special significance or importance – that would be idolatry! It doesn't matter that God created the world – I still don't have to pay him my respect unless he agrees with my moral sense. If he <u>gave</u> me my moral sense the case is really no different. A moral sense must be autonomous. A thing is good because it is moral, not because God says it is. And so in the case of art. If I have an art sense it must be autonomous. A thing isn't good art because an artist or a politician says it is. There may be practical confusions and difficulties in understanding art, just as there are practical difficulties in sorting out what is the right thing to do: but these don't destroy the conception of good, even though 'good' must be a guide to practical activity.

Now if art is a discrete, autonomous 'compartment' in human nature (I mean the ability to create and recognize art) this doesn't mean that art should exist on its own, like a clear pool we dive into when the weather is hot. Obviously the problems of human life are so pressing that one uses all ones experience and ability to deal with them. Art isn't just a mirror reflecting itself. It will reflect the whole of our concern. Morality has a sense of urgency. The cool pool exists in a burning forest! We use it, surely, to put the fire out – since, in the excluded nature we're giving art in the particular argument, there is no possibility of living in art – it is a rarified compartment not related to practical life and not influenced by it. It is something we <u>use</u> in opposition or contradiction to everyday life. Such an art didn't have a moral element. It would be above morality, or indifferent to morality. Yet how could we satisfy, or alleviate, or escape from, our moral pain in the world ('your pain is my pain') in a non-moral retreat? But put at its best, this wouldn't be what is normally meant by escapism. It would be more like a retreat we need now and then to confirm our sanity in a painful, destructive world. Would it strengthen us to go back into the mould – presumably to try to change it? Then surely this must have a moral element? In itself a non-practical moral element? – but how can this be? Where would we get the moral insight to make it practical, to use it in practical ways – and if we didn't what use would it have been to us?

You mustn't think of it as a 'rest' – just as soldiers are sent to 'rest-camps' during a war, so that they are refreshed and strengthened. It can't be merely quietness. It must be a sense of ordering our experience – giving the chaos a pattern so that we can look at it coherently. It must therefore predicate meaning. It doesn't create a serene stupor. In this case art couldn't teach us anything – it would only create the circumstances in which we can learn. 'Can' then becomes a further problematic. If art teaches it presumably can't lie. But if the 'can' is thrown back to us we have to identify a further ability – a further function of perception, art from any moral necessity to follow it, or retain it. Because art doesn't 'convert' us – now we see, now we understand! It isn't like a religious conversion. But we retain it in our lives. It becomes a sort of glass ruler – through which we measure our dim experience, and which guides our reactions.

If art exists in the abstract in this sense, then it is in a one-way mirroring into which we gaze. It isn't made up from our day to day experience. It doesn't share a common nature, or structure, or development, with the rest of our human nature. It isn't an attribute of our mind in the normal sense of the working, functioning mind, which is intimately connected with our practical living. It is a thing apart.

Morality is practical and therefore political. Just as a moral sense tries to bring order and harmony and truth into the world – and some of these things are not necessarily always immediately compatible, truth and harmony for example – does a work of art reflect the same things in the arrangement and use of the art materials and elements? If this is so, then art isn't an abstract 'thing-apart' – its method is identical with the practical, moral sense – which (for me) is in origin biological.

If you give priority to the practical moral sense; this doesn't mean you identify yourself completely with the politician. The politician is a psychological entity – the moral sense really isn't. Our grasp of the moral sense – whether the moral sense becomes a necessity for us – may have a psychological determination – but the sort of altruism we mean by 'morality' is a logical structure and a rational structure. The necessity may also be shown logically – just as the necessity of love may be, in order that the race continues, but that demonstration isn't the same as the psychological necessity to love. Moral necessity in this sense is, by the way, intuitive – it is only love that is blind. The moral sense is psychologically acute at sensing out suffering. The logical political morality may regard this as a weakness because it makes persistent, consequential, long-term moral activity in an immoral society impossible.

But a thing can only get a character, a nature, from activity. This is true of art as much as a moral sense. Only very simple things have a complete 'nature' – such as elementary particles. Out of the activity of these come other things. And out of the activity of these things come higher, more complicated things. Art and morality are later constructions. They 'reflect' biological rhythms (if the reflecting of rhythms is the construction) not elemental, physiological rhythms – not the basic energies of creation in this sense. They reflect the basic energies of men being human animals.

July 1973

Art has to be thought of as an ability or disposition of human beings, but the art work must incorporate something – unlike the moral act, which is a rearrangement of other things, altering nothing but the arrangement between them such as food and people. But the art work must contain something more. The art activity is partly the cleaning away of the unessential – the removal of chaos, so that, at the most, only the essential or required chaos remains. But even this cleaning away of the irrelevant isn't a purely negative activity, because it must be guided by the positive pattern or order that is to remain. How psychologically clear this pattern is to the artist, doesn't matter. He may arrive at his pattern by using accidents. But the pattern always has a relationship to society. Art is always a thing in itself, but it can't exist outside its social relationship. So when the artist asks the public to look at his art-accident, he's asking them to look at the accidental in a way in which society doesn't generally do – or ask for. The element of criticism in art may vary. One artist may use art as social criticism in an obvious, polemical way. But all art has an element of criticism of the everyday in it; and when art is looked at in this way it is understood and enjoyed. Art has also, very often, been enjoyed as a possession. But then bourgeois politics are taking precedence over art in the mind of the possessors.

Yet this seems to suggest that the criticism can remain very anodyne? How, then, is it an important element in all art's moral element? This simply means that art-possessors don't see the objects they possess, they see them as mirrors in which is reflected their own self-satisfaction. Then the artist probably wants to make the criticism overt – but this for a moral reason. Even then the criticism may go unseen. The obvious case is Goya and his royal patrons.

Is the criticism inherent in all art's moral element? In the sense that society is always imperfect, it must be. But this seems merely accidental unless we say that art (to create and enjoy it) is essential to human nature; then there is a human aspiration to express itself in this way, just as a child likes to measure its height against the door post.

Yet there seems a gap between the merely 'passively-critical' (which all art is) and the 'positively-critical,' which is more morally intended and political art. It is, perhaps, like art calling attention to itself.

There is a distinction between a good politician's speech in which he attacks certain evils, and an etching by Goya attacking the same evils (or what are apparently the same evils – it is difficult to say what the content of a work of art is; its specific content can't perhaps be sharply distinguished from its nonspecific content.) Of course, the politician underpins his speech with action. But obviously the speech is different from, say, a poem. The poem may also call for specific action, but it also exists in itself – as a poem or work of art. Most speeches don't – with the exception of certain pieces of oratory – and one should probably say, only a _few_ pieces of oratory.

Partly this must be because the poem universalizes the particular, of course. Just as it makes the moment paramount. Then we live in the art of the artist's perceiving or understanding or even perhaps just creating the X which is the specific subject of the art. It isn't necessary to say that the artist recognizes, 'creates,' the eternal or permanent in the act of identifying and surveying the individual (and this might take the artist years or seconds as an eternalizing act!). To say, I will now see this as the eternal and generalized is non-art. Art is always specific and intimate and individual. It almost seems as if politics were more generalized than art. Art is concerned with the eternal individual, politics with the generalized specific. But this only refers to the necessary methods of politics, not with its aims – or the human motivations of politicians.

If this is so art has to do with the justice of each individual. It portrays the justice which is the right of each individual – or rather, it portrays each individual's claim to justice and his right to it. (What expresses this right – the 'passively-critical,' the 'actively-critical' – what?) This means that art makes claims on politics, of course. Politicians can use art, and artists can use art for partly political ends, but the art must be true to its own integrity and methods. It can't be used as a means to convey objectives selected outside the integrity of art. In this way, when art clarifies fascism during its efforts to convey a fascist sentiment – it destroys that sentiment; or it becomes itself an empty gesture, a method without an artistic context.

Art isn't one specific thing – but it is a specific activity. Art works aren't the core of the apple, they are the whole apple surrounding the core. Each part of the apple faces outside to the world but is also connected to the core. And all works of art are connected to each other. It is the 'ambition' inherent in art to make the whole world its art-work – though this is finally meaningless and impossible.

July 1973

In a work of art the contents are allowed to exist for themselves. A spot of red paint is a spot of red paint. It is given full justice. But it would be banal to say that a work of art simply makes you look at everything new and see it clearly – as if you were seeing it for the first time. There is no particular virtue in looking at everything in that way. It is the usual experience of people who are lost.

And yet we are reminded, by art, of what things are – not just what we use them for. My fingernail exists in itself as well as for me. My class and my work may decide whether it is short, long, dirty, painted, or chewed down to its root. But it is still a fingernail which is given to me to use: the 'offer' transcends the 'use' I make of it or am forced to make of it. The 'use' may become its reality for me. Art may remind me of its 'offer' – and so may describe to me the way I use it. We may see so many red wounds that we don't understand them till we see them as a mark of red paint on a canvas. (But this is very unlikely. In fact if you cant see wounds you'll hardly be moved by art!) By 'seeing through' to something we can understand our role in its creation. But we should expect the work of art to draw attention to its contents. Surely this is what Rembrandt does with the lines on an old face? By reducing them to paint, canvas and texture, we understand what they really are. Accidental and surrealistic art is doing the same thing. It exists in relation to other art. When a urinal is shown in an art salon, it comments on other works of art. It attacks sentimentalism in art – whether the sentimentalism of a watcher who misunderstands a Rembrandt picture, or of an artist who incorporates the sentimental into his picture. It isn't as great a work of art as the Rembrandt portrait, but it may act as a very important artistic effect. Art exists also for the hermit, but it's important to think of art in its social context. It's in this context that the art–urinal works. Both the urinal and the Rembrandt portrait refer to injustice in society. The urinal is more reduced to polemic, however, it is an attack. It isn't a humanist description of certain values in the way that a R[embrandt] portrait is. It is more a piece of propaganda, more a political act. Of course, the exhibition of the urinal (even the concealing of it) draws attention to the thing in itself. The artists intention is implied rather than shown. Rembrandt's art shows his intention. So the urinal, oddly enough, allows us a freedom Rembrandt doesn't. We don't know the urinal artist's intention. He may be a sectarian, arrogant fool. Of course, he may have issued a manifesto, and we may know from this and various political acts of his, what his intention is. Even so, we're only obliged to trust him as much as we trust any other politician, and we can only know him as well as we know any other politician. He may be lying to us – and himself in some way. Rembrandt doesn't lie – indeed art can't lie. It must always tell a truth. Artists such as Rembrandt tell a lot of complicated truths.

Art has various ways of attracting the spectators' attention, but it cant force the spectator to accept the truth; anymore than sentimental works will make everyone feel reassured.

The urinal is more a political-work, a propaganda-work, than a work of art. And as a work of art its most important function is a teacher of art – as a teacher of how to look, @ [at] the thing in itself, and so to reassess one's own activity. In what way does a Rembrandt portrait differ from this? – or more exactly, what does it add to this?

1. A moral ordering of the artists experience.

2. A classification of the things themselves so their moral design becomes apparent. But I mean 'moral' really only in the first sense, since this is a real article. In the second sense, things are shown as 'opportunities' for human use and enjoyment. There is no inherent criticism. The criticism is the artist's and spectator's acknowledgement of the distance between themselves and these things, of their misappropriation of them and of the false ideas we attach to them. I don't mean to the physical materials the artist uses, but to their attributes (colours and textures) and to the shapes and designs he makes from them, which remind us of reality in the everyday world, either by direct representation (copying) or by 'abstract suggestion.'

July 1973
One can find a moral justification, for the political use of art, outside art – and this can be done very easily. The artist finds the justification just as any man finds a justification for moral action, on a point in acting morally. When the world is deformed, and being more and more ruined, and when people are suffering – then the artist ought to use his art as propaganda against these things. The faults might be so urgent that he abandons art for more direct political activity; but in any real, lasting social situation that we're likely to be in or know about there will be a legitimate function for the artist in this way. So art can always be morally justified – artists cant. The justification for art as politics is a common sense one.

But is there a justification in art itself? By becoming deeper art does it become a clearer moral expression? This would, of course, avoid the dangers in propaganda – that it becomes banal and inhumane. Propaganda does often teach people to hate other people; not other ideas, but other people as holders and representatives of these ideas. Can art ever be used to urge people to hate other people – as opposed to hating their ideas or actions?

A point to note: propaganda is successful when it appeals to most of its potential audience and produces a pre-determined effect in them. But this isnt, at least not completely, because of art. Art may appeal to many people, but it may appeal only to a few (particularly at a certain time) and still be great art. Yet one feels that it will appeal to many people, and potentially to everyone; but the artist may not be able to describe this appeal in another way (other than it's expressed in the work of art) and its appeal is probably broader – not restricted to immediate, specific goals for action, as propaganda is.

The important question is: is there a moral justification for art which can be found in art itself, and by expressing this moral content more clearly, does the art become greater? This isnt, of course, art for the sake of art, because the justification refers back to human experience, to our daily lives. When art holds the mirror up to nature, does nature only see a reflection of itself, skilfully copied, or does it look into its own true face, not at a 2-dimensional copy? Art does more than hold its mirror up to nature – it uncovers the face of nature, and of human nature as part of the common nature.

All the familiar, dangerous questions are raised again. Obviously there can be a political guide to propaganda. The lines can be clearly laid down and, if the artist thinks the circumstances are appropriate, he will follow them. But when we're concerned with a moral element in art that is peculiar to art (though it reaches out into human society) – who can lay down the guidelines? Surely these can only be discovered by the artist working at art. Propaganda decides the content of its artist's work and also the appropriate method: this is, always, implied. And also it will require, or the authority requiring the propaganda will require, that the artist will be a certain sort of person. The artist will not be allowed to live for his art – his art will be part of the general life, and so must the artist's own life. The style of both art and life will be laid down.[44] The question is can the peculiar element of art be incorporated in propaganda. I imagine this element to be diffuse, like a sunset, and it reaches into all aspects of artistic creativity – style, materials, form, subject, as well as the painted attitude and feeling towards society. So propaganda can certainly be artistically stylish, and exploit materials in a pleasing or dramatic artistic way. But the attitude, the feeling of the artist, which has to embody itself in a work of art, identify itself with something <u>in</u> the work of art – how can this be dictated from outside the activity, if indeed it exists at all? The artistic activity is itself a search for the truth. It happens in a process of constant risk, where the truth can always be missed, vulgarized, sentimentalized.

I recognize that the meaning of all this is unclear. But I don't want to

[44] I think Bond means by 'the way of life,' the reason for living, morality etc.

describe a merely psychological process. I want to say that art embodies
an objective truth. Perhaps it is only the artist being objectively true to
himself, reaching an objective judgement about himself, one individual –
but how important this is to society; because what is objectively true of
one person is morally true of everyone. The act of judgement is really a
recognition of what standards to judge by. When you have recognized
those standards the practical judgement becomes clear and obvious. This
is what is hinted at when people talk about the purity of art. Now
politicians may deviate from these standards. That may be a practical
human necessity. But it must be recognized that the deviation is a
deviation and isn't the embodiment of the whole historical purpose, or
the ultimate truth. A politically minded person will argue that necessity
is the ultimate truth, because its in the sphere that the wretchedness and
suffering of life occurs, and that if the politician doesn't respond to
necessity he will propagate more suffering and wretchedness; and he will
pillory the artist as an idealist, looking out from his ivory tower like a
god saying 'yes, the gods also weep over you – but we must remain true
to our godhead.' But the artist will say: 'you are concerned with practical
difficulties, but in the middle of these difficulties how can you maintain
your standard of justice? You will always be under pressure, you will
always make mistakes, you will always compromise with your own
weaknesses. I, as an artist, ask you to be practical and acknowledge that.
Left to itself every political foray will become a hell on earth.' And the
politician will say 'Hell is always on the earth. That is what we, as
politicians, are trying to change.'

[. . .]

22 September 1973

I am living in a time when the slack is being taken up. Decisions are
not isolated anymore. The questions dont concern style, attitude, or even
temperament – in so far as temperament is a choice. We are no longer
smoothing out little rucks in the cloth. We have to bear the consequences
of our decisions; probably we can now be judged by our immediate
effectiveness. Unless we are effective there may not be later times to
judge us, or a continuing culture that is able to use us.

I feel old. I'm not yet forty, but people twenty, fifteen years younger
than me – they belong to a different culture. I suppose as people get
older they've always felt cut off from younger people. But I feel
something stranger. I lived through the last seconds of an ancient, dying
culture: the horse and the smith. That makes me contemporary with the
Greeks and the Persians. You dont feel Homer unless you've seen a

smith at work. At work not in a museum, but when you looked in on the way home. See the horses waiting at the stream outside the smithy. See the sparks as it got darker, and heard the 'locals' talking: they often gathered at the smithy. I also remember the horses going to the fields to work. I remember the horses working in the big cities, delivering milk, coal, bread. Great living ghosts, always breathing heavily, standing like rocks, always prisoners, always patient. This gives one a sense of belonging to the past. One wasn't completely surrendered to novelty and innovation.

People, then, had to programme themselves for the future. They had a culture that enabled them to maintain the land, the houses, their relationships, in good condition. They had an idea of the future, and so a responsibility for it. They tended (I have to use that word) the details of the future. They equated time with growth – with destruction also, but that was the melancholy or tragic aspect of time – but with growth, so far as they were responsible, so far as things were left in their hands. They learned how to help things grow. All this was inherited before exploitation, before profiteering. Most of the culture isn't recorded history. It didn't build churches; it painted utensils that were used and destroyed, it used straw and flowers and dances; it had no literature, it had an oral tradition; perhaps there were ten thousand Chaucers, and only one who survived his education and wrote.

I touched the skirt of that culture before it disappeared into the grave; and so I learned responsibility for the future. Now the decisions about the future are made by specialists. Their education is limited to their own lifetime. They don't even have one century of experiences and companions. Life has become an experiment, not to produce a morally willed result, but to see what happens.

We live in an age that has less security than any other in human history.

We have to give responsibility for the future back to the people. Otherwise they will have only a sort of instant humanity, that can be used by specialists. Everything we use comes out of a mysterious slot. Life and death come packaged, already assembled. Our actions don't teach us anymore, they are only rewarded repetitions. We have a consumer society; I want a creative society.

For a life to be sane the details of creativity must make objective sense, they must be part of a general pattern: there is this paradox: the slack's taken up everywhere except in our personal lives, and these are all meaningless slack. For the people the error of feudalism is that political imperatives interfaced and disrupted their private meaning; in a 'total-society' (which is produced by technology and its political institution) private meaning is abolished, and the personal becomes the trivial. I see that in a sane society the details are joined intricately with the universal, these details have the rhythm of the universal.

I'm like a peasant, I cant be disillusioned, because I've never got anything out of illusions. Don't confuse naivety with self-deception; naivety can become educated innocence, self-deception is associated, sooner or later, with guilt, and it becomes rigidly doctrinaire. Most western communists are spiritually at home in the 19th century, eastern communists are working hard to catch up with the 19th century. The communism of the 20th century hasn't yet been thought.

[. . .]

18 February 1974
Dramatists' Problems

A work of art is a social object. It will become the experience of people in society. A writer has a responsibility for this fact; just as a supplier of water or the manufacturer of cars should not produce something that is not socially beautiful, or not beautiful to individuals or groups.

A writer should present problems and dangers, he should clarify the particulars of these so that his audience understands them better. He should make them urgent, so that solutions become imperative. But he must also turn his attention on the solutions. Compassion for the suffering is not enough.

In the west, at this day – I say day and not time or generation or age, because the situation could change quickly – it is the problem of change that's becoming more urgent and more critical, small changes are least of all a help in a situation where the connection between things is at fault. The relationship between men and the materials from which they live, and between man and man in society, creates difficulties of its own. Our problems are not only how we scientifically grow wheat, but how we (irrationally) distribute it, and use it to maintain the institutions of society.

It isn't enough to point out a political or economic injustice or to criticize reactionary ways of 'containing' as injustices, rather than dealing with them. Social organization doesn't work, and a writer should try to find the ways of making it work.

What sorts of things have gone wrong?

Perhaps the most important is that we have H-bombs. We have the ability of total destruction – an incredible extension of the instinctual-physiological capacity to use force that people have had in the past, – and (in a way) which they didn't have to learn how to defend themselves from, because the limitations of that instinctual-physiological capacity were themselves a protection against it. Further limitations, through political and humanitarian efforts – these were in response to compassion. But the need for control over our present nuclear power – this is basic sanity. We have a social structure that can ignore this danger, we're like the Romans living on the side of Vesuvius.

Another danger is the institutionalization of ignorance. This can be unnoticed because everyone goes to school and we spend a lot of money on education. But it is inherent in city life, unless effort is put into correcting the fault. Young people in cities live in a dream. There is no cause and effect – or if there is its of a limited sort. They see the world as a slot machine, and to make it work all you need is money to put in the slot. The machine itself is magic. The education of most people wont provoke them into asking how the machine works. 'I had a funny dream last night – but I won't waste my time trying to make sense of that.' Their ignorance is this: they don't know that life, the physical and emotional world, is a system of mutually supporting and changing systems. They believe that you can change a component of the machine without altering its whole design and structure.

An education in technology doesn't promote this sense of relations, of independency. It is concerned with highly concentrated relationships inside an artificial universe, the machine. The solving of specific problems creates a sort of near-sightedness. Primitive people have a much clearer view of total situations (as far as it affects them, and that's quite far) than civilized people. But as people's understanding of the whole becomes more restricted, their 'involvement,' their physical contact, with it, becomes greater. This is because of cars, aeroplanes, building machines. The atom is a great power! – but when you've seen a giant earth digger working, you realize the impact that an army of these is having – and in such a short span of time. The danger of all this is that piecemeal improvements create a universal destruction. There's nothing romantic in worrying about this. No artificial cherishing of the past that was comfortable for us few but miserable for most. We have the responsibility of all acting people to consider all the results of our actions. At the moment we're forfeiting the future.

So we have to say, how do we get a fair and generally acceptable distribution and use of our resources, without jeopardizing the future happiness of new generations?

Another problem is the divisions that exist because of the classes in society . . . But the economic and cultural realities of these divisions between classes haven't changed. And so the masses of people are becoming psychologically unsuited for the culture in which they live. Its as if an eskimo was suddenly transported to the jungle – suddenly! The idea of suddenness crops up again and again, it is a determining factor in so many of our present problems.

The psychological pattern of subservience no longer controls the actions or attitudes of the working and lower technocratic classes. There's no longer the old mental obeisance before authority; the moral authority of authority has gone. Rightly so, of course. The old authoritarian class ran society for its own benefit. Incidentally, while it did this, it established firm relationships between the members of society, so that people knew where they were, and what they should do. This is no longer so! Everyone has genuine democratic (or rather democratic-style) expectations. They want what the next man has (not necessarily what the next man wants!), democracy becomes the ability to acquire. But there is no real considered choice, because there's no real democratic ability to affect the range of choice; the attitude is to get a fair share of what's going. This is, of course, only surface egalitarianism. A democracy is the organization in which the members have the right and ability (I mean the structural ability) to change the nature and details of the organization; it is not merely the organization in which people have a fair share of what's going, or the right to use their own force (or numerical strength) to obtain as large a share as possible of what is going. You could have a very efficient society in which there were no genuine poor, but that still need not be a democracy. A democracy is about the way affluence is achieved and that will affect the conditions of life in the affluent society. A non-democratic affluence will not produce happiness – unless people are rats! And there is also the further question whether or not genuine affluence for all classes in a democracy can exist if all the members aren't fully represented in the democratic process, whether a society not representational in this way wont tend to become an economic fantasy-land. Representation isn't enough: there has to be genuine responsibility by every member – not delegates but electorates have in some way to be accountable.

In our present 'demoquasi' representation is really the handing over of responsibility. This, however, doesn't produce freedom of mind. We are content to hand over responsibility for the total society, but suffer when the generalized view 'infringes' on our private happiness; for example, our job and the sorts of entertainment we accept, or have to accept, or want, may make increased transportation necessary, but we may suffer from ill-health when a motorway is built near us.

Accepting responsibility means limiting generalized social activity. It means taking power from centralized users of power, and therefore limiting generalized activity that infringes on our private good. There is a political argument against this. Power then doesn't go back to the people, it goes into a few hands with even less political surveillance and responsibility. That was so in the past, but it doesn't necessarily have to be so again. Perhaps the centralizing of authority was a necessary step towards democracy, but by itself it can only lead to demoquasi. Perhaps authority must now be devalued. Presumably what would be necessary to prevent a retrogression like this, would be sufficient technocracy to maintain a free flow of public information. In this way abuses would become known and presumably could be dealt with by some political means. Of course, we assume that the ability to act effectively in this way entails our present degree of central organization (I mean the vesting of responsibility in a central authority). This is a central issue, it depends what is possible. Presumably there is a technological answer to the present centralizing effect of technology. I assume that it is not only that technology itself is centralizing in tendency, but also, more so perhaps, that centralizing is the way to make profits and the way to increase political surveillance – actually to increase it in the interests of technology, unless you assume that totalitarians like Stalin were motivated only by evil. So there should be a rational solution to the ratio between technology and centralization which could work for the good of people in the community.

I've started to talk about change and I'll go on to talk about the future. This is important, when we think about change we have to think about 'change to what?' In the past left-wing politics have concentrated on getting representational power for people. But while this fight was going on another set of problems have been posed – by technology. They are concerned with the question, given x number of ways in which it's now possible to organize society – so it produces m in n ways – which is the best or appropriate one for the species? The old left view was that technology would increase in quantity, and this would destroy bourgeois political structures. This is, in fact, happening though whether it would lead to genuine political activity isn't yet clear. But the view is based on this assumption: technology would multiply quantitatively and this would multiply qualitatively in people's attitude. But when technology multiples quantitatively it seems to imply certain qualitative adaptations within society, and in any case you have to answer the question: when has technology multiplied to a degree that it itself becomes socially unacceptable? Technology is not a mythical cornucopia. It is a finite arrangement of finite resources.

Technology is, within its own universe, so powerful that we now have to impose a direction on it. We cant just see it as the old left has done, as a means to opening the door of emancipation. Technology <u>can</u> step outside the limitations of hitherto human reality and create a fantasy world, <u>but</u> it will then create a world which will exist for itself, not for the sake of the happiness of the people in it. So although technology (and industrialization) have destroyed the old bourgeois ethos, we mustn't think of it only as a cause of political development, we must find a political control for it. Otherwise we're freewheeling. Certainly we destroy the old political forms, the reverence for traditional (and self-interested) authority goes; but as this happens the old interests create a consumer society where allegiance, law and order, acceptable behaviour, isn't obtained by moral influence but by affluent enticement. Of course, the enticement doesn't work, because the working class want as much as the bosses, it becomes an assumption of democracy. The only basis for a solution is responsibility, in which authority is in general hands.

A party of left-wing leadership has to exist in a situation of trade union initiations. Its job isn't to make the working class politically active, but to direct its political activity into new channels. It isn't to create a feeling of group consciousness, trade unions have done that: it's to create a generalized social or class awareness. There is already general political activity, in the limited sense that's possible in demoquasi. Left-wing politics have now to say what democracy is in a technocracy. Change must be related to that, not just to the seizure of power. If workers have only limited activities they can express these through the T[rade]. U[nion]. struggle. Real left wing politics can't avoid the question of what sort of society can be truly democratic. This can't be separated from questions of seizing power, or at least it shouldn't be. Otherwise how can you mobilize T.U. activity so that it becomes radically left-wing and isn't limited to obtaining a just share of what's going? We have to criticize not just the unjust relationships existing in society, but the inhuman society that at present is being created by technology.

Chapter Six
Great Wilbraham Papers

Great Wilbraham Papers 5 March 1974

A writer has to deal with this problem, if he wants to develop he has to solve it: does he continue the ancient tradition of writers – which is to talk about a better society which remains impracticable but which is an ideal in people, which they can perhaps anticipate in the tension and repose of art, and which they can 'keep alive' in themselves, so that the tradition is handed on to the generations who come after them – or does he compromise with the artistic experience, and expression, of this ideal world, and become overt propagandist for a political movement outside art, – and make more practical steps towards the attainment of the ideal in society?

The artist who lives in the ideal, anticipating the ideal society in a non-political contemplating of something that's not yet obtained, is always in danger of becoming a dreamer. His ideal society may in fact just be another world that will always be impractical and so he's writing not as a prophet but simply as a day-dreamer. Writers like this often believe that the world can't be changed, or if it is then not by art. They are sometimes nihilists, more depressing even than christians who believe that this world will always be destructive and aggressive, but that there is another world in which this ideal is also the practical. For them, art is a cry of despair or pain, or a work of misery. I don't see any virtue in making people unhappy if all happiness is an illusion based on triviality or ignorance.

It can also be argued that the ideal mustn't be contaminated by realists. That it must be a guide, a distant star, to which people must aim in their practical life. Like the donkey's carrot it can never be reached, but its practical use is obvious. Perhaps it just inspires hope, perhaps it increases dissatisfaction. The portrayal of the ideal might be achieved indirectly through the description of the sickness and ugliness of hell . . .

The ideal isnt often portrayed as a straight-forward utopia. We, the audience, understand something about the ideal from what the writer

says – its portrayed through hints, criticisms and inferences that have to
be drawn. We don't see a society in which the ideal has become practical,
we're shown people, individuals, groups, moving towards that ideal. The
author is, very often, portraying the practical world as it progresses or
changes. The writer isn't saying this is <u>how</u> you live now. So that what
he says about the Ideal is also about how you should live now in order to
achieve the Ideal Society, or at least make its achievement a greater
reality for the people who come after. The writer is always practical in
this sense. He is like an awake man shouting to sleepers, and they hear
his voice breaking into the dream of their everyday life.

I don't think a writer can avoid having practical effects; and (unless
he's merely being trivial) he holds up the Ideal to daily compromise and
failure. If he's a Nihilist his only social justification is that people will say
'That's not true.' But people often don't want to say that. A nihilistic
view of society is a justification for one's own predatoriness and
aggression. Its said that the Theatre of the Absurd has a progressive
social function because it is the humanistic and coherent criticism, that
creates and vilifies a picture of absurdity, which controls the experience
(of seeing these plays) in the minds of the audiences; and that its by the
way of portraying the world as absurd, that the standards of this
criticism are maintained – they're not compromised by reality, by the
imperfections of practical activity. Art remains a distant star: it wilfully
and forcefully condenses the audience to live in the world of need and
compromise; this is perhaps alright, if the audience is very knowing and
clear-sighted and can think and behave in this way. But absurd plays
may just be depressing. Nihilist plays may result in people making <u>less</u>
effort to make the Ideal practical.

[. . .]

Gt. Wilbraham Paper 11 March 1974

Every change is the summation of other changes. Some changes are
more radical than others. They are like a weight being dislodged or a
pressure exploded. But they can only occur when they have been
prepared by previous changes. You can't do very much in the way of
planting explosives in the path of human history – to direct or rearrange.
Historical effects are the results of the impressions of the human species.
These impressions are like a ground swell that insists on the fundamental
rhythms and shapes. To alter this you'd have to alter the <u>functioning</u> of
human nature. That can partly be done – but only partly and
temporarily. Perhaps in the future technology will make it possible to
alter human nature more extensively and permanently. Our robot

enemies arent machines, they are technological-scientific methods of seeing and adapting people. People could be made into machines. The captured psyche would be more efficient than electric and steel robots.

You can partly control people and so change this technical development, by using the elements of human nature against each other. So you can make a man so frightened of you that he will become your fanatical supporter. This must often happen in totalitarian states. You can also indoctrinate people when they're young. But the only really effective method is terror: this will give you fanatic support. Education will always in a number of cases produce a tension about authority. There is in human nature a tendency to question everything, on one's own behalf, truth as well as lies. And when even the truth is questioned, its obvious that someone will always find out the lies. Information is conveyed through human relations. Its the nature of these human relations that reflects the truth or falsity of what's being taught. People who live lies are not easy to live with, they're not likeable. There is no such thing as a happy lie, or a trustworthy lie: everyone learns critically – people's critical sense is usually more developed than their credulity. Obviously, this can be overstated – but enough people have enough scepticism to prevent falsity being entrenched. Sometimes people think its prudent to live a lie. But they'll only believe it when they're terrorized into doing so. Therefore, to stop a society being propelled forward by purely bourgeois motives – ambition, greed etc – it is necessary to subject it to terror. But in the long-run 'enthusiasm' (in the sense really, of fanaticism) is inefficient. It doesn't propel a society forward, or redirect history. Terror is always based on lies, I think. There's no reason to inject truth by terror, because truth has its own evidence. This means that history has its own sense of timing, and it cant be radically speeded up. Surprisingly little can be done about this, short cuts are geographically shorter, but the ground is marshy!

If what I've just written is in many ways true, it follows that truth is its own solvent of opposition. Its important to realize that force mostly functions in society through consent. The army maintains its discipline by the idea that the officers are more intelligent than the soldiers. In fact this isnt so, they've only had a more expensive education. The same can be said of workers and managers, labourers and squires. If you can demythologize the relationship, you withdraw the consent of the politically weaker half of the relationship. The politically stronger half then either uses the will to power, or it displays its naked force: the mythological relationship is reduced to mere violence. Then the truth is exposed to political stress, instead of political stresses being used to cover lies. History is a continuing process of demythologizing and therefore truth is always moving into the political theatre. But the social structure, which depends on political tensions, need not develop slowly and cautiously, because we have to deal with 'dislodgements and explosions.' But these climaxes cant be stage-managed from outside; they come at the historically appropriate moment. They are eruptions from the bottom upwards. Revolution from the top can only occur in a state of terror. The historically-appropriate moment is decided by several factors:

1. The relationship between the bulk of people (the change is from the bottom up) and how they live. This is their practical teaching about how the world behaves and how they have to fit into it. Its the logic of rain and the rain-dance. If a feudal lord told his peasants that God is good he might be believed, if he told them that rain was not wet they wouldn't believe him (unless they were fanatics living in a terror). This also teaches them how to relate to authority and power.

2. Accepted ideas: these are based, of course, on the state of ideas in 1. – but they often have some independence of their own. The idea, for example, that the world is flat. This has to be discovered as false – and it will then affect men's attitudes to their own life and their own segment of the earth.

3,4. The tools of change. Perhaps these become more important as technology develops. There isn't only the terror of progress, of course, there's also the terror of the status quo. A false authority will secure itself by violence. As the myth supporting it is whittled away, the violence is exposed and must become more obvious. So a pressure must be built up against the resistance of authority, to change. The moment will be decided by the amount and type of force the authority can command!

Its not change that makes violent revolutions but the authoritarian resistance to change.

A committed writer can thus do two things. He can convey the liberating ideas, the demythologizing of the old lies. He can also prepare his audience for the role they must play when change meets resistance: that is, for revolution.

[. . .]

Chapter Seven

The Bundle, *Stone* and *The Swing*

The New Road[45] 1 July 1977
a 2 hour play

Basho finds baby by river. Deserts it. Poem on the cruelty/absurdity of the world.

Child rescued by peasant or his wife, who is touched by kindness.

Basho continues to live by the River and he works for the landowner (and riverowner).

The banks of the river are neglected. They break. There is a flood. Cattle and people drowned. The landowner sends out a couple of rescue boats, but you have to pay to get into the boat.

Scene of the peasant family and the child sitting on the roof. They have no money. In order to be rescued they have to sell the child – who is now a young man – as a slave-worker to the land-and-river owner.

Perhaps the boy is set to work for the bachelor poet Basho – and he has to work very hard!

A local gangster terrorizes the countryside. Boy deserts to him. Persuades him to fight for the people. Could be a scene where the water surrounds the land-and-river owner's castle and he asks to be rescued. The gangster makes Basho sing to him.

The currency is 'bowls of rice.'

[45] *The Bundle* or *New Narrow Road to the Deep North* opened at the RSC Warehouse, London, on 13 January 1978 and is published in *Edward Bond Plays: 5* (London: Methuen, 1986).

Boy runs away from the slavery at Basho's house and hides in mountains. When he is exhausted he is found by gangster. Gangster makes him a member of his gang. The boy converts the gangster. The gangster isn't a psychopath but an 'opportunist.'

Oedipus was abandoned on the mountainside with his legs fastened together. Gangster could tell a story about a king's son who was abandoned on his mountainside in ancient times. How the son was rescued and became very wise. But how everything he tried to do well turned out badly. He had been cursed by the She Dragon.

The abandonment by the water need not lead to the creation of a monster, though it can do. It can create a self-aware person, who learns to recover himself. (Depends who picks him up and how he's treated.)

Perhaps the peasant refuses to be rescued from the roof? Rescued for what? Its not a life worth living. And now that I've sold my son I don't even have him to support me in my old age. Our corner of the field only grows enough rice to support one person properly. Let my wife eat it.

Gangster used to farm on the mountain. But because they stole cattle from the lowlands the landlord's sent troops into the mountains and destroyed their farm.

P[erhaps] gangster and boy/son are defeated – and the son is captured, tried and killed. As he is taken away he addresses the audience. Then Basho and the L[and]/O[wner] could thank the audience for their cooperation at the performance.

P the gangster isn't necessary? The son and the gangster could be the same person. The son, when he runs off into the mountains, finds someone sleeping by the road – or pretending to be wounded – and instead of helping him he robs him – because he is starving.

My name is Basho. I am – as you know – the great 18th century poet who brought the Haiku verse form to perfection. It is not necessary for me to give you an example of my Haiku since you will already be familiar with them. Nevertheless I will quote to you my most recent Haiku. It has to do with this baby that I have just found abandoned by the river.

Its better if the son and the gangster are not the same person. The thief he joins up with is a comic Tiger-man – keeps growling to imitate a tiger. Should be small and wiry.

3 July 1977
The son is rescued by the Ferryman. Later the F[erry] M[an] has to sell his boat – this is before the Flood.

TO COMBINE SHOGO AND KIRO.

Are events against this? Even if Shogo consciously chose to incorporate Kiro. Would this become a tragedy for S[hogo]/K[iro] – corrupting him and giving him self-knowledge of corruption. Or – if K chooses to incorporate S? Could K then be-the-one with the tightrope of necessity – knowing that he has not stepped over the boundary and is therefore still in control? But the problem is the reaction of the crowd to K/S – not their cognizance of themselves.

Does a democratic play have to deal with crowds – not individuals, except as they are members of a crowd, and receive their moral current from the crowd? The forces of history are certainly mass forces.

[. . .]

From dawn to dusk
I ferry man and woman
On this river

Merchants going to sell
What they have
In Kyoto
Women sent to marry
Actors and Lawyers
They pray when they step
Into my boat

Some watch the water
In silence as we pass
Some chatter
But my son
I ferry him across
For no purpose
Backwards and forwards
From dawn to dusk . . .

Tiger is a fool rogue – often laughing. But would he stab his best friend in the back if his worst enemy paid him to? He is certainly killed in the end – he is a Man-child.

The play should end with the execution of Tiger – and the survival of the Son. He is the force <u>that is seen</u> to be creating the future.

In a play we have to show not merely the consequence of any action – but its cost. The cost is shown in financial, emotional terms or in terms of human suffering – or in a combination of those things. Nothing appears from nowhere on the stage – it has to be paid for in humane-artistic currency.

The play is a comedy because although it shows weaknesses, of progressive forces, it also shows strengths.

Is tragedy to do with personal life – or social. Certainly social movements and events are often tragic. But tragedy (to have any creative value) must be a learning experience, or a maturing experience. But can it teach <u>social</u> lessons? It <u>can</u> change the individual to give him a greater understanding of his own existence. It describes the limitations of his life in terms of necessity – but like a hedge, these limitations can enclose a rich pasture. But moving large social forces requires intellectual understanding and as these forces have power of their own – what freedom may a man have when he sets out to control them? Can he only bow more and more, to necessity – or refrain, and in this way slow down the inevitable forces of history? Will history have <u>its</u> blood, that is?

1. Boy abandoned/left by Basho, rescued by F[erry] M[an] (against his inclinations. He comes back twice before he takes him and knows his wife will be angry).
2. The FM and son. Ten or more years later/ FM reports on the gossip he hears on the boat. Landowner increases his share of the tariff.
3. The river banks have collapsed through neglect. FM, son and wife sit on roof. FM can't afford to pay to be ferried off. Barters son for passage.
4. Son in service of Basho. Son overworked. Runs off – although this is a capital offence.
5. Son meets Tiger. Tiger is pretending to be wounded. His mates are in hiding. But son apologizes and robs from him. T and his mates are so impressed (they can usually count on the sentimentality of the rich

merchants) they ask him to join their group. They are so impressed with the wisdom of what he says that they make him their leader.

Song about how after the flood everyone must go back to their old place. Soon the rich were rich again, the poor stayed poor, cobblers became cobblers, lawyers lawyers, and beggars beggars. Only one man tried to change. He soon gives up and went back to his old business of selling shark meat. What is it in the mind of men, that makes it difficult for them to change?

Lo-Chu the clock maker said he could hear the rivers ticking.
The community of fishing people who live by the river – the son must set out to change them.
Scene of meeting between them and the Son?
They then repair the walls of the river themselves – when they have dispossessed the L/O.

4 July 1977
At one stage the F/Ms pole must be broken – perhaps by L.O.

Fish by Night.
    Dark stage. FM and son in boat. A lantern hung from a bent pole. Talk, while FM fish. Boy asks, answer FM direct, straight forward, 'stylized.' Avoid charm. At the end of this scene LO breaks the pole. LO closes ferry because he thinks FM may be ferrying rebels across the river.

Son's Address to the Rebels:
That their violence is uncoordinated. They are as bad as the LOs they rob. They are merely bandits. Each scene to be built round a physical Haiku – in this way a house is built round a den.

The son survives (at the end of the play) but he is not a superman. He should be shown to be vulnerable – and in a song of the future he notices the dangers.

Heaven did not create the people for the prince. It set up the prince for the people . . . The prince is the boat; the common people are the water. The water can support the boat or the water can capsize the boat: – Hsun Tzu.

[. . .]

Actors/writers/directors should first study and understand the characteristic behaviour of a class: how they eat, sit, walk, what time they get up, what time they go to bed, and how this shapes their general behaviour. When this is discovered, then the story should be applied to these people. It is true that in the class there will be types – but what is relevant is the reaction of the types to their situation. A poor man walking upright moves differently from a rich man walking upright.

Enemies are tied together like a river and a sea.

5 July 1977
A good cook changes his chopper once a year because he cuts. An ordinary cook once a month because he hacks.

The real problems of our species are social. A dramatist deals with individual characteristics. This poses a problem. How do you pose the general through the particular?

History is like a waiter. He serves up the future on a platter. You may choose from the menu. But you must pay the bill.

Basho should be drowned in the river – perhaps trying to swim to freedom.

                                    [. . .]

8 July 1977
Fishing scene: perhaps scene ends with B[asho] calling in the dark to be ferried across the water. He is on his way back. He could then join the discussion between FM and S, giving pseudo answers to S's questions – or getting annoyed that they should meddle in higher matters.

LO comes to B and asks him what his enlightenment is. LO approves (good, good!) and asks B to speak to his peasants – who fish and farm. They make sensible criticisms – but B is able to counter this with 'brilliance.'

Sequence:	1. Situations before people
B returns	2. Compulsion before will
Flood	3. Determinism as the
S into B's employment	grounds of freedom

Could Tiger meet a real tiger?

A scene in which S refers back to his infancy. Looks at the water and says that water could have been my grave. One day it broke its banks. The whole earth from horizon to horizon was crowded with the water.

[. . .]

There is nothing worse than to stick the iron mask of the past onto the present.

Ask not who is buried under the hill
But who walks on the grass

When the Watchman in the night says
All is well
Get out of bed and take to the streets
The hawk out to murder
Had a hard time of it
Buffeted by the winds

And I as I watched it
Swing like a pendulum on the wind
Along the edge of the copse
When caught in the rain

New Road 5 July 1977[46]

The rescue of the baby by the river is a humane gesture by the FM. It costs him something – but not a great deal, not too much – he has a job and the family won't starve. I'm certain he has the happiness of being a father. The later gesture – of helping the rebels to smuggle arms – requires more. The final gesture – warning the son – requires his life. The gesture is this: he drops his pole in the river. The son knows his father is such a good boatman that he would never do this unintentionally. Therefore it must be a warning.

The son is rescued as a baby. For him this is good. He escaped from the dangerous water. But he lives by the water. The water gives money – to the FM . . . <u>and</u> to the LO. The son must cross the water – to work as

[46] Many of these entries actually precede earlier sections. The entries come from a separate notebook Bond was keeping at the same time as the current notebook. Rather than attempt an integration of the notes, the editor has preserved their original order.

a rebel. On the water he is exposed. There is no cover – only the night, and that also hides the enemy.

If Basho commits one atrocity (by leaving the baby) he will commit others. Perhaps an account of him at a burning house worried about saving his diary, not a baby. Of him walking through a famine, a drought, a riot – and concerned only with writing beautiful poems (it would be a paradox if they were beautiful). Of course it would seem as if his poems, his concentration on beauty, protected him from fire, flood, famine, robbers and murder – which isn't the case, even via money (that is, even if the poems sell well they'd still only enable him to buy a limited amount of protection).

If F[erry]M[an] drops pole in water the LO would have no reason for killing him – could have been an accident. Could Basho denounce him – because B would understand? (I have written 12,000 poems and there is not one ink blot on any page). Perhaps: FM drops pole, its recovered, they go on to the shore. By this time son has fled. They search for him – and go away angry and frustrated. Then: At a later scene B denounces FM and says that their son is getting army information across the river. They threaten to hold FM hostage. FM says that his son would not help him or surrender. They say: you must be sad about that. He says: No, glad. FM and his wife are killed.

Possible image: In the flood a group of people are stranded on a hill. The hill is the village burial ground – so they are stranded among the graves of their own families. Each has to pay before they are taken off in the boat. F[erry]M[an's] W[ife], and son are left on the hill last. His boat has been swept away in the flood – because it was quite small. (They laugh at the FM for being without a boat.) He can't afford another boat – so his next boat is the property of the LO. (Good; keep in play.)

[. . .]

When son addresses the peasants meeting he says he was abandoned by one of them. I am the son of someone that's poor – unless my parents have died. Therefore listen carefully: because you are talking to your son. There is an old saying: if the abandoned child returns to the house he should be kept. Perhaps the god brought him back. Nature of the rebellion: the rebels will fight if they can get the new weapons which son can buy from the south. So he is slowly arming the peasants with rifles – they are being shipped over on the FM's boat. How does he pay for the rifles? Would son have to prove (to the peasants) that the river god doesn't exist. For example: Son says: If the river god exists and all I have said is untrue, then god (river god) strike me dead.' There is a silence. The door opens and the LO slowly comes in. The peasants get the point that it isn't god who decides about their lives but the LO.

Peasant: Who sent you?

LO: No one sent me. I've come to collect the rents. (Couldn't actually have come for the rents – just heard they were at a gathering).

There should be a scene of <u>disguise</u>.

The play must be very <u>theatrical</u>. Its reality is analytic not descriptive (normally). Live incident.

[. . .]

Realism is naturalism gone ripe. N[aturalism] is R[ealism] gone sour.

[. . .]

17 July 1977

There is a small thin man	Moral exhortation
Who ferries the boat	Functions only within a system
Over the water	To change the moral nature of men
As if he were poking	The system must be changed
The eye of god	
With his pole	

1. Rescued
2. Caught in the boat.
3. Flood/rescued from hilltop graveyard.
4. With Basho.
5. Escape: Tiger and a gang of thieves.
6. FM asked to ferry arms across river by son. Agrees.
7. LO. Tiger has been caught. FM threatened with death of wife. Agrees to get son on boat – perhaps to send a message the wife/mother is ill.
8. River: father drops pole in water. Son escapes. His hunters frustrated.
9. Denunciation of FM by B. FM is drowned in the river he spent <u>his life working on</u> (?)
10. Son and the peasants who live by and from the river.

P[ossible] in 4: Son waits on B and LO while they discuss the situation over a meal – son's reactions shown not because he drops plates, serves wrong person etc – but because he does everything perfectly – but when LO and B have gone he sits down and cries by the table as he cleans it.

P[erhaps] FM has always had a 'clean' boat – ie, he's never trafficked in contraband or arms or secret messages – unlike X and Y – perhaps he tells S this in 4. Therefore the son changes the FM's attitudes.

Arguments shouldn't be discursive (as in Shavian theatre) but simplified into Haiku-ness, sharpness, something between a slogan and a short poem. But the substance of each argument must be shown in an action – in a decision being reached, this <u>clinches</u> the argument, or rather resolves its complexities. Note, all the same, that decisions aren't necessary in all elements of change – people can act irrationally. But then there is an emotional reaction which is the form of a judgement (though this can be redirected, as in racism). Because of this redirection <u>decisions have to be made by someone somewhere sometime</u>.

Why does the son become a revolutionary? Why does the father decide to help him? (From this it will follow why he decides to save him.)

When Tiger informs on FM, FM says its natural that under torture scum like that (actually he now sympathizes with T) would denounce anyone close to son. He denies ferrying rifles. There could be a western business man who sells arms to both sides?

The son becomes a revolutionary because he was abandoned and then saved. He understands loss, but he also understands that things can be changed and prizes won. He is positive for change: he means to win, he will find out how to win. He is a rational hero.

Perhaps the peasants, at the end, decide to build a bridge over the water. This is not a denial of the FM. The FM's life is the basis, foundation, of the bondage.

FM tells the S a story. Once, years ago, he had set out in the boat in the dark (on some urgent errand), he had poled and poled, but he couldn't reach the farther shore. He knew the feel of the bottom on the end of his pole – but <u>soon</u> the ground underneath was strange. He didn't reach the far shore. The river had flooded and the boat was in the middle of a lake – so he found, when morning came. P[erhaps] instead of songs and music there should be (or not <u>instead</u> of, perhaps, but <u>also</u>) poems.

[. . .]

A scene when S talks to two people who have abandoned their son – or are going to. This should relate to 4. P[easant's] son has been carrying B's writing utensils by the water. He is made angry by S's questions. Goes off. Then the two peasants appear with their bundle, S talks to them (as if they will keep the child because they feel sorry for it.)

S: they'll give it food – this will harm the other children and they will die from undernourishment. So they abandon this child to save others. As we leave this child here we are rescuing three boy children and five girl children (part of their family). B could observe all this. S is asked if he will feed the child. Says B feeds him very little (for reasons of asceticism!) and if he should save the child he couldn't feed it because he would be tired and B would sack him. So, when the P's are gone he throws the bundle into the water.

But the bundle, coming up in the air and falling in the water, becomes an image in the play. The bundle is like a stone that sends out ripples – and when S thinks of it, 'the ripples become shivers in my flesh.' It is this that makes him a revolutionary, and for him it is made concrete in the sailing bundle. They explain that the river is slowly eating away their land. First it was as large as ten houses, now it shrank to the size of a handkerchief. If the bank were reinforced . . . !

S is frightened about the bundle. Once he sees the whole world as a bundle, a stone, being thrown into the deeps of space. But there are no ripples. Perhaps they will come in but they must first run over space.

The whole world as a stone
thrown into the worthless deep
of space
An echo losing itself
Confined in a ring.

In such a world
What is the use of saving a life
When a life means the death of another
A roof over your head
Means someone put in a coffin
As if the world had ceased to turn
One half always in the dark
The other in the light

The object of poetry is to take simple things that everyone knows and use them to identify imponderables (to most people part of the time) – the movement of life, the moral cause and effect of life, act and consequences. The surface images refer to, and conjure up perhaps, the rhythms of existence, the yet largely unorganized processes. So, a spoon can represent a turn of the world, or a tragic love affair – one only has to use it properly, so that it doesn't appear frivolous – love is not a spoon, but a spoon can make the meaning of love clear. If I saw Christ walking on the water I would throw stones at him. What is the use of walking on the water? The world can't be made decent by a circus act.

The 'psychological' relationship between FM and son is well developed. The 'political' relationship between S and the bank-dwellers – or S as a bank-dweller – needs developing. I put 'psychological' in quotes because its basic human characteristics are abstract and political – it needs economic and social involvements to activate a psychology, to be part of it. 'Psychology' cannot exist in a pure way: it is like drops of water on a living creature. The pattern of the drops is decided by the shape of the creatures.

[. . .]

When the S throws the 'bundle' into the water he says 'this world is not yet ready for acts of kindness,' or [for] 'saints such as the FM'.

Psychological characteristics can blur the edges of economic facts. A factory owner <u>can</u> be decently paternalist to his workers, sponsor artists, have good 'tastes'. A worker can be a 'good' man and yet beat his wife when he is drunk. But in general, happiness and kindness are not attitudes to facts. Happiness is the result of facts, and so is kindness. A poor man may be benevolent. But that psychological attitude does not excuse economic suffering inflicted on him and his family – malnutrition, educational neglect, whether in a slum or a modern architectural concept, and so on.

Do not love your neighbour if you live in the shadow of the landowner's castle, but love your brother even if he lives a thousand miles away.

What is the core of the play? The fishermen and farmers who live on the banks of the rivers are 'slaves' to the LO – they pay rent and labour.

This is unjust. The LO doesn't even keep the river-banks in a safe state. Why not? LOs don't – it costs money. They only make the essential repairs. In order not only to be free of debt and waste, but also to have a safe life, the people who live on the bank must get rid of the LO and make the bank theirs – then they can keep the bank in good repair. The LO lived in a fortified house on a hill. If he had lived down below with the peasants he would have repaired the banks. The play's core is this: that each man can only properly look after his own affairs, no one else will do this for him, but to do this properly all men must work together. Hierarchy can only be justified as part of the organization necessary to do this. For example, only <u>one</u> man can be the anchorman on one end of a rope in a tug of war, but all men in the team are equal and pull together in the same direction. Hierarchy cannot be justified on moral grounds – as a means of persuading people to take part in an organization. Membership must be based on reasonable grounds. Nor can hierarchy, in a society which is not caught up in the passing crises of a Revolution, be justified on political grounds – when it is again a means of exhortation or inspiration or coercion – co-operation in political matters must also be voluntary and rational (but people are really acting in free will <u>only</u> when they act rationally. Human assent to the irrational is achieved by emotional coercion only) . . . the core of the play is the increasingly rational understanding of their lives by the bank-dwellers.

B's role is to preach the harshness of life, the absurdity of it, that it is only a painted veil, and that the people must endure quietly – for the sake of escape after life.

Why isnt the FM a farmer or a fisherman? Some deformity that incapacitates him.

[. . .]

The S learns from the scene in the graveyard. He sees the condition of the peasants and that the river – which is the reason by which they live – is also the means of keeping them in economic subjection. B says that the FM and FMW should be glad to give their son or someone says this on B's behalf because he will be in contact with an Enlightened man, will have the spiritual advantage of serving him, and will also learn from him. The S, when B is on his poetry expedition, repeatedly asks B why the banks burst – why the gods let this happen or make it happen – and B always answers him politely but not satisfactorily. It seems to the S that the banks should be repaired. Then there wouldn't be these periodic catastrophes. It's when he sets out to suggest this that he runs into trouble – and begins to learn. He first wants to tell Basho, who fobs him off. Then he tries to tell the LO, and is given a warning. He has to run out of the village or town. Then he meets T and the other outlaws. He could throw the bundle into the river on this journey (before he meets T and the OLs).

Part II Son reasons: if LO wont repair the banks the bank dwellers (BDs) must. To do this they must get power from the LO. (If we are to have a good culture which enables men to think and behave rationally, we must get power from the elite. The elite of any culture always debases it.) Note: a poem or chorus on the number of people who are drowned in the flood. When the water rose the living take refuge on the graveyard hill. When the water went down they carried their dead to the graveyard hill. Could there be a water vendor?
S has been rejected by B, LO and BDs (all in part 7). He must convert BDs by explaining their situation to them. But he must also show them that its practically possible to remove LO's power and to see through B's observations.

Scenes for Part II
1. ?
2. Son visits FM and FMW and persuades him to take arms. FM at first refuses. FMW tells S he will – (?) – because she says FM is only shielding her(?).
3. ? LO/? B/? – on capture of T
4. LO visits FM and threatens him
5. Scene on river – FM drops pole B denounces FM. FM drowned.
6. Death of Tiger – B lectures the BDs.
7. Son.

[. . .]

In a Utopia people would not need to learn from experience – they could be taught rational behaviour. Until then they will have to learn from the fiascos of history – fiascos because history will always be influenced by reaction (till utopia) and from time to time (till utopia) reactionaries will have authority and power.

[. . .]

The Stone 16 February 1976[47]
A man carrying an enormous stone on his shoulder. Naked except for white pants (Y fronts) and a long black coat. He is somehow conned into carrying the stone. But later he wont give it up. He carries it on his back by day. And on his chest by night. The man has to have a very direct friendly nature. Open, frank. Perhaps at one time he comes to an inn called The Seven Deadly Vices – and its there that he sees the dance? Associated myths are Sisyphus – and the man condemned by the devil to empty the sea with a leaking cup. The stone could get bigger all the time. At first its only a pebble. The thesis is that conduct and behaviour can be imposed on us, and that we came to need them like a prisoner needed his chains.

Associated images are birds in cages, prisoners in chains etc.

Scheme of a journey – but perhaps the man's going somewhere specific or has some definite thing to do?

17 February 1976
The stone is the burden of social conformity. This is an artificial imposed conformity – and not real community (which is taught and found). The conformity is required because it imposes function.

The man who gives X (or sells him) the stone, later sells him a chain so that no one can steal it. He also stamps it with a number.

[. . .]

18 February 1976
It is always necessary to tell the truth but it is sometimes tactless to repeat it.

Inspiration takes the form of second thoughts.

[. . .]

Song for The Stone 4 March 1976
The fisherman has his nets
The farmer has his plough
The student has his book
The soldier has his gun

The fisherman catches fish
The farmer harvests grain

---

[47] Bond's notes for *Stone* are published in *Edward Bond Plays: 3* (London: Methuen, 1987). The reader is referred to the previous footnote regarding chronology.

The student learns his trade
What does the soldier do?

[. . .]

20 March 1976
Revolution is politics not utopia. For this reason it can't avoid political
necessity. But it is sometimes claimed for it that it should avoid political
compromise. That makes revolution a very strange form of politics. If
only the cultural revolution could precede the political one, if only
personal change of heart could precede a political structure! In a way
they seem to, because a revolution must be desired before it can happen.
But that is the dark crux of politics – that a revolution must begin not
merely by imitating its opponent, but by intensifying its opponent's
methods. At least, that's been the story in the past – and this is true even
of the Glorious Revolution because this had really been won, in blood,
by Cromwell. The question is, has affluence, technology, and demythologizing, made a difference? When I say a revolution intensifies
the methods of its opponent, I especially mean that its forced to use its
opponent's more crude methods. The opponent will have learned how to
sublimate and moralize its oppressive methods – at least till the 'run up'
to the revolution. None of these subtleties are available to the
revolutionaries. The reason why there has been so little physical
opposition in this country to the ruling class is that the ruling class has
been so successful in moralizing and sublimating its methods of control.

19 March 1976.
The play is getting too complicated for its short length.[48] It will be all
exposition of plot!

19 March 1976
   Brecht wanted to show the function not the character. People are
reduced to a function – but not precisely so, because if their function is
irrational (which it must be in class society) this affects their individual
behaviour. Its because of this irrationality that there is progress. It's a
mistake to show people as entirely embodied in their function. One must
also show their irrationality – which drives them to exceed their function
and this introduces the grotesque. You cannot show a function, you can
only show a function breaking down.
   The irrationality of the ruling class weakens them – the irrationality of

---

[48] Bond refers to *Stone*.

the lower class (whether its hate, as in Victorian England; or the aggression and bewilderment of affluent democracy) is its strength. For example, present social relationships create hooliganism. This hooliganism isnt politically directed – it occurs on football terraces or is straightforward vandalism – but it weakens the grasp of authority because it forces it to move from myth, moralism and sublimated force – to naked force. This reveals the true situation. It becomes apparent when Tory MPs want to put hooligans in public cages, when the police demand to be armed, when the public agitate for corporal and capital punishment.

[. . .]

You can tell if a man is afraid from the way he eats.

[. . .]

5 May 1976

You work to live and eat and sleep and love.

[. . .]

17 December 1976

In our own time this inability has led to silence: to the pause.[49] In the pause there is the centre of the play – and this is left for the audience to speak to itself. This implies a common knowledge which it is impossible, or impolite, to express in words. 'What can this mean?' That we have no language for our most important truths, no way of expressing our deepest thoughts, our most precise illuminations. Where does Shakespeare complain (seriously) of the limitations of his pen? But Shakespeare was a man who found the truth convenient. The writers of the pause – the hiatus – do not find the truth convenient. The pause indicates the bound eyes, the gagged mouth.

Drama is not fiction. A character in a novel may invent a lie, or rather the author of a novel may invent a lie, to explain that he, the character, is a creature of causes and consequences. But an actor must demonstrate this truth: it is not possible for an actor to <u>persuade</u> any one of anything – any more than a scientist can <u>persuade</u> you that nitrogen is heavier than air.

Language is very important. You must learn to speak before you even tie up your shoes.

[49] Bond comments on *Drama from Ibsen to Brecht*, Raymond Williams (London: Chatto & Windus, 1968), 112: 'an inability to speak out – an inability of which almost every notable writer in the last 70 years has complained'.

Chapter Eight
The Rothbury Papers

Rothbury Papers 30 November 1978

Men inherit much of their biology from pre-man animals. This biology is largely deterministic: it enables the animal to survive by instincts. Much of it is even unconscious. The machinery of the body works unconsciously – breathing, metabolism and so on. The animal does not need to observe an event and react to it. Very primitive animals – half plants really – dont even have to consciously monitor their environment for food, shelter and sex. Relationships between more complex animals – both interspecific and intraspecific – require monitoring and response. One cannot say willed response because the response may be instinctive. Perhaps one could say that in all vital matters – sex, food, shelter – the response is largely instinctive. Outside these vital matters the animal may sleep and play more or less at will.

Human beings must inherit something of biological necessity. If the social organization of animals could be shown to be (always) merely a matter of instinct, it would also have to be said that human society is based on instinct (or it would have to be shown that human beings are in this respect radically different from pre-human life). It seems that within herds of primates there are different sorts of social organization depending on the nature of the environment. Primates living in open terrain need central leadership. Those who live in forests do not need this so much. The open terrain requires large societies. In sheltered terrain the society can be smaller. The elements that make this choice of society possible may of course be instinctive. That is, the choice may be achieved by patterns of aggression, identification and submission. There may only be the appearance of choice.

Human beings are one stage more advanced. They often invent their environment. Not merely by farming but also by inventing technology. Thus, although men may not choose to introspect themselves and change themselves subjectively, they do, as a community, change their environment and therefore their relationship to it: this necessitates subjective change. This later change may, however, be merely mechanical: that is, someone who was aggressive or rapacious before (within a feudal technology) may be the same within an advanced technology, using this technology as the instrument of his aggression and rapacity. The earlier technology required him to behave in one way in order to survive, perhaps. Does a more expansive technology, one which provides greater and more general affluence, necessarily mean that he will behave differently? Surely it will depend on how it affects his relationships with others. A man in armour on a horse will behave differently to others than a man working with others in a factory. This is especially true if we think of the relationship between the armoured horseman and an unarmed yokel standing on the roadside. A technology must be processed through social relationships in order to achieve a qualitative change in human nature. The rewards of affluence will not themselves change that nature. When men were poor and openly exploited they could still behave with charity, care and solidarity towards each other. That is to say, some could – since there are character differences between people. Human culture can only be created by relationships between people. It is not changed because people react to new toothpaste, more food, warmer clothes in certain ways. Human nature cannot be derived from things. We do not become better, our world does not become safer, because we have more and different things. Technology can only provide quantitative change. Qualitative change is caused by relationships between people. How? A man is not a social thing. He is a thing in society. Outside society he is almost nothing. But this still does not mean that he is a social thing. His thingness is his biology. His culture is social. It is his culture that relates him to his society. He is given to his society (by birth) in an act of which he is not conscious and which he does not will. (This does not mean that birth traumas – or happy births – are not possible.) He is a biological thing. His lungs relate unconsciously to the atmosphere, his stomach relates unconsciously to food, his bowels to excreta. (Culinary preparation of food, and continence, show the interaction of the conscious and unconscious). I said above that the mechanism that works out the social relations between primates may be made up of instinctive responses (not instinctive determinations, as in unconscious breathing). No doubt the relationships between people involve the working of instinctive capacities: to love, hate, reassure, test, identify etc. This may be said in a different way: that the social relationships between people work through their 'thingness', their inheritance of pre-human biology. Or, their later relationships with their world are based on, involved, their earlier relationships – that one strata rests on another. Our social nature involves our animal nature. For example, a human being in some way excluded from society could still eat and experience the satisfaction of stopping hunger, 'it' could still have sexual experience, even if this were only to masturbate. It would still be involved in these experiences, and they may be called experiences of the vital.

Death, suicide, murder: these are the ways in which we end our lives. Most men die naturally, some kill themselves, many are killed by others (in wars), death is an aspect of the thing: suicide and murder are aspects of society. Life is an aspect of both the thing and of society. (Im talking of human life and death.) Human beings exist as things and as characters: both aspects are vital. The human mind is not created by society, it exists as an aspect of the thing. But it is only a potential, like the potential to hate, love, aggress, care. The possibility of mind contains the possibilities of hate, love, aggression, care and so forth. Consciousness is the assembly of these potentials in a specific way, which creates a character. We may often read the character in the thing, in postures, expressions. These reflect a relationship of the thing with society in a specific way, as much as clothes or customs do. The relationship moulds the thing. Men in non-tropical climates have white skins, men in tropical climates have dark skins: the thing expresses a relationship to an environment. Some men wear purple, some men wear rags: these express a relationship with the social environment. One man has a pleasant face, another man scowls or foolishly grins: these express relationships with the social environment. Men do not relate to the environment, as animals do: they relate to the social environment. An animal is a thing among other things (though animals grade into humanness, there isnt an abrupt change – as if god had dropped a soul into men – but an accumulation of changes which develop from quantity to quality). A man is a thing among men – and this changes him into a man. It is as if the egg-thing burst. But if this is true of the world of appearance it is probably true of the world of subjectivity: the mind is a consciousness of the thing and of society. The face scowls because of a relationship between the thing and the world (the scowl may become a permanent expression). The mind may also scowl. I speak as if the man-thing were passive in society. Of course this isnt always the case because society provides opportunities for different sorts of action to different people. If a man scowls you could say that is what society sees when it looks in its mirror to see what it is. If the mind is a series of potentials it only becomes 'autonomous', develops

its character, through the work of relating the thing to society. The thing
is given (there may be innate characteristics but the variations are small:
phlegmatism, joyfulness, resilience, over-caution). There may be variations between people but we recognize what a person is physically. We
cant mistake him for a wasp or a giraffe. The social environment
changes. Hence the need for a manipulable consciousness, or the
opportunity for it. Is the mind an aspect of the thing or of society?
Neither, it is merely potential: just as water may be steam, snow, ice, a
waterfall, a calm lake – so mind, or rather character, varies. In theory the
mind might be the projection of whatever innate tendencies the
individual has (phlegmatism, joyfulness etc). But men dont exist in
theory but in fact. The mind is usually born not merely within an
individual but also within a society. So the person experiences the act of
receiving his mind both from this thing and from his society.

6 December 1978

As an individual grows older he forms the elements of his nature into
a character. A younger writer must include part of this process in his
writing. Because of this he will write in a certain way. The denial of self-
consciousness or self-involvement will also, of course, affect (often
strongly) what he writes. When the writer has resolved some of the
problems of his life – and made them fruitful – he will probably write in
a different way. In understanding himself he will have come to a better
understanding of others and of the common society. He will therefore
not see himself as a special individual – the particular characteristics of
which must or may prompt him to write in a particular way; instead he
will see himself as part of society. This new relationship will be as strong
and close as the relationship between the individual's mind and body. He
will see the world in a general way. Just as, earlier, he had been aware (or
even if unaware had nevertheless been involved in) the problem of his
own individuality and in trying to create a workable life and a just
assessment of himself; so now he will be concerned with achieving a
workable society and in clarifying social justice. The individual reflects
society in himself in many ways, he is created by society in many ways;
but just as he achieves a sense of purpose, responsibility and will as a
person, so he will relate to his society in a moral way – creating truths for
the use of society. Of course he can only do this as himself. He may have
compromised himself, he may be without self-understanding: then his
understanding of the world, and his dealing with it, will be false. He may
have had some advantages: he may have been born into the working
class, or (if into a 'higher' class) he may have great creative intelligence,

the ability to understand and interpret reality. When he writes, he must devote not merely his conviction but his intelligence to what he writes. All this means that he will be able to write with greater freedom. He will not be driven by the demon to express himself. His community will be as essential to him as himself. He will be driven by the desire to express his community. His experience will be general because he will experience his community.

Note on Brecht

Brecht's problem – like that of everyone else – was capitalism and socialism. But that problem changes. Brecht was faced, in the thirties, with the immediate collapse of civilization (even capitalist civilization). Possibly the advanced world could have entered a long period of barbarism. The violence of the capitalist state against the individual was obvious. There was brutality on the streets and there were also special places of brutality: these were not battlefields, as in the past, but the special sorts of prisons called concentration camps. He also saw the man in the street turned into a baying automaton at mass political spectacles. He saw books burned, language debased and emotion and prejudice let loose on his country like wild beasts. And he also saw resistance: when capitalism and sovietism joined forces to fight nazi-capitalism. Again, states were fighting – each other. The problem is in many ways different for us – though the cause of the problem remains the same. We should think of capitalism not as a particular social disease but as the source of several diseases. Indeed, when cures for some diseases are found it is possible for this source of disease to find other social weaknesses. The violence of the state against the individual is, in our time, rather well concealed. We have hooliganism, strikes, social unrest, inflation, disunity. At the top the government promises law and order and provides a high standard of material living. Of course this sort of living isnt shared by everyone. But the poor are not so poor as they were – unless they have fallen into the cultural-trap, that situation where the relationship of consent between society and individual is totally collapsed. Then people become apathetic, virtually sick. But the SS will not be sent to round up such people to take them away to concentration camps. Books arent burned and what may be said or shown in books and films – this is interpreted more liberally most of the time. The diseases of capitalism are more insidious for us because they are newer and more exotic. Those ancient curses of starvation, plague, religious hysteria and other sorts of fanaticism, of flood and fire – these dont threaten us so much anymore, if hardly at all. Nor are we threatened with an immediate war – or are obviously in a war – as Brecht was in the thirties and forties.

Hitler was a disease of capitalism. That the capitalists could recognize him as a disease and help to remove him indicates that in comparison with other diseases he was not a very serious disease. He is diagnosable pretty obviously, and – unless you were in close contact and subject to the hysteria he created – not dangerous provided you were prepared to fight him. War is an ancient illness and an ancient cure. War is understood, men know how to fight it and they can recognize victory. But we live in an age when the ancient concept of war is, or ought to be unthinkable. How do you recognize victory in a nuclear war? The struggle in a war, the waging of battles, the ruses and strategies – all these are understood: they are the substance of war. But a nuclear war has no substance: when it occurs the war is lost because no victory can be recognized. So the ruses, strategies, tactics, subterfuges, resistance, posturing, threats and propaganda have been transferred to peace. If there is to be a third world war we are involved in it now, as much as people bleeding and crawling with lice in the trenches in 1918 were involved in their war. Peacetime has become a tactical stage of war: we do not live in the ancient peace, we live by making threats and being under threat. So we are now actively struggling for the future of our species and our day to day living must be seen as a form of militarism. We live in a time when peace requires its pacifists – who will try to remove nuclear weapons from our history. But this does not state the problem clearly, it is more paradoxical than this. Our own weapons are as dangerous to us as the weapons of our enemies. What defence can we have against ourselves – in traditional ways? We are now involved in a silent war. But it is not seen as war – it is not recognized in the way that Hitler is recognized. Traditionally people have assumed that war would not suddenly come out of the blue. The threat would increase, there would be time for discussion and perhaps compromise. Failing this, there would be a time of armament, training – and then a time of actual fighting. But when our situation occurs it will develop rapidly and it will not lead to a crisis which will involve fighting when we can then test our strength, courage and patriotism. The crisis will end when it is created. So instead of war being a time of danger, peace is a time of danger – provided the conflicts that lead to the creation of nuclear weapons are still active. The only way to avoid nuclear war is to resolve those conflicts. This means the passing from capitalism to true communism. There can be no nuclear peace between capitalist nations because although capitalism could still recognize a Hitler it could not go to war with him if he had nuclear weapons. Any future Hitler would use nuclear weapons.

It seems to me that the circumstances in which we live are greatly changed from those in which Brecht lived. Really we live in a time of greater and more insidious danger. How does this affect the methods we use to analyse and change it for the better?

Brecht could use traditional rhetoric – and in some ways traditional forms. Anyone writing before the war is writing of and for pre-atomic man. The horse has been the main form of locomotion – and especially of rapid locomotion – on land for the whole period covered by literature till the present century. Greek metaphors, similes and descriptions involving horses had an immediacy for the greek, the renaissance and the nineteenth century men that they lack for us. For us they become poetic instead of being, as they formally were, poetry. They are a description, now, taken from a special stock of images etc., that we no longer constantly renew – as it was renewed when horses were commonly used, when their eyes and hooves and shoulders were seen every day and when the sound of their hooves was heard. And also, when people were constantly seen on them. The horse and its rider were an image connected with social intercourse and labour. The horse was also a beast of burden – a creature of flesh and blood, like men. Images of horses, then, involved readers and authors in reality: they summed up an action and its cost, an objective and the endeavour to achieve it. The resting horse, the horse at the knackers and so forth – all images of flesh, blood and bone. The writer may have been sitting on a chair stuffed with horse hair when he wrote his image. A modern equivalent might be the aeroplane. It is not immediately flesh, blood and bone – it doesnt eat smelly oats and excrete smellily. When it stands alone in a field it ceases to be, unlike the horse. The horse relates intimately with the rider – one learns to ride a horse by talking to it with special physical signs and with sounds. One learns to fly by reading and moving instruments – often there is judgement, but a pilot can of course be talked down so that he lands blind. We are less and less surrounded with a natural library of imagery and reference that is biological and more and more by one that is mechanical, electronic, one removed from human. The world of nature reminds men that they are human, that they are created by and extinguished by those forces of nature which are imaged about them in the natural scene. A flowing river becomes an image of life in a visible way in which a current of electricity cant. How could I say what pre-atomic men achieved from this surrounding natural imagery? Perhaps it enabled them to live in their time in a particular way. History develops, men developed, through technological development. Do we need a constant imagery to remind us that we are human? The imagery of technology presumably reminds us of our ability to control and develop nature. When technology breaks down we have spectacular new imagery – perhaps equivalent to the imagery of Lear's storm, Zeus' thunder and so forth. The pre-atomic natural imagery had a lyrical aspect. Can there be a true lyricism in the imagery of technology? Lyricism: the human consciousness as part of the natural world, a mutability within a mutability, mortality within change, age within seasons. There is also the lyricism between people: young lovers, old pairs, parents and off-spring. We wish to share our humanity with one another not merely a common-membership of an organization. Membership of a society, a community ought to be the sharing of humanity. An organization can exist for a specific finite purpose: to redirect a road, to ensure standards of competence and propriety in a profession and so forth. A community – society – does not have an objective of that sort. A community – or society – must express the nature of our species. Technology is only another tool that is made and used by human beings. The classical world had the imagery of weapons, boats, farm implements. Renaissance writers had the imagery of the crafts: the awl, the plough and so forth. Is technology so extensive that quantity becomes a change in quality? We change in response to our man-made technology: that is, we change ourselves indirectly. A surgeon uses tools appropriate to the operation he is doing: a knife to cut this flesh, a suction pump to remove this blood and so forth. He operates to achieve specific effects of an operation. He changes the form before him in a direct, intended way. This is not the way technology changes us. We make the technology for specific purposes: to supply heat and light, to plough fields, to lay concrete. These operations result in immediate effects. The total of these effects is a changed environment and a changed physical relationship to it. We make cars, we will not walk to work but ride there. We become an immediate part of the operation that has been affected. But the whole of our environment and our activity in it – that is, us as part of the environment – changes. But we remain something called people. People need a culture, that is a mind and mental attitudes and expectations appropriate to their behaviour (which changes) within an environment (which changes).

Changes: men make technology. Technology changes human work and recreation activity in two ways: it makes them do new physical things (riding cars instead of walking, working on a small part of an object instead of making the whole object: note, this could be modified but not rechanged back to a craft world). New activity produces new human work and recreation experience. Also, it requires new attitudes to work activity. (Mind of man working on conveyor belt differs from mind of craftsman at his bench. Craftsman requires varied skills and also judgement. Mechanic requires minimum skills and virtually no judgement more than a patient ape could use.) These new attitudes are purely functional changes. This results in new attitudes to self and to society. Oddly, as mechanics do less and less (compared to craftsmen and artists) they develop greater self-autonomy. Their minds cease to be feudal. They cease to be the major creators and the minor consumers: they wish to become major consumers. This is because collectively (as opposed to individually) they produce very much more – there are more goods. Also, they are brought into closer contact with their equals, and those who have power, wealth and authority are more remote. But at the same time they can be more easily called to account – and can be seen on television where they often defend themselves in the way a squire would not have done, he would have felt insulted if asked to justify himself.

Sport 7 December 1978
There can be an acceptable elitism in sport because the body cannot lie. Elitism in matters of the mind is more dangerous. The mind can be used to fabricate illusions which are as destructive and wasteful as the behaviour of those very intelligent children who, for emotional reasons, use their intelligence to behave stupidly. Elitism in culture is the most dangerous of all because it substitutes lies for values. A culture may divorce itself almost completely from reality. Values assist the long-term welfare of the species, not necessarily to the always immediate welfare of the individual. They are normative in that they prescribe a certain sort of future for our species: one which ensures the continuance of our humanity as well as our physical competence and energy. Elitism in a culture is based on the idea of an elite class and a culture owned by it. Culture is a unified community where value is present in each member.

Rothbury 7 December 1978
I WILL DIE FOR YOU
There cannot be one love affair or one marriage in which one or both partners have not said to the other: I would die for you. Yet I suppose not once has anyone done so. People do not die for each other, except by

coincidence when fighting wars or resisting tyrants; they kill for each other. And they do not kill for those they have married or make love to. They kill for love of country or god. In most cases, then, they kill from fear. Men join armies because they are afraid of the social consequences, of the obloquy, of not doing so. Some men die out of idealism. They may join a small group of terrorists that is itself socially ostracized. But even then they do not die for love but for an idea. Having written this I must qualify it: nationalists may die for the liberation of their country, and this could be called dying for love. I can only say that the formula 'I would die for you' is not a sound basis for living together.

Brecht notes (continued)
In order to understand human behaviour Brecht wished to demonstrate the class behaviour of people. In all matters of social relevance people's behaviour was determined by their class position and their understanding of class. This is true. But if I go back to the analogy of class as a disease of our species, will this help us to understand how we should write? A man suffering from a disease sees himself as a patient. The sufferer from class-disease (that is everyone in a class society) is not an ordinary patient. His cure lies in his own hands. A political-doctor may enlighten and instruct him. But it is only when he exercises his will or power of choice that the actions of curing become possible (at least when men are seen as a mass; some passive individuals may be changed by the actions of the mass). So in politics the person must become aware of himself as a man suffering a disease: as both man and diseased-entity. The disease is not an object that enters him as a virus which then takes over part of his body and its functions. He performs, he is, in part the disease. The disease should be seen, perhaps, as a mental disease (with objective consequences in the form of behaviour). The man must come to see himself objectively. That is, he sees himself as the disease: he becomes the spectator of his own abnormality. He cannot, however, see himself as only disease, as total disease. He sees a performance which does not accord with natural behaviour. He sees himself behaving illogically, wishing or willing one thing and doing another. For example, he wishes to be free but sees himself living as a captive. He does not see himself as a role but as himself in the role: he sees himself as both the actor and the role he is acting. This nexus between role and self is his reality. He may not see all this analytically but he bears the psychological and emotional (and behavioural) consequences of this split or contradiction. If the two sides of the split are drawn apart he may not recognize the reality which he experiences. The medical doctor separates the

disease from the man, isolating the invading organisms as enemies to be extirpated. Abstract analysis of reality may not produce the image of reality.

The old question reappears: how do you show members of different classes. Suppose you have to portray an aristocrat. This aristocrat is both person and class-role. But the class-role is historically redundant. The social world has progressed from the stage where it produced and had a need for aristocrats. In remaining a member of this redundant time the aristocrat lives in at least two epochs: the present and the past which created his social-role. His present-self is therefore a perversion manipulated by his dead-role. He may be seen, as a totality, as a person, as corrupted. He may therefore be portrayed in a unified way: he should be shown not merely as an antiquated-role but also as a character deviant. If the antiquated-role is shown on its own it appears as a caricature, as unreal, as a manipulation of the facts, as a gloss on them, as a satire. We should show not merely the antiquated-role but the human cost of that role. This is not to arouse sympathy for the antiquated-role. Sympathy is an emotion appropriate to repose. We are concerned with action. One may sympathize, of course, and I think it is better to sympathize: because hatred is not a wise 'choice' for motive. But sympathy is irrelevant and is only a danger if it affects necessary action (not self-indulgent action). In order to promote action we have to show the character bound to his role. If the character were merely a role the role could be changed by abstract reason or liberal legislation: an antiquated-role produces an evil-character, that is: a dangerous character. He is not sub-human, he is a special sort of human. He is possessed by his role (class-role). We think of the class-role as something applied, rather like clothes put on to a person. We have to see the class-role as it is interiorized. In this way we show how it makes different sorts of men. So a class-role becomes truly three-dimensional, an existence in depth. It is not merely a facade, nor can its description be reduced to a facade.

There is another special reason for this. When the audience sees a person – figure, face, gesture – they respond in a special way. They know they are watching a totality, are being signalled to by a totality. The appearance must indicate motive and intention. We spend, in our daily lives, a lot of time learning how to interpret what is going on inside the others. To give a simple example, a man in a uniform indicates something about the way he behaves (i.e., the uniform indicates it). But we do not expect the uniform to behave in this way. The uniform is not the actor. The class-role is also not the actor. The man in the uniform is uniformized as a person. The uniform on a dummy does not influence us – except perhaps aesthetically or sentimentally. What is dangerous is what the uniform does to the person. It is the same with the class-role of the aristocrat. As a character he retains dispensation over certain normative values: charity, restraint when possible, kindness, sensitivity to certain things. But these will operate only within limits prescribed by his class-role. It is the class-role which predominates; and when his life is finally assessed it will have to be in terms of that class-role. Only if he freed himself from his corrupt class-role could it be judged differently: because his character would then have become different and his 'personal attributes' (charity etc) would operate in new ways and have different effects. So the class-role determines man, forms character. Character is not abstract, the possession of certain faculties and tendencies – it is the relationship an individual establishes with the world.

No one is a true representative of their time but they can represent the future (just as many of them represent the past). We do not live immediately with our technology. We live with the social-structures inherited from the past. In this way we are all distorted. Take a communist working man. As a worker he relates, immediately, to his work in a rational way: he works the machine in the way the machine was designed to be worked. But in his social relations he cannot cooperate (as he does with the machine) but must struggle, fight, resist, attack. This means that he must behave in certain ways: the corrupt aristocrat may, as a character, be able to indulge himself more in gentleness and in acts of charity than the worker who must struggle. The worker has reason on his side whereas the aristocrat does not. We therefore (if we are to describe the worker rationally and that means sympathetically) have to have a way of demonstrating the humanness of reason. We know that reason can often be cold and destructive: it is so in the administrative reason, the functional reason of the aristocrat. What the aristocrat can never have is reason in a human sense – that is proscribed by his class-position. The aristocrat cannot understand himself or others. The worker can understand. The aristocrat is bound to see the workers as more or less animals. (Aristotle said it was impossible for slaves to reason). (Of course the edges of these attitudes are in our time not merely blurred but camouflaged.) The unconscious worker may see the aristocrats as, at least partly, leaders. The conscious worker will not make this mistake: he will simply see them as the monopoly holders of most administrative forms, most information, most force and so on. The worker may appear like an animal and even be deformed by labour and malnutrition. In order to improve his position (which is also to carry out the prescription of his history and our species) he may show to the outsider the characteristics of animals as defined by the aristocrat: he may be aggressive, he may use violence. (These are animal attributes unless they are sanctified by the state.) Yet we have to show him as the carrier of reason. Unconscious behaviour of workers (striking for self-improvement etc) may have beneficial social consequences, although no personal reason is present in them – I mean the worker could be acting for purely selfish (though legitimate) reasons. His actions are not part of a philosophy or understanding. But men do explain their existence and the explanation of our age is communism. That philosophy exists as a fact and actions can now be derived from it. When actions of this sort are performed they are characterized by reason – not necessarily by kindness, charity etc. Abstract virtues have no real moral worth until they are seen in social and class contexts. They should be seen as enabling possibilities: an elastic band can bind papers together in a useful way or it can sting you.

[. . .]

Notes on Art 16 March 1979

There is no fundamental difference between the making of the blade and the decorating of the handle of the dagger of a neolithic hunter or farmer. Both are to establish a relationship with the world. The blade-making is (if one could isolate it in practice) a mechanical activity: it is a thing behaving like a thing in relation to other things. It is a thing which changes other things. But it does this through human agency. Why should the hunter or farmer decorate the blade? It seems (from the point of view of things) a waste of time and labour. It establishes a special relationship between men and things: men decorate things. Men decorate the world. This establishes a special relation. It makes the world familiar to him – in that he doesnt relate to it mechanically like another thing, but that it connects his mind with the world. You could say that the dagger blade teaches the farmer to carve the handle. Men order and interpret their experience. Once the hands are used the mind demands to be used. Once the hands are used the mind thinks. Why doesnt the mind think: it would be a waste of time to decorate the handle? Men appropriate images of the world. As men have to make decisions, sustain efforts and refine ideas – so as to enable them to live and to live better – they are involved in the problems of will. It seems we have to decide, whether or not this is an illusion. To strengthen his powers man, consequently, expresses himself as a creator. All human activity can be seen as a form of creation. Man creates.

Pre-human animals are not creators in this sense because they do not have the experience (illusory or otherwise) of free will. Pre-human animals are controlled by their instincts in all significant matters. Men create significant matters (by the process of their lives) to which there are no instinctual guides. Much of the activity of a dog seems random: but this applies only to activity between significant events. Significant events, for a dog, are limited in type: its relationships are stereotyped. The dog doesnt create them even when they change: it fits into them.

Art is the expression of the relationship men have with the world. It is the tools of consciousness. Art demonstrates men as part of the world, creating creatures. Art is an expression of the difference between human and pre-human animals, it expresses the different sort of relationship that men have to one another and to the world. The body expresses the physical relationship. The mind expresses its relationship through art. How does art differ from abstract ideas? For example, the mind needs ideas to organize society in certain ways. These ideas result in administration, they are not expressed in art. There can be administrative skills. Again, these ideas and skills can be mechanical. Art is really the expression of the non-mechanical nature of human beings, of the non-mechanical part of their nature. This doesnt mean that art is concerned with the non-material. All human activity is a form of materialism. Only when materialism is seen as depleted does this become deadly. The basis of the relationships between human beings are material – they are economic, industrial, agricultural, and therefore social and political – but the relationships between people are not mechanical in the same way: we have emotions, temptations, depressions, exhilaration, loves, devotions, hates. We can express hate through the use of a dagger or through a painting. We are wrong if we make a decisive distinction between formal art and the art of living, of buying bread, or boarding a bus, of behaving in a traffic jam. If we cut art away from human activity in this way we're behaving as stupidly as if we invented and used a machine that made nothing. But as mental phenomena are not subject to many of the immediate tests that physical phenomena are, the mental non-machine can pass unnoticed. Of course if all human activity were subject to immediate physical tests (to test by the mechanical ways of nature) then the scope of human activity would be very limited: we would be animals and we would have to depend on instincts. We have art because human beings are a different sort of thing from other things.

Art has to do with the part of human beings which is non-thing. This non-thingness is a more complex, more highly advanced, more efficient, way of dealing with our relation to things. We cease to be things in order to enhance our relationship with things. Art is not a reality existing for itself. It is materialist in that it concerns our relationship with things, which is ultimately the only relationship we can have. It is not an alternative to this relationship. During this process of relationship other people can cease to be things and become persons like ourselves. The egoism of things is then superseded.

Art does not follow its own inherent laws. The development of art comes through its relationship with the human's world of things: that is through the economic, industrial, agricultural relationships men build between themselves and the world. As men do this in union, and not as isolated beings, social and political relationships are also involved. These relationships are established on the non-thingness part of human beings. Art functions in this area. Art has therefore to do with the social and political relationships between men. There is a logic and disciplined development in these relationships. Art has a corresponding structure. Art is not a freewheeling imagination or fantasy – it is logical and rational.

Human consciousness must have some structure, some ordering of memory and acquired knowledge and experience. This is necessary just as a physical structure must have a shape and an establishing functioning – metabolism, respiration etc.

Art is a form of knowledge of the world. Men are in a city or a field. Consciousness is in men. Consciousness takes the world into the individual. We are conscious of the world in which we are. But just as we cannot invent new physical laws – cancel the law of gravity, for example – so we cannot arbitrarily alter that relationship, cannot change the world by a self-sufficient act of will. Nevertheless human beings may, notoriously, be deluded about the world. Human history may be seen as a proceeding delusion, in that what men often thought to be fact (in relations and politics etc) may not be so. But it was a fact, and therefore not a delusion, in this sense: that it enabled the community to operate, that it was a way in which society-individual-environment could relate in a mutually sustaining relationship. It was not necessary to know the world is round in order to walk on it, it is sufficient if it at least appears to be flat and stable. To travel in space it is necessary to know that the world is round. We think we have relationships because human beings have certain innate attitudes – devotion, loyalty, resistance, pride etc – and relationships are the only way in which these innate attitudes can be expressed. Therefore, we relate in such and such a way because that is what human beings are as individuals. Not true. We develop attitudes to the relationships in which we find ourselves. Our attitudes may lead us to want to change, and be able to change, these relationships. Human creativity is not fixed either by human nature or by the nature of the world. Human creativity concerns the changing and betterment of that relationship between individual–society–environment. Although the environment limits what is possible to human development it does not create it – since it could maintain human beings (as it does other animals) in a static state. But as the relationship between human beings and their environment is so thoroughly dialectical there is hardly any sense in talking this way. To all intents and purposes, as human beings become conscious they make the world conscious – just as tools take life from the hands of their users.

Art is concerned with, arises from, the nexus of the individual and the community. Finally, the individual does not have a purpose that differs from the community's. This is not the case, though, in class society – because in such a society the relationship between things is introduced (or maintained) between people. Art can be used in that relationship. It appears to be a means of stating the thing-ness of relationships between people in classes. This is the case when the means of art are owned by the ruling class. Historically this has been the case. Just as the politics of Pharaonic Egypt, Athenian Greece, the Renaissance, were imperfect when compared with the politics of socialism – they belonged to a more primitive state of the relationship between individuals–society–things – so the art of the past must be considered inferior. Yet this seems to contradict general belief and experience – including Marx and many marxists – that the art of the past is not merely appreciable by us but is often superior to our own art. Here we come to an apparent paradox about art: it seems to stand outside historical development, outside the progressing relationship between individual–society–things, outside the development of politics. If this were so art would not be connected with the most important parts of human experience – it would be either trivial or false. Of course we can make moral judgements about past actions.

We can say that one ancient king was good and another evil, or that one Roman emperor was better than another. We feel that these judgements make sense, although from the standpoint of socialism royalism and imperialism must be judged bad. But we can say, given certain circumstances then act A is better than act B – it is kinder, more generous, more noble – even though it will not abolish imperialism or royalism or any other elitism. Really we are making a moral judgement about a changing situation as if it were a static situation. Only in socialism could these judgements be whole – that the good party member did a good act, or that the good citizen of a socialism did a good act (acted well). Other things being equal it is better to be kind than unkind. But the morality of actions can only finally be judged on rational grounds, and this implies a rational understanding of the human state and of the nature and potential of human beings and the world we're in. We could say of the good emperor, his motive was good and those he helped benefited from his help – although as a political force imperialism was cruel and destructive and merely progressive in its era. Within that situation we can see that an emperor could achieve moral goodness. Whether any of them did is a pragmatic matter: in theory they could.

Art is a record. It shows the skills and attitudes and perceptions of the artist. The skills, attitudes and perceptions concern the artist's world and his relationship to that world.

I have now defined the area in which art functions. I have next to say what it is, what is permanent in it and why it's changing and developing. Men make themselves in a way that a pre-human animal doesnt make itself. Pre-human animals merely reproduce themselves – they evolve only very slowly. But men create their own consciousness just as they increasingly develop and extend their relationship to things. Consciousness is the settled relationship between experience, memory, knowledge – and all the impulses that go together in a human being, the aspirations, indignation, happiness and so forth. Human beings are sensate beings in a world of things which they appropriate. They are sensate and conscious and they must organize their experience into patterns. Human beings develop and change – as history progresses – but at any one time human beings must know what it is to be a human being in that time: otherwise they couldnt function in that time. Their various capacities and responses, and their knowledge, experience and skill, need to be organized into a working whole: I must know what continent I'm in, what country, what county, what city, what suburb, what street, what house. I must know how to relate to friends and strangers. I must be able to judge where I am in order that I can function. I need to do this just as much as my body and mind need to draw oxygen from an atmosphere which is largely lethally poisonous to my organism. Consciousness is of self, society and things – and of the relationship between these things. It is the relationship which supports me.

I now come to an important part about art. Art is dynamic and not static. It is an appetite and a fulfilment – as eating, playing games, relaxing, working, solving problems are. But I think it is a dynamism of a very special sort. The relationship between the individual and his society must be in part a moral one. If one is in a group one is immediately involved in questions of the rights of that group. If this werent so we would all be totally egoistic. The relationship between people has a moral slant. This moral slant exists within the political, economic, social framework at any one time. There are conventions for deciding who goes through doorways first. There are laws about property and inheritance. There couldnt be any society between people without some laws, some consent between them, or some response to force. We know that in fact the laws at any one time are usually unjust. The laws serve particular class interests. In capitalism, for example, it facilitates the exploitation of the worker: law and order is there not merely to protect, say, an innocent child – but to see that the worker can go to his factory in safety and the owner can go to his bank in safety. In a class society there cannot be one law for all – this is logically impossible if we say that the purpose of law is to ensure justice. It is impossible because the different classes will benefit in different ways from the same law – and therefore it is in practice not one law but many. It is only one law in the statute book. The moment it operates in the street, shop or factory it becomes many laws. Law in a class society is therefore a source of injustice – in spite of the good Caesar, of course. It seems to me that art is not concerned with law of this sort, but is concerned with justice of a more moral sort. This seems to lead to an immediate contradiction. Most art has been commissioned by the owning class – and, like most others things, has been owned by them. How then could art be concerned with the moral? And so many of the elements of art – colour, wit, shape, design – do not seem specifically to do with moral questions. The answer to the second point is easy, art is not to do with these things but to do with the organization of them. We can get pleasure from watching a sunset. The pleasure we get from looking at a painting of a sunset is different – though in practice we may see the real sunset partly through eyes conditioned by paintings. Art seems to record the truth and it can do this in a world of lies. Abstract art may record the truth as well as art that reproduces more nearly the normal appearance of things or people. In art we state our experience of the world in a form which states that it is our experience. We would have to say that art sometimes records the truth in spite of itself. Thus, religious pictures do not have a meaning only for religious people. The truth has been placed in a specific or special, localized form – just as Caesar did good – and this form can be a corruption: nevertheless, the truth is displayed. I seem to be saying either a) the truth in art doesnt always meet the eye (the owner class cannot really see the art it owns) or b) that the truth is seen but not acted on. In either case it seems to limit the value of truth. But this needn't be so. Paintings may have been acquired for the wrong reason. Nevertheless, they may have a real value. What the owners have frequently valued them for is not the real value that they display. Certainly most art has been commissioned and used as decoration or for prestige by the artistically imperceptive. Yet at other times people have clearly got much out of art. This would seem to be the case with the theatre and the Greeks. When art is created in time of social change, conflict or crisis – then it speaks directly to most people because most people are involved in that crisis – obviously they are, if its a major crisis of political, economic and social relationships. Art is the desire to express rational comprehension – which is why, in a society such as ours, its often created by mad men. But it need not be. Art, therefore shows not merely what it tells – but also the effort, the desire, the discipline to tell it. Art always seeks to tell the truth. Now a witness may lie – but he may only be mistaken. So, the Greeks believed in nymphs and godlets – and when they stopped believing in these things they could still use them as helpful metaphors. Plato wanted a static society and therefore he banned the arts from it.

Science has always had certain disciplines of truth, certain standards of evidence, certain axioms of comprehension. The workings of these disciplines appear in the results produced by science. Art has the same disciplines, but it shows these things in the work of art itself – the seeking to create a work of art is revealed in the work of art, is part of the image, or the story. This doesnt mean that the artist can as it were ignore the facts so long as his blind seeking is honest. He has to see what there is to see, he has to live very much in the cold light of day. Just as a scientist must know previous science in order to do science. Art that ignores this particular discipline becomes sentimental, gimmicky or fey.

It is not good art. Art is good when it demonstrates knowledge and seeks further knowledge. The knowledge is of a particular sort since it is finally this: what it is to be a human being in the world at any particular time. This includes a knowledge, which can be rationally accepted – that is, engage all one's faculties and apprehension – of how we got to a point in history, knowledge of what is happening then – that is, a rational awareness of so much of the political, economic and social realities it is historically possible to have – and at the same time a sane consciousness of meaning and purpose in existence. If this isnt there, why bother to write or paint. If it is there, and yet you seem to say that life is meaningless and absurd, then the work of art will display this duplicity and will be sentimental or cheap. Of course, it could be said in the past that an artist might display this: the world is a place of misery and despair but I say that it should not be so, I shout in the dark, I protest against this injustice – even if it comes from god. To take this for artistic display, now, would be sentimental – since rational knowledge makes it clear that injustice is created by men and not by god. Therefore, to display truth the artist must make this clear. Art isnt the arbitrary play of imagination. Its agreed that the phantasies of mad people do have a clinical meaning. That there are understandable causes for the frenzies that have historically swept societies. So human behaviour is susceptible to rational apprehension. Art is based on the same rational cogency. To work, the imagination must know not the head its in – the name of the artist that signs its products – but the economic-political-social relationships its in. What one discerns in a work of art is a rational relationship to the world – an understanding of what is, and also a critical relationship to it – of what should be. In this sense Christianity was once a progressive force – with repressive attributes, certainly – and its art revolutionary; though it must be said that religious art is always implicitly anti-religion. This seems a paradox, but it is clearly so. A judging god over Caesar is better, from most points of view, than a Caesar who arbitrarily behaves as god, who calls himself god. To remove God out of the world at least takes some power from his hands; this power is then appropriated by the bishops. The timeless record of art through this states the potential humaneness of human beings in a time when they are treated as things, when the relationships between them are based on thingness. We can see what art can do and also what it cant. It cant change the world – but it is part of the process of changing the world. Human beings need an image of what it is to be human – art partly creates this, and its a creation that is free from the controls of education – education being another source of the knowledge of what it is to be a human being. Much education is concerned with skill, the ability to use the thingness of the world; but education is partly to do with the relationships between people. Who could paint a Jew: Rembrandt or Julius Streicher? The creation of and participation in the created images of what it is to be human – this involves a lot of human time and effort. The stories told at a canteen table at lunch time are as much art as the plays at the national theatre. More so very often – because they relate more rationally to reality. Art is most different in that it takes a common daily activity and places it in unusual surroundings – so that it may be observed more closely. But even if you could carry on a conversation in a breadshop you still might not understand a main-stage play. The play isnt dealing with anything different. The conversation in the breadshop will involve economic and political and financial and other relationships. So will the play. But it can make these relationships clearer – bring out their contradictions, just because the artist can concentrate more time and effort on them. The artist is a specialist in the ordinary – which he shows to be truly extraordinary. All artists draw on and from the street. Economics and politics are often bolstered up with a lot of metaphysics – and society has often been held together by the glue of metaphysics. Art has also often been put into the framework of metaphysics – but it has always denied or superseded this framework. The discipline of creation pushes away the limitations formerly imposed on the work created. The rigorousness of that discipline, the conscious involvement within the work created of as many of the determining factors from the real world (that is, economics-politics-social organization etc) as possible – these things are displayed in the work of art and increase its value. That's why a classical statue from fifth century Athens is superior art to a fascist imitation of it in Nazi Germany – although the German artist was theoretically in the position of knowing more. The artist mustnt merely know the truth, he must love it, seek it, be energized by it: its this that connects art with justice.

We must not only produce socialist art for the barricade, the banner and the placard – but also for the kitchen table, the bedroom, the school room, the park. When, however, say in drama, the play is dealing with human nature and therefore with the political economic and social relations between men – then these relationships must become the subject of drama. This isnt propaganda but high art. Propaganda will not be sufficient to create socialist consciousness and judgement and socialist ability to assess and act. We have to show socialism active in all spheres of life.

What is Art? 16 March 1979

1. What is art? A vital expression. To understand what art is you must understand what human nature is.

2. The world of things. The world of people. The world of evolution, development. World as change. Changing structures of animals. Nature of human change – evolution in history. This creates human consciousness, which itself develops.

3. Structure of change of human consciousness. Not arbitrary. Develops in parallel with development of human activity and organization.

4. Nature of human consciousness. Conscious of self and otherness. Is not merely an observation but the creation of relationship. Note also human emotions, drives etc.

5. A consciousness appropriate to each historical era. A corresponding art.

6. Human consciousness/human social character – enables the social/political/economic structure of any era to function – and also to develop as the basic relationship alters. Human consciousness is comprehensive – not a set of mechanical formulae that can be called up in situation X. But a self-extending judgement. Art related to buying bread or travelling in a bus.

7. Problems connected with art. Class owned. But this is 'high' art. Art is not universal – art objects seen differently from a class viewpoint, just as other relationships and things are. Beauty has a use, a social use.

8. Art is nevertheless not subjective. It is objective but often seen subjectively. When objectivity and subjectivity are one you would have the furthest development of art we can at the moment imagine: pure socialist art. Our stage is transitional – it is the development of socialism.

9. Art has always contained an imperative. Consider Greek art: it deals with the elements of the basic relationship which founds consciousness: politics/economics/social/individual. Relates art to these questions. Compare Greek art with Nazi copies of it. If art is 'knowledge' the Nazi copy should be superior to the Greek original. Not the case. The imperative of art: like science, a discipline to tell the truth – it will tell the truth as it is then possible to know it, therefore it is rational. Imagination is an exact science. Science, however, doesnt record its discipline, its standards, as part of its object – the standards are merely those by which it achieves its object. Art incorporates its method, so that the demonstration of truth in art is not merely what is discovered but also the act of

discovering it and the means by which it is discovered. Art demonstrates the inherent rationality of human beings – in the sense that in operating the world we make a distinction between mad and sane behaviour. If human sanity were not possible then art would not be possible. (Paradox of madmen making art.) This is because the world is always more irrational than the art it creates – and will be so till there is a socialist society. You cant say of any one piece of art that it is necessary for human development. But art activity – and rational art with its association with justice – is. We couldnt develop consciousness without language. If you have language you need art to go with it. It doesnt replace the material relationships, but its one of the modes or terms in which that relationship must be worked out.

10. 'Set' art is merely a specialized, heightened form, of an everyday activity – not something different in nature but in degree. The ruling class has always imaged and recorded its sensibility in order to know itself. All the imagery is also the method of relationship. Relationships dont copy the 'high art' image – but it (the ruling class) develops the diurnal image in a higher form. As most free Greek citizens took part in public discussion of Greek affairs its art was concerned with wide political-social issues. When the ecclesiastical relationship between individual and state was destroyed in the Reformation, and people's religion was changed, so art again widened its scope. In socialism we see the affairs of the man in the street broadening from buying bread and boarding buses into a wide concern with political and social relations. Art will reflect this. But there is a continuity between buying bread as a socialist and fighting or voting as a socialist. Politics is not an external manipulation of life – once you have power – but the way you live. It is always that anyway, even when you dont have power. But when you have power or are working to take power – then politics is willed consciousness, not the consciousness of endurance. So that to buy bread properly you must understand the political relationships of power. Obviously not in the sense of reading white papers or government reports on how to buy bread. Human beings become autonomous when they can exercise judgement rationally. So art shows people in various situations and crises so that generalized forms of behaviour can be seen – and these become experience for the spectator. Clearly the traditional – or rather bourgeois – boundaries between art and spectator have to go – but there'll always be artists who are specialists, just as there are specialist sportsmen.

11. Aesthetics. Wide scope of socialist art. Art and propaganda. In intensifying the political content of art the artist is only responding to material reality, because we live in an era of political crisis.

12. The art of the greeks, renaissance etc – were transitional to socialism. Socialism is now a rational idea – wasnt in earlier art-eras. The discipline of art – the imperative of art (formula for this: . . . .) – showed the rational human situation at earlier periods. It uses the same means of discernment now: just as the standards of truth in science remain constant, though they become more sophisticated: but one truth is based on another. In science a thing cannot both be and not be. Socialist art would record socialist man and socialist consciousness. In a socialist society there would be no class enemies – therefore no struggle against them, therefore all men would then be brothers. But we cannot reflect that utopian consciousness, its not for us to say what it would be or what its art would be: we're transitional, we have to create socialism. At what stage in the transition are we? If in actual revolution then artists would become propagandists – to serve the immediate needs of the seizing of power. Job now different. Its a matter of tactics to say what front you fight on and what methods you use. Yet art is a strict discipline. Art doesnt however dictate the form in which it shall be presented. Artist can choose – if his skill is adequate for it – to write plays for factory gates or for main stages: in which way will you infiltrate your ideas more into society and what are your particular skills best suited to? The answer to the question at the front of this paragraph: the artist will choose those subjects which best demonstrate the nature of the social-political-economic relationship which creates consciousness. He will not write about gods, myths or uncontrollable forces of irrationalism. Art does this – in the theatre of the absurd and the west end, and the results are dangerous – and corrupting when they're taught in universities. But he can still show a wide spectrum of human concern – since politics will enter into all human relationships. He will want to concentrate on those points in the web where power is knotted so that everything holds together – so he might write about strikes, riots, revolts, the relationship between labour and beauty, work and ruling authority – all subjects I've dealt with. His objective will be to hasten the revolution – but there are many ways in which this is done. An army needs many sorts of troops – spies, guerrillas, cooks etc.

13. The art of authority: to create a self-pleasing image and to impose an image on others. But there has always been a people's art – perhaps

till industrial revolution. The ruling class saw art as a record: the ruled class saw it as an enigma, since there was a discrepancy between art and reality or they didn't see the same thing.

Art Questions Rothbury 19 March 1979

Art helped to create the human image – which human beings need in order to incorporate morality into their daily life. Yet most people have no direct acquaintance with art – not anymore. If the images are created they are then diffused through society. What is the relationship between the breadshop and the main stage. The behaviour in the breadshop: we can put on certain performances, certain expressions, gestures, use certain phrases. So we <u>conduct</u> ourselves. When some cant do this – when they are obsessed or behave in an over preoccupied way – we say 'they're not themselves'. So when they are themselves they are their socially competent self; its accepted that they have more intimate or personal behaviour. The relationships in the breadshop are kept at a certain distance. (We dont expect every loaf in the breadshop to have a secret file or hacksaw in it.) The formal patterning of behaviour has been learned through education and practise: it has been tested out. We behave in the breadshop in ways that we're told work and which we have tested. Untested behaviour is the behaviour of children or idiots. The behaviour involves the staff of life (bread) but its limited in its references: prices are involved rather than direct questions of moral values.

The main stage: you could show manners (breadshop behaviour) and compare it with morals. That is, argue about values in the conversation about prices. Examine normal unexamined conduct. This means that the behaviour of the breadshop is unexamined – in what way then is it art? Its art because it enables people to live socially – but it needs to be subjected to a further process of analysis and inspection and development. The world of appearance is also a world of art. Second use of main stage: more directly analytic and polemic, in that you bypass (more or less) the world of manners and try to deal directly with the world of reality – you dont show just the breadshop transactions, but the growing of wheat, the baking of bread, the maintenance of society which is necessary if wheat is to be grown and bread baked, and whether these things are done justly. But to do this you must reproduce the recorded reality of the world – that is, manners. In order to survive in the day to day world you must learn the art of manners (I mean this very broadly, the art of social relationships). This involves not merely forms of politeness but also the ability to display one's deeper emotions and one's convictions when this is appropriate or seems desirable to the actor. So 'manners' is the world not merely of formal behaviour but it also licenses some exhibition of 'private' behaviour – it is not merely a place of convention but a place in which the truth can be told when this is appropriate. So the whole person is engaged in the world of manners, one takes one's soul to the breadshop. To buy bread the whole human being must be involved – must be potentially there, this is because the breadshop may become a parliament or a slaughterhouse (if a bomb is thrown) or a place of mourning – if the baker's child has just died etc. Manners, conventions, guarantee that one is not merely a creature of convention and manners but that one is a human being: or rather, manners ought to guarantee that, ought to assure others that one is a civilized, moral being. (Again, I mean manners in the broad sense of appropriate and effective behaviour.) The main stage takes the forms of manners and conventions and subjects them to deeper search and analysis and test. So in order to buy bread one needs politics, philosophy, aesthetics. Bread becoming the substance of the eucharist is an earlier version of this idea, perhaps. Its necessary, to civilized beings, that all the moral and political subjects of art are implicit in the behaviour of the breadshop – that the breadshop behaviour is a way of understanding the underlying political and moral experience. In our present society this isnt so. The forms are merely formal – even when they're observed. They dont guarantee a civilized consciousness. So, some formal behaviour is necessary for any social living. But for that behaviour to guarantee the continuance of society it must be analysed completely. You can have formal behaviour in a concentration camp, in the foreign office of an imperial power. Yet for higher morality to work it must be reducible to the conventions of the breadshop – be judged by the same awareness and sensitivity that is used in the breadshop – not by some supernatural or supernormal standard or sensitivity. Only what works in the breadshop can work in utopia. The key to art is in the breadshop. That is how people live from day to day – the performance is social and is required of them if they're to live from day to day. But from year to year – a deeper political responsibility is necessary. So the stage elevates or moves the breadshop to the public theatre. It then examines wider social relationships.

[. . .]

The Jew in his cell
Looks at the window

It was from there
One morning
The gun protruded

We have to work out knowledge and experience in terms of our sensory nature: in doing this we create a character, ourselves.

[. . .]

On Dramatic Method Little House 29 July 1979

The German's [Brecht's] theory says that we must discard as irrelevant everything that does not immediately demonstrate the analysis. But there is no schema of history that can be got at in that direct way. The analysis must be clear – but its embodiment must also be clear, because it must go through people's lives to the reality. It is the difference between a plan and a building, or a diagram and a picture. The plan must be shown erected into a building, otherwise the truth it conveys is incomplete: this is because the method in which the building is built is important. The plan without the method is dead. The method involves people living, working, and co-operating together. They learn and organize in certain ways, and because of this they become certain sorts of people. What they do is what they are. You cannot show what they are unless you show what they do. The plan must be given those dimensions which are specifically human, which have to do with feeling, sensibility, taste, discrimination, judgement and so forth. Unless you show people becoming people you cannot show reality: you cannot show it unless you show people becoming builders. The general draws up the battle plan: the soldiers fight it in the trenches and in aeroplanes. The plan must go through the human mould. It must be translated into a different dimension: the ontology becomes human, mundane, intimate, heroic, trivial and so forth. Human beings are always related to those two things: the trivial, the bread on the table, and the philosophical and ontological, the state of their city and their era. The two compacted together make up the human character and 'read off' as in a computer the sum of the facts.

[. . .]

The writer dramatizes action. Therefore he does not dramatize the analysis. He dramatizes the problem. The problem arises from the different worlds. He dramatizes the abrasure between the various worlds. In this matter, to show what is the same is to show why it is. Why it is is because of what human beings are: the consciousness, sensibility, responsibility towards each other etc (of the working class). This is the force of history. Machines change men, but men make the machines, and the men who make them are full characters searching for change. If you try to dramatize the analysis directly you cannot say 'why' (give history a force and not merely make it an embodied-logic as if logic could will itself). The motive of history is the consciousness of its people: history is their (often) unconscious. It becomes conscious when their motive is to understand it and act on their understanding. This seems to conflict with what I said in <u>The Bundle</u> introduction about dramatizing the analysis. But it doesnt contradict it. Really I am now talking about the way the analysis should be dramatized.

The audience's dramatic experience: if the audience remain objective in a way similar to the objectivity they might have when they read a report they are using the stage and the actors as a substitute for a book or paper. It is all right to do this. But there is a different theatrical experience. We see the actors as commenting on – all the while – what they are doing. I dont mean, now, primarily their intentional comment: I am playing a bad character. They are using the sub-language of gesture, expression and tone. These sub-languages make up a form of human contact and comment. They are the concretizations of what it means to make and understand a value judgement. Without this sub-language human beings could not possess values. This is because a value is not a mere intellectual thing expressed verbally – and has no possibility of being that. Judgements are about people: what the sub-language expresses is that people are about value. The sub-language is a (more direct than speech) contact with the innate person – not merely as an individual but as a member of the species and of society. The sub-language is often unconsciously (more or less) expressed and as equally unconsciously (likewise, can be more or less) received. We're dealing with the difference between words and the tone, force, rhythm in which they're expressed; with posture, with expression; with movement of the whole body or parts of it and of groups of bodies and so forth. The analysis is the over-language. It is analytically clear. But the enactment of it involves the use of over-language and sub-language. There is, or should be, no such thing as a sub-text: a secret behind the appearance which the actor makes accessible to those subtle enough to perceive it. There is, however, a sub-language, and it is this which energizes, vivifies, evaluates the text. The sub-language is like a light shining through from behind a stained glass window. (The idea of a sub-text is that of a sheet of glass through which you can peer into what had been concealed depths. It is a false sensibility.) The analysis is the stained glass. It is also the story. It is also the first area of the actor's performance. The sub-language is important because it is the language by which people in daily life size-up and reassure and assess each other. It is partly the way they judge formal assurances and statements. (Textures and fashions of clothes are also part of the sub-language, just as are blushes and palings.) As the actor is consciously using and commenting on the analysis the sub-language can be called a comment on a comment. It does not wholly verify the analysis, which must be intellectually and factually true. It is closer to the nature of value. I will try to make it clear with an example: the analysis says 'and after this we will all be happy'. The sub-language shows what it is to desire happiness, or the actress might show us what happiness is, by anticipating it with her smile. She could smile in conditions which would normally produce despair. The actor cannot choose not to present the audience with a sub-language when he is on-stage. He has his own sub-language (which is the personality he brings from the street). Can he shape this into a sub-language for his character-role? Can the actor divide his own sub-language? I think so: the sub-language is not a mystical, essential self – so that if he entered into his own sub-language he would be possessed: i.e., becomes his words and gestures etc. It is a two-way mirror. The actor who unconsciously always takes a small step back before moving forwards has a sub-unit which shows us something of the actor's own cautious or hesitant or even timid nature. But he may be more conscious of the way he smiles or gestures to us to gain our acknowledgement and assurance. The sub-language is not the self but part of the relationships with the world – but it is often more direct than over-language because it enables us to see further into a person. Note that just as the actor may be unaware of the step backwards we may register it but only unconsciously instead of (as would be quite possible) consciously. If you are playing Iago, then Iago's analysis of himself is clearly inadequate. Nor is he Verdi's pure evil. The sub-language of the actor would enable us to see more directly into Iago and so relate him to an analysis. Thus we might say that Othello represents a black bourgeois and that Iago is a primitive type of working-class attitude to the upper classes. We might then act Iago's quick wittedness, persistence, contrivance – and even the patience with which he lets the pot boil between stirring. Instead of using a sub-language of evil we use a creative, vital, joyful sub-language. Othello need not be shown as a white-nigger or Uncle Tom. He is a victim of Venice more than of Iago. (Note William Shakespeare's brilliant use of vowels: O in Othello, the twisted painful i-a-o of Iago. Both names have three syllables. Iago backwards begins with an o: Ogai. Othello has the pure open vowel at both ends: Othello – Oletho. This is to drag up much of the sub-language into the over-language.)

Certainly the author prepares the sub-language in the text and so it might appear that there is a sub-text. But there is no sub-text without language, no sub-text that can be played as if it were the analysis. The analysis is on the surface of the text.

The exact use to be made of sub-language can be discussed later. In one sense the actor always retains his own sub-language (though he can, as we've seen, exploit his capacity for sub-speaking to illustrate or concretize his character-role) and it is his personality – his reason for being on-stage, his actor's pre-stance. But I have discussed sub-language because I want to make it clear that a play or performance can never be reduced to an objective demonstration of an objective analysis: the performance always involves a sub-language statement of why it is being performed. There is the presence of human value on the stage, not merely human logic (and of course the two cant be parted: an illogical analysis will produce false acting. The audience may be content with the false analysis and the false acting, but their experience will not be profound, will not be art.) The audience's reaction to a play will be complex and on over- and sub-levels. We should use that complexity and not assume that it is a confusion. Its the use of this complexity which makes sensitivity and subtlety and wit possible. These qualities are processes of clarification and evaluation. They become possible when art is rational, that is when (at any time in history) intellect is used to describe and understand the situation of men in the world and not obscure it in ruling-class mysticism. Any ascending class, in order to achieve power, must be rational (in the optimum degree appropriate to the historical moment). It can therefore unite sub-language and over-language, analysis and the affirmation of value, thus uniting the individual and society. At those moments the good of society and the good of the individual are one: society improves the lot of the individual and vice-versa. After this the ruling class begins to falsify reality (mythologize) in order to justify the static role it assumes for its leadership.

So the analysis is abstract until it is made art and then becomes not merely an expression of logical truth but of human truth. (Note that history is logical in its development but that there is a history only because human beings have and create value). Now I return to the argument of 'the worlds'.

Both worlds are real forces. Otherwise there would be no conflict. The opponent world is hollow only in that it is empty of value. It cannot, furthermore, maintain itself except by intellectually debasing the other world. This other world resists (for various reasons) this debasement. The other world claims its own functional freedom, its own autonomy. Conflict ensues. Both worlds are the products of the same forces although each world revolves, if you like, in a different direction. It is necessary for the working world to understand the opponent world, which is for the moment the ruling world. It is on this level that 'we're all human' – not that we're all entitled to forgiveness but that we are the products of historical forces and all their processors. You cannot schematize one human being without at the same time schematizing all human beings. You cannot know yourself until you know others, just as you cannot know yourself till you know your class. The problem must be seen entirely from the point of view of the working class, which is the source of value. But its view can be accurate, it has no need of distortion – indeed all distortion is a mythologizing. In order to retain power the ruling class must distort and mythologize. The working class has no need to do this: indeed, its 'destiny' of communism is lived truth. It cannot show, always, the ruling class in a cynical form for this reason: the ruling class is itself not cynical, it believes in the truthfulness of its own motives. It does not see itself as cynical and therefore doesn't act cynically. Its relation to analysed truth is of course not merely ironical but decadent. We have to show the diseases of the ruling class, and this cannot be done by reducing the class to a caricature. This disease is present in the reality we portray. We have to accommodate it in our portrayal. The project of the working class world is to comprehend the total of the worlds. This is because really the working class world encapsulates the opponent world, although it does not share value with it. It's the working class' possession of value that demarks the boundaries between the two worlds.

[. . .]

Notes for a Short Essay 'Acting a Life' 26 November 1979
Commonly said that one should act a 'character'. The character shows what he has in him. In a crisis he shows certain moral strengths or weaknesses. It is true that the actor must show a character in this way, in the epic theatre as in other forms of theatre. But a character doesnt give

us knowledge of a man. Goodness, kindness, restraint, magnanimity, perseverance – these are not abstract human qualities which 'include their own truth' or 'tell the truth about themselves'. A man who exploits others in a social system which condemns his employees to malnutrition and ignorance may nevertheless donate kindly to charity. A Nazi general may be steadfast and persevering. To have knowledge of a character we have to put the character in its historical situation. (Social situation.) The individual is a member of society. His characteristics arent judged as one would judge water spouting from a stream – having its own natural purity or impurity. We have to consider the nature of the act not its motive. We have to see how it interacts with the others in society. There are no psychological solutions to dramatic problems. To discover the characters' psychology we have to study the society of which it is part.

So we show the characters interactions with the others rather than its (psychologically motivated) actions. The actor needs a 'content' – something which he uses in the dramatic interaction. Its usually thought that this content is a self-sufficient character. But we should ask 'to what use does the actor put his role?' The actor must study the relationships he has with the others in the play. From this – the collection of relationships – he will be able to discover his character, the character he is playing. He will find himself in the situations. These situations are not arbitrary. They are historically defined. Its because of this that objective judgements may be made about the character. The character will be seen as a member of society in a moment of history. We will not then be tempted to judge the character by its incidental characteristics – but by the truth of its historical situation. Our judgement may then be moral and normative and not merely a matter of taste or appeal. If the play is not written with much historical understanding, then the actor has to supply this understanding – even if it seems to go against the tendency of the play.

An epic play will be written in a certain way. By epic we dont mean the specific story of any one play. Epic refers to the history of men. We are dealing with men as they make themselves under historical pressures. The play isnt so much an epic as part of the epic. In a sense even modern dramas have to be historical dramas, because they have to place men in their history if they are to be art. The epic play takes nothing at face value. It tries to show the character from various sides, in different lights, from various angles. This makes it dialectical. In drama dialectical means seeing the character and event from different angles so that judgement may be discriminating. The epic writer will try to show all relevant aspects of a character. The character will not know its own psychology. Its behaviour will be constantly uncharacteristic. The actor must know more about the character than the character knows about itself. The situations will show historical truth. They will contain political understanding. Human history is to be morally judged in terms of politics. The situations will be intended to reveal historical truth. In relation to politics we must ask not what a character is but what it believes, what it thinks, what the ideas in its head are. At the root of the character is the character's opinion about history and the world: that is, we have to play the character's political consciousness. We do not have to think in terms of metaphysical good and evil, heroes and villains. We have to ask what their relation to the political situation is. Only then can they be judged and only then can we see how to play them. The 'psychology' of the characters is their 'political meaning'. Note that this doesnt in any way mean reducing the characters to schemas or ciphers. They will be rounded and full, complete and complex. The truth, the judgement, will be exhibited in many facets. The audience will encounter many things they meet in the street, shop, factory, office, playing field, arts centre. Truth will not be an abstract statement but a texture. Once we grasp the truth of a character – once we establish our political judgement of the character – we can demonstrate that truth in many ways. We must delight our audience with that demonstration. The audience cannot be persuaded of very much unless its discrimination is involved. Slogans are valuable – but we must show them embodied and enacted. We give the character, instead of a metaphysical or abstract characterization, a full politico-historical character. Then subtlety and nuance are not wraiths or dreams, they are reflections from concrete certainties. Sensibility is a reflection from the concrete. Sensibility can never be a substitute for the concrete. There is no acceptable self-sustaining sensibility. The meaning of the character is its historical-political meaning. The character's biography begins long before he is born ... history has no privileged spectators.

On Philosophy

What is the use of a philosophy? A philosophy is not necessarily what one thinks but something that tells you what you think. This is surprising. But a person who has a philosophy thinks about things in a way which he would normally hardly ever think and arranges them in a coherent pattern. This means that X is not a subject of like or dislike but its a relation to Z and Y. I might like the taste of strawberry jam but if I know that it is a poison the taste will change: I will prefer nonpoisonous cherries. Its true that people often do like things that are bad for them – but they like the 'good' aspects of those things. For example an alcoholic will like the way alcohol simplifies his (immediate) problems even though he knows that alcohol harms him. Often one's likes and dislikes are influenced by one's philosophy. One's opinion concerning X changes because of what one knows about Y and Z. In other words a philosophy organizes the experiences and phenomena of the world into their 'meaning'. Then one sees that one is often not free to respond in a random way to many things – that questions of taste, for example, must often be subordinated to understanding. We might like the barrel-organ player, but if he always murders someone when he comes to our street – we will take the sound of the barrel organ as a sign of danger and drive the organ player away. Often what passes as matters of taste are really matters of fact. So what you are as a person depends on your philosophy. This means that you have to make inquiries about the world. To say (in however elaborate or genteel a disguise) 'I know what I like' does not entitle you to claim understanding. It can be of the order, I know I like the taste of this poison. Often a philosophy will probably surprise you at what you think – can I, must I, really believe that? But that has never occurred to me! Nevertheless, your philosophy tells you you must think it. In a philosophy you can examine something by looking away from it.

You can then compare the different philosophies and try to come to some judgement of them – always bearing in mind that this isnt a question of likes or dislikes. An unphilosophical person cannot love the good. Those innocent souls, the naturally good, who are beloved of folk stories and children's stories – they are not good. To be good there must be understanding. The naturally good try to control the world (if they bother about that) by virtue of their goodness. Their smiles will have a good effect on the robbers – or on the rescuers, so that they come to the rescue. That there is no understanding in all this goes without saying!

Can a philosophy guide one's likes and dislikes in a rational way? Often a 'philosophy' is merely an excuse for what one likes and dislikes, an explanation for how one wishes to behave – not an understanding of what one is. A philosophy ought to relate men to the world. A philosophy is an act of understanding of relationships, of understanding the understander. The reason why the question 'what am I?' can be asked is part of the explanation of what I am. A philosophy, if its to be a guide to all occasions and problems, must include everything in its explanation. It must relate one thing to another, otherwise what is being dealt with is not philosophy but faith. A philosophy which requires something outside what has to be explained in order to explain it is not a philosophy, but a myth or religion. Thus god is not able to form part of a philosophy. Only what the various things that have to be explained can give to each other can count in a philosophy. It is the relation of these things to each other that founds the philosophy. More of the same things may be added by science, of course; but an explanation outside of what is, used to explain what is, such as the spiritual being used to explain the physical – this is not and never can be philosophy. We do not have to search outside and beyond the things to be explained for their meaning; though we do of course have to search into the nature of the things themselves, but in terms of their nature. What is can never prove what ought to be. Similarly, even if there were a god he could not be the explanation of anything. The gap between god and man cannot be bridged and therefore god cannot serve as an explanation of men or their world. You cant get an ought from an is, you cant get a world from a god. So why something happens has to be understood in terms of the relation between things: no other sort of explanation is relevant. If 'something goes wrong', if men behave brutally, there must be an explanation in terms of men and their relations to each other and the world.

Animals are to a large degree mentally fixed. They are guided by their instincts. Their relationship to the world is permanent (unless men alter it). They develop in evolution. Men change their world by their industry and therefore their minds must be open-ended. If their minds were fixed, permanent – then they could relate only to one political, industrial and economic form of the world. This is not so. So human nature consists in this relationship between men and their society. Human nature is not the creation of the individual apart from his society – any more than his language is. There are however constants in all human behaviour. The need to sleep, to eat and so forth. But human behaviour is not human nature. Human behaviour is a social product and human nature is the socially created (or interactionally created) foundation of this. There is no human nature outside society. The constants – the ability to feel anger, love, to eat and sleep and so forth – are not the foundations of human nature or human behaviour. They are merely the means of it, the opportunities of it, that make it possible. We do not do x because we are capable of anger, we do x because our society uses our anger at that point. We are not directed by an unconscious in any significant degree. What is taken as the important unconscious is merely the engine ticking over in sleep or abstraction or preoccupation. The world is not shaped by the unconscious, our behaviour in the world is not so shaped. The subconscious is really the unknown, and that is: what is unknown about society, the meaning of the relations that structure society, the lack of openness or recognition between members and classes in society. Yes, we live in a world of the unknown and unseen – as the bushman lives in his own world of mythology. But by 'worshipping' the unknown we do not bring into use all the richness of hidden personality – we use it, but we do not relate to reality. The secret reality of mystics and hippies is really the raw material of reality, the possibility of reality, which has no structure until its related to this world (in epic form) – the richness is there, but its there to have meaning, that is its biological and ontological function: so it shouldnt be short-circuited into knowledge of itself. It is the great potential harvest of man, but the hippie and mystic merely turns himself into the mouse that feeds on this harvest, not the man who does so; just as the fascist turns himself into the rat who invades this harvest.

Acting a Life 22 August 1980

The problem is how to act a life rather than a character. A life has to be acted in order to describe what happens to an individual. We are concerned with his history and not his character. The character is only part of the history; even more important we must remember that in many important respects character is determined by history. Character cannot be reduced to temperament. Character is of no interest outside situation. It is the conjunction between character and situation that creates the events of a personal history.

We must see individuals not as individuals reacting to society but as part of society, as both cause and effect – perhaps, structurally, as the brick in the wall. It is a brick, yet it is part of the wall, and being in its situation is 'wall'.

It is possible to use players like counters. They can then demonstrate, rather like markers on a map or, say, flowing lines in a moving cartoon, the structures and processes of society. This is not a good use of actors. Such work is better done by other means of teaching. Human societies do not exist because coal is mined at Y and moved to Z. They exist because there are people able and prepared to mine, drive lorries, own, sell and so forth – and this means people able and prepared to live within specific social structures. The theatre is not good at diagramming the mechanical facts of society – it is better at portraying the human facts. Of course these portrayals must always be based on the physical facts and must not become part of the mystifications with which the physical facts are commonly disguised.

The human mind is open-ended and not finalized by instincts. This is so because it must accommodate itself to the rapid way human beings change the world. There is no constant human nature – what is constant is the human ability to create new forms of consciousness in new conditions. It is this area – the creation of new consciousness and the inappropriateness of old forms of consciousness in changed surroundings – that is the real work of drama. And its final work is to show how, in the new world, we can be human. Human consciousness is the point of conjunction between society and the 'givers' of the human being. The need for warmth, food, sex, the fears and panics, and the happiness.

We have to understand the subjective qualities very clearly. All men must do certain things in order to live. They must breathe. This is automatic and many of the things they must do are automatic. They must eat and engender young. Digestion is automatic. The earning of a living is social. The physical erotic enjoyment is automatic, the forms it takes are social: this is true of marriage, courtship and so forth. But society is also imbedded in psychology. In one society children will fear their parents long after they themselves are grown up, in another society they will not. In one society parents will batter their children, in another society not. We have to say that many natural experiences – such as erotism – can become tinged by society: and the means influenced by social structures. If the whole world were a nunnery or monastery everyone would associate erotic feelings with guilt or defiance. Just as there are powerful forces demanding obedience in society – such as obedience of the law, politeness in public and so forth – so there are strong forces within the individual that demand obedience. Even many of these are subject to the control of the will. For example a hunger-striker may starve himself to death. Nevertheless he couldnt hold his breath till he died. Someone might asphyxiate themself. But it would be difficult to stop yourself dreaming by an act of conscious will (if not impossible). Usually we think of social living as accommodating the needs of the individual. But we must think of consciousness as a meeting point which looks both ways: at society, and at the given of the self. We must not think of these given as determining the individual. The individual is the meeting of the two. It is the construction that results from the individual being in society. The individual may exert his will against society or for society. We think of the 'given' as determining which he will do. We have to think, instead, of the social situation as determining in all vital respects. It is frivolous to say that a man can survive in Auschwitz and so prove the strength of the human spirit. A man might admire the distant exploding of an H bomb before the blast reaches him. What is determining about the species man, now, is the social. So a man must be understood in terms of his social situation: a) his experience, and b) what he is taught – the way history, society and man is explained to him. We know that in class society the description may be inaccurate.

We cannot say that morals are guaranteed by god. Morals are created by man. The class society says that morals are what are good for maintaining the given social structure – or what are needed to change it in a certain way. (In feudal society it was good to honour the king: in the bourgeois revolutions it was good to cut off his head; once this had been done – and kingship radically changed – it could again become good to honour the changed kings.) If one could work out a pattern which described the human mind changing, to accommodate its changing activity in the world, a pattern which enabled the 'given' needs of men to be most adequately met without infringing the needs of others, a pattern in which the human mind could be used to describe the world as it really is, and not depend on mystifications which enabled men to act in ways which did in fact often infringe on the 'given' needs of some of them – then this pattern would describe a rational understanding of history and would be socialist.

Index

NOTE: Writings by Edward Bond (EB) appear directly under title; works by others appear under authors' names